the lonely letters

Duke University Press *Durham and London* 2020

the
lonely
letters

ashon t.
crawley

Printed in the United States of America on acid-free paper ∞
Designed by Aimee C. Harrison
Typeset in Whitman and Neuzeit S LT Std by Copperline Books

Library of Congress Cataloging-in-Publication Data
Names: Crawley, Ashon T., author.
Title: The lonely letters / Ashon T. Crawley.
Description: Durham : Duke University Press, [2020] | Includes biblio-
graphical references.
Identifiers: LCCN 2019033500 (print) | LCCN 2019033501 (ebook)
ISBN 9781478007760 (hardcover)
ISBN 9781478008248 (paperback)
ISBN 9781478009306 (ebook)
Subjects: LCSH: Crawley, Ashon T. | African American Pentecostals—
Biography. | Loneliness—Religious aspects—Christianity. | African
American sexual minorities—Religious life. | African American
Pentecostal churches—Social aspects. | Church music—African
American churches. | African Americans—Race identity. |
Experience (Religion)
Classification: LCC BX8762.5.Z8 C73 2020 (print) |
LCC BX8762.5.Z8 (ebook) | DDC 289.9/408996073—dc23
LC record available at https://lccn.loc.gov/2019033500
LC ebook record available at https://lccn.loc.gov/2019033501

Duke University Press gratefully acknowledges the University of
Virginia, which provided funds toward the publication of this book.

epigraph

1—". . . some tail or trace of her voice's yet to be
bodiless thrust caught in his throat like sand,
a precise powder perhaps (as of a moth's or even
an angel's wings) cautioning breath itself."

2—"Somewhere a curtain had fallen away, a cape
of moth-eaten silk."

3—"He'd been nervous for days, weeks, months.
It thus came as no surprise that during the drive to
Burbank there had been moths, not butterflies, in
his stomach and that his stomach might as well
have been wool."

—Nathaniel Mackey, *From a Broken Bottle Traces
of Perfume Still Emanate*

contents

and³

Dear Reader,

And it begins this way. I was sitting at the corner desk where I always sat in Woodruff Library at Emory University. It had to have been the summer of 2006, or maybe the early fall semester, but not much after that. I went to Woodruff almost daily for study, to read and write, to socialize and figure out who I was in this new world of academia. I was in a master's program studying theology and queer theory but was introduced to names like Hortense Spillers, Saidiya Hartman, Daphne Brooks. I began reading what they were writing and diving into their works cited to read more in Black studies, performance studies, and Black feminist studies.

As fate would have it, a friend suggested I read an essay in *Loss: The Politics of Mourning* by the then-unknown-to-me Fred Moten titled "Black Mo'nin'." This friend knew I was interested in the intersection of performance studies and sound studies and thought this essay would have something interesting to speak to me. So I found the collected volume and began to read the essay about Emmett Till and his photograph. But at the very beginning of the essay, before I could finish it, there was a passage from a book titled *Bedouin Hornbook* that was about the Black singer's voice, falsetto and the gospel moan and shout.

. . . I'm especially
. . . One point I
. . . new word, new world.

I was undone. I put the essay down, searched the library's website to find this book, this *Bedouin Hornbook*. I locked my computer, left my desk, found the book in the stacks, checked it out. I returned to my desk and began reading it immediately. It changed the way I thought about music, about writing about music, about dreams, about writing about dreams. It has remained with me, all these years later, the way Mackey happened upon a poetics that could create such a rupture in the way I consider worlds. And for that I am thankful.

In some ways, I have always written letters:

I never thought that I would be tossing and turning late at night, t-shirt slightly moist from sweat, unable to sleep because you keep popping in my head. The truth is I kept trying to blame you solely for the reasons our relationship didn't become what it could have. But this night, I realize that I am partially to blame as well. You are to blame because you feared love in me. I am to blame because I allowed myself to fall in love with you without defining lines before our emotions were too attached to each other.

A year ago, in September, I never thought that I would long for you as much as I do but shit happens and I fully realize that what happened between us transcends all boundaries of ordinary love. Damn, in September 2002, I didn't even know you and now, November of 2003, the only one on my mind is you Love—and I miss you.

Dear Love, when you told me after months of interactions and flirtations and gazes and smiles that I was unequivocally crazy to think you loved me, or even liked me in any regard romantic, you crushed me. I went away believing that you lied to me but finally gave in to what seemed to be the truth—that what I felt for you wasn't reciprocal. Then we became cordial once again after a period of not speaking with each other because I was too hurt to hear your voice. Then you informed me candidly that you didn't want me to be around you

2

because you didn't need any distractions and I was definitely a distraction for you. How the hell is someone that you don't have any romantic feelings for a distraction?

I've learned that we were both confused by our communion. I call you Love because that's what you are and that's what we do and that's what we have. Ours was never a physically based relationship. Not in the typical sense of the word, at least. Our physical was defined by sitting close to each other—really close, but not really touching. Our physical was found in eyes, the movement of our mouths, the scents of you and me intermingling—doing what we never did—make love to each other.

But I know dear Love that what we had and have is nothing less than the strongest love, even in our separation physically, emotionally, and mentally. You need time to figure out that you really will only be happy with me. You want my arms to hold you at night no matter how much your mind fights it, your heart knows it is truth. Our love is stronger than most because we never needed the physical to validate our feelings. We only needed location and voice and time with each other.

Love, I know now that the love I had for you was and is reciprocal but you choose to represent it differently from me, which is frustrating. I cannot understand the intricacies of what we have. Love is spiritual to me—something that meets on a plane much higher than our temporal body-physical realm.

This connection we had is how I knew you would call every Thursday at around 6 p.m. to see where I was although you knew the answer to the question. This connection is what allowed us to spend countless hours together without watching the clock—without caring about anything else in the world. This connection is what made me smile even when I was mad as hell with you. It is the reason we could walk around late at night and talk about nothing and follow up on the phone or the internet with more rambling about happiness, sadness, and love.

Although we spend no time together these days, largely because of your fear, I still know that you love me stronger and harder now than you did before because I love you all the more. Indeed, fear is what is keeping us apart. You feared falling so hard in love with me that you shunned the very idea. You tried to forget me but it isn't possible. We are connected so much that there is no way to forget me. I am not one of your acquaintances or friends that you have met along your life's journey. I am much more—I am the first true love you had and have. You can fight it but we both know the truth, unspoken though it may be.

As you have told me, this year has been an up-and-down ride for the both of us and we are both better people for it but we have not attained the level of what we can be because we are not finished with each other. We met in spirit and our souls are making what our bodies await. I become sick to the stomach when you are not well. My voice is ingrained in your psyche and your touch is what I taste. Instead of fighting the urge to be with me, acquiesce and find the greatest joy you've ever had.

One cannot say I did not have a sense for the dramatic, for the grand gesture and desired articulation, even in my very first moments of trying to live more fully into a blackqueer life. In 2003, I ended my letter to Love with the invitation to share in the practice of joy. He declined. I still search. Not much has changed since that time, though joy today is actually more important to me than I could have then realized. When I reread the 2003 letter, I am often stunned by how precise it was about the feelings I'd felt, but also stunned by the boldness of address, the clarity and conviction of force, and the fact of sending such a thing to its recipient. It was a questing for noncoercive communion, a questing for *consent to be otherwise than a single being*, a questing to move from *unity to multiplicity.*[1] Yet it was a questing without the necessary language or guiding ideologies gained through the years of necessary work against sexism, patriarchy, misogynoir, queer antagonism, empire, colonization, and antiblack racism. The questing was sharpened by engaging Black feminism, queer of color critique, necessary for a more robust, full, and non-coercive, reciprocal life. In 2003, I felt anomalous, that only I would write something with this searching and restive yearning, with this heartfelt but also excessive and superfluous and hyperbolic flow. Could I find refuge in writing? Could other writers help me practice gentleness and care? What was this desire about beyond the object of its affection?

2003. It was the year I began accepting blackqueerness as a way of life, when I began to separate myself—even if ever so slightly—from doctrine and theology that said I, and queer folks in general, were fundamentally flawed, sinful, in need of change. It's taken me a long time to figure out that the letter form allows me to reach for feeling, allows me to feel something close to what I felt in my churches as musician and choir director and preacher, as praiser and worshipper and believer. The letters are written to a composite character named Moth, and each is written in search of portraying feeling and mood and disposition.

I found Mackey's letters, *Bedouin Hornbook*, and I realized that letters can be about love—certainly—but also friendship, music, and, indeed, joy. Writing *The Lonely Letters* has been an exercise of return, of thinking again about all that was compressed in the letter to Love in 2003, compressed and thus able to be expanded, extended, and—today, happily—critiqued.

I am fundamentally a Blackpentecostal, I believe in repetition as a means for discovering something that is below and beneath and behind what appear to be flat surfaces. At church, we'd sing songs for ten to fifteen or even twenty minutes, just a verse and chorus, and the spirit would fall. And it's because the repetition allowed us to stay and linger and wait and tarry and think and imagine, repetition as limit became also possibility, delimitation the occasion for meditative opening and vulnerability. I am fundamentally a Blackpentecostal, the way I think worlds, imagine sound and music, are because of the force and verve of sound and music from within that world, a world with its own sonic epistemology.

Style.

Sound.

I am a musician of this tradition, was a Hammond B-3 musician first in my church in New Jersey growing up, then in Philadelphia and, later still, in the greater Durham area. These two words—*style, sound*—mark how Hammond organists in the Black gospel tradition discuss the differences in chord changes that accrue to certain cities—the Brooklyn sound, the Chicago sound, Old

School, New School—differences that are *not*. One plays the same song in Chicago during testimony service that they play in Brooklyn but the chording might be different. This difference is not denounced, it is celebrated. It is a difference that does not necessitate categorical differentiation, a difference that announces a sonic epistemology that is not grounded in western philosophical, theological, and musicological ideals.

It occurred to me one day that my writing is like my journeying as a musician, often playing the same thing but constantly reaching for chords and arpeggios that could say that sameness with difference. Baraka's changing same. In *The Lonely Letters*, readers familiar with my first book *Blackpentecostal Breath: The Aesthetics of Possibility* will find that many of the same objects of analysis are used: some of the same sermons, the same music, the same concepts are worked again and with and over and through. I am still trying to discover something about the lifeworlds of Blackpentecostals and *The Lonely Letters* gives another occasion for such a thinking with. Thinking with? It is important for me to continue to underscore the idea that I am attempting to *think with* the Blackpentecostal world, that it is worth thinking about, wrestling against, engaging as if there is life there, as if the world is one of complexity. Much of Black life has been relegated by the normative register of western thought to that which is not worth thinking with. I not only resist but contend forcefully against this. And *thinking with* Blackpentecostalism means that the world continues to shape me, continues to gift me possibility against limit.

Semiautobiographical, at thirty-nine years old, I have not yet had the occasion to sit across from the table, or hold hands on the couch, or lay next to someone and have the words "I love you" uttered in the ways we call romantic. And I have never had occasion to return such words and affection. This fact could lead to embarrassment and shame if it were not for friends that practice love and care with me. Yet and still, I experience loneliness. How does one deal with disappointment? How is one to live when one feels that so much has been so heartbreaking and difficult to comprehend? To desire to feel, to desire sensuality, this is what *The Lonely Letters* explores, but in ways that are improvisational and stilted, not on but kinda under and a bit behind and also then a bit ahead and then also over—marking a different relation that is not linear to—the beat. It is an autobiography of loneliness with fictional characters A and Moth as interlocutors, an exploration of heartbrokenness through a kind of Audre Lordean mythopoetics. It is an attempt to write in and through Lorde's theory, through Mackey's line and root, through Black sociality. *The Lonely Letters* is in a Black feminist and blackqueer tradition of struggling to make sense of—by producing a fundamental critique against—the normative world, and it practices a restlessness of word and phrase that seeks ways of existence otherwise.

But it would be unsatisfying, I think, to write a bunch of letters about the personal, private, individual experience of loneliness and aloneness and desires for romantic love. Though I do not shy away from this being a very real factor that animates this autobiography of loneliness, this mythopoetics approaching but shying away from "what really happened," the letters are about so much more. I found the more these worked on me, came to me, spoke to and with and through me—these voices, these friends, these tales—the more I found the narrative, if there is one, to be about the severance from community. They are about the complexity of thought and movement and spirit that emerges from how it is to feel abandoned by communities of care and concern, about being left behind by churches and institutions that were once integral to life and love. These feelings of severance, abandonment, of being left behind, come—and are felt deeply—in nonlinear fashion, they are not given to progressive temporal measures. Rather, they are experienced repetitiously, in cycles, in fits and starts. Can one consider loneliness to not just be, or to not primarily be, an experience of the individual but of a social world? What happens when blackqueerness is what one experiences as connecting to others, but living such a life is what creates or occasions the distancing metaphorically and materially felt from family, friends, religious communities? What is *that* but loneliness of and from and in the desire for social worlds, for sociality? And can anything be made in the distance, at the border, in the margins? This distance marks limit, but limit marks occasion or, as Nahum Chandler would say, *possibility*.[2]

The letters attempt to stage the complexity of thinking and performing the limit and possibility, they ask about and linger over these concerns. The experiences of severance, abandonment, of being left behind are not experienced on a straight line, which is why the letters attempt a mood but not a linear narrative that has a beginning, middle, and end. The experiences of severance, abandonment, of being left behind are limit, but also occasion, each enclosure an opening and unfolding to what could be *imagined to be possible*. A and Moth are placeholders for desired connection. A wrestles with limit and what it means to be *of* possibility on the interpersonal and social levels. As much as I have met people similar to both A and Moth, and though A is based on my life, I do believe they also *are* types, they are not empty vessels—no—but they do serve as signposts for feeling. Feeling has resonance in various disciplines and allows for an approach against disciplinarity, toward and through the interdisciplinary, in the service of an alternative epistemological possibility altogether.

In *The Lonely Letters*, I attempt to think the relationship of quantum theory, mysticism, relationality, and blackness together by considering the sound and noise of Blackpentecostal spaces. Building on the work in *Blackpentecostal Breath: The Aesthetics of Possibility*, *The Lonely Letters* are written to think together what might seem to be disparate ways of thinking worlds—known and unknown, worlds religious and scientific, worlds noisy and musical—with hopes of considering the epistemologies of these varied worlds as Blackpentecostal. It's about love and heartbreak and hope and joy and how what is thought scientifically is part of a range of *sensual* capacities, that the scientific is a misnomer.

I began writing the letters in this project which you now hold either in 2003—the letter to Love—or in 2010—a letter to another person of interest:

if i were unafraid, i'd tell you that a chance encounter with you in
august at your church and hanging out with you later that week still
makes me smile

    if i were unafraid, i'd tell you that i think what you do is amazing and
courageous, and literally has inspired me to do more

    if i were unafraid, i'd tell you that even though i don't know you, i
feel you and your struggles, and care about your well-being

    if i were unafraid, i'd tell you that though you are doing a lot of stuff
right now, i hope that you take time for self-care

    [. . .]

    if i were unafraid, i'd tell you that i wish i could hug you, hold your
hand and tell you everything will be all right

    if i were unafraid, i'd tell you that i want to be your friend, with whatever possibilities exist there

if i were unafraid, i'd tell you that i simply wish to get to know you
but of course i am afraid, so i couldn't possibly tell you any of that,
though i hope that somehow you discern these things.
thinking of you,

I have been writing in the letter form for some time now, each with the hopes of establishing connection. So perhaps then, too, *The Lonely Letters* is a search for a claim to connection with you, reader, with a desire to be in conversation, to think our worlds together, to figure out a way to practice justice and care with one another in order to alleviate the suffering of the masses. So, you choose, 2003 or 2010.

Organizationally, you might perhaps notice something similar to *Blackpentecostal Breath*. The letters are organized into five sections: Breath[3], Shouting[3], Noise[3], Tongues[3], Nothing[3]. There is a superscript with each section, a 3, meant to mark performance. That is, I think of *The Lonely Letters* as that which was written previous to, during, and after *Blackpentecostal Breath* and I sometimes describe it as the semifictional version, a different though not categorically distinct genre, of that first book project. *Blackpentecostal Breath* is a performance studies analysis of Blackpentecostalism and, in so many ways, was already on its way to being performed, was already being performed in letter form.

People have contacted me to say that passages in *Blackpentecostal Breath* compelled them to breathe deeply, to sigh, to sing, to praise. I wanted that text to capture something of the breath of blackness, of Black *pneuma*, of the choreosonic force of Black performance. But *The Lonely Letters* is more intentionally about three-dimensionality, the 3 superscript is to mark the relation to movement, verve, the resistance of the object. *The Lonely Letters* has been performed, both textually, choreosonically, paintedly. So you can think of the sections of *The Lonely Letters* as correspondence—literally, letters to and against and in conversation—with the chapters in *Blackpentecostal Breath*. But as in the first book, the categories of sections are illusory at best, the concepts breathe into one another, they are porous, the chapters as categorical distinctions are not pure and cannot be maintained.

The Lonely Letters is about the capacity for that which we study to work on us, to transform us, to change how we inhabit the world. Not dispassionate nor disconnected from the fact of the flesh, *The Lonely Letters* is about detecting connection in the most disparate of ways. These letters attempt to resist the epistemology of western thought that privileges so-called critical distance, abstraction, rationality, the dispassionate, the neutral and does so by moving intentionally and intensely with and into the feeling of the flesh, the way one can be moved to tears and joy and happiness and heartbreak. It is not an escape from the social but a withdrawal into the density that Black sociality—blackqueerness—provides. There is safety in that tabernacle. There is protection there. What if it were possible to resist the enclosure of emotion from thinking, to resist the enclosure of the flesh from the mind?

The letters are in epistolary form, a poetics in the tradition of and heavily influenced by Nathaniel Mackey, allowing me to explore the relationship between blackness, sound, and quantum theory, not as an analogy but a way to think epistemology. Roughly one hundred trillion neutrinos pass through each of us each second. Passing through us yet not typically the stuff, the material, of thought. Blackpentecostal believers often talk about "feeling something," where "something" cannot necessarily be described with precision. What if what is being felt, what is being registered on and in the flesh, is the resonance of a kind of matter uninhibited by gravity, like neutrinos; what if what is being felt are vibrations that technologies like those found at the Sanford Underground Research Facility (SURF) consider the foundation for the universe, though we cannot detect these movements with our finite sense capacities? Or can we? Things that occur on the quantum level go against common knowledge regarding time and space. Actions of particles are often unaccounted for, cannot be controlled nor guessed. In quantum states, time and space do not produce causal effects between particles and, yes, it appears that particles' behaviors in the "past" are determined by their "future" behavior, counterintuitive claims for temporality. Just what is history, and the relation of blackness to history, in such a world?

"I want a consensuality with you," A says to Moth. And this is important. Given the world of sexism, patriarchy, misogynoir, queer antagonism, and femmephobia, and the inequitable practices of power that produce harm and coercion, what is most grounded in the letters is a desire for noncoercive relationality, a friendship that sometimes spills into—because it always is—eroticism, a relationality they must recommit to over and over again. It is important to seek consensuality, a "continued consent to be together," A says, because the letters cannot be about trying to convince Moth, cannot be about attempting to convince anyone, of value and nobility and honor in the service of inequitable practices of sex and relation. The letters are about the attempt at consensuality, a sensuality of mutuality that is continually being inflected, changed, opened, closed. Frustrating, at times, but also necessary.

The kind of love A seeks with Moth is about the celebration of the antagonism to and renunciation of sovereignty, an antagonism to and renunciation of an individual, individuated, modern liberal subjectivity. No cartesian dualisms here. And similar to how one must attempt to touch a moth delicately lest it disintegrate away into a kind of powder, A's ruminations on love and mysticism and renunciation of the one for the social, his ruminations on the renunciation of the subject for the entangled folds of blackness, a being together with others as the grounds for experience, are in the service of a delicate grasp of the other that withstands the risk of disintegration. A ruminates in the service of holding while being held within Moth. He wants an experience wherein they both are changed. And perhaps as you read and hold the words, the words will read and hold you. A reciprocity of a being held way of life. A consent for the words to work on you, for the worlds interior to allow withdrawal into them. A noncoercive way to be together with others. In text and sound and song and dance and paint. The choreosonic, centrifigutive motive. The choreosonic, centrifigutive movement. Hold this while you are held in it. A holding of sociality, density, love. And breathe. And breathe. And be.

This is the desire for friendship as a way of life,

Ashon

breath^3

Dear Moth,

It happened again and I don't know what to make of it. Not staring but the sorta moment you feel someone looking at you from across the room and you look up from the convo you'd been engaging and, sure enough, there he is, looking. You make brief eye contact, he takes a deep breath and looks away. It's almost as if his looking—the very fact of his doing it—stunned him, and that stunning took place in the space and pause between inhale and exhale, so he also was not immediately able to look away. You're the trainwreck. You're the fire to which the moth is attracted. Beautifully so (or, at least, you convince yourself; and you think this word, *beautiful*, when he does this because that exchange, that brevity, that pause, had so much space in it, so much capacious possibility even if only, maybe *especially* if, you'd imagined it; the word beautiful just kinda echoed in you at that briefly there gesture; the word beautiful, you hope to describe what he thinks upon seeing you, noticing you; it's that look he gave, that look that was full of sound and touch and smell, the look of feel).

But he's also very cute. So, the hesitant averted gaze, the stalled look away after the look, the wary worry which announced, before any "hello," the emergence of problems? I heard it, felt it, went for it anyway. It resonated. Kinda like a bass note, a bottoming, felt, throbbing. Almost.

It was at Calvin's art opening a few weeks ago, his first gallery showing in fact, so things were abuzz and he was rather excited. Wine was flowing and there was genuine giddiness in the air. I was pleased to be able to support and met all sorts of folks: people I'd only heard him talk about, folks whom he'd tell me I needed to know; new people I'd never heard of; and was finally able to meet folks that I'd only known from their social media presence. It was cool.

Anyway, Calvin's artwork was nothing short of amazing. Called it his "music and movement" installation where he'd taken all sorts of oil and acrylic paint, pigment sticks, cutouts from magazines—whatever he could find—in order to create various swirls and strokes, all based on the music to which he'd be listening at the time, all abstract. He said the pieces he created were supposed to approach a kind of sonic referentiality, were a type of metaphorization of the sounds, of the music. It made me question the concept of abstraction because they were not theoretically removed, they were material manifestations of the music. An idea for later. Maybe.

I was moved by the colors he used, mostly darker gradations :: deep purples and blues, dense, full-bodied reds, and lots of black. He used a variety of surfaces, he said, *to bespeak the everydayness of our encounters with music. This is a piece about the sublime's relation to the ordinary.*

I sorta laughed a bit at his description because it's just so different—abstract in the different kind of way I talked about above—from our ordinary conversation. And it sorta felt like it was on the edge of a kind of self-congratulatory "look at this cool shit I did and now please pay me!" manifesto implicit in the self-referential descriptions. It becomes easy to misread motives of artists if we only rely on their narrative constructions regarding their work. I guess that's why exhibits are important, not because they validate and justify but because they can open up to a social community. Then again, Adrian Piper kinda hates the artworld and often makes it the subject of her criticism, so maybe I'm wrong. Aside from his description, it truly was amazing. Couldn't deny it. The problem, of course, was that there was this hella cute dude there with his girlfriend-ofthreeyears (he said it, rushed just like that, while she was in the restroom).

Calvin wanted me to meet this guy because he's likewise interested in mysticism and is a sometimey church musician, so he thought we'd hit it off. Dude was definitely glancing at me even before the official introduction, when I stood across the gallery space talking with some other folks. So when we were introduced, of course I was surprised to learn that the young woman was not just a friend but was, in fact, the girlfriendofthreeyears. Nice guy; he and his girlfriendofthreeyears were, in fact, cool as hell. The three of us talked for at least an hour, conversation moving through all sorts of terrain, from theology to the presidency. Needless to say, I got along with them very well, so Calvin wasn't wrong at all. The problem?

Well . . .

You know how I tend to get a bit on the edge of loud, and insistent, when I've had one too many glasses of wine. Not a belligerent volume but just a kind of emphatic speaking, a sorta intentional and forceful kind of saying of whatever is on my mind, no filter. It's kinda easy in those moments to remember that I was serious about preaching at one time in my life, that I wanted folks to be convicted by the very way the argument happened. The whooping, the force of breath, the clapped hands to displace air. All of it was so fleshly. Anyway, talking to him—to them—I felt like those days in the past. It made me miss preaching.

Told them, "I voted Green Party the last two times! Not even gonna vote the next time around if things keep going the way they're going!" And though true, it's always weird to sorta feel that comfortable and light with folks you'd just met. Anyway, girlfriendofthreeyears went to the restroom but saw an old friend and stopped to talk to her for a while. So dude and I kept talking and it was nice. It goes without saying that I noticed how handsome he was and how, had there been no girlfriendofthreeyears present, I would've overtly flirted. I might've *been* overtly flirting.

He's kinda pretty, kinda soft, some would say feminine and his clothing was eclectic, artsy, cute. His voice low, he had a kind of playful bashfulness that I enjoyed, a kind of gender performance that some would say isn't manly or boyish or whatever those categories are supposed to mean. These lips and voice and eyes. It was a lot. I felt it. Between the convo and the charm and, thus, the very real and there charge between us felt in the held then given breath, all my buttons were being pushed. But I'm not desperate. And I'm needy but only in a way that I hope can be ethical, I don't wanna go down that road again and you know what, and who, I mean. But things did cross my mind. His smile, his eyes, his lips? A kind of shy and curly smile. A voice that whispered but, also, bottomed. Conviction. Comfort. Care. All there. Like we'd known each other and were meeting again. It was so good.

After we talked and girlfriendofthreeyears returned, I moved on so I could talk to other friends I hadn't seen in a while. We Facebooked each other and I scurried away. Whispered to Calvin "oh my god . . . he's cute! ugh!" He laughed. I settled on a new group of old friends with whom I could catch up. But while drinking this newest glass of wine and having convo where I laughed a lot and made several points, I looked up and saw him. Not quite staring but definitely looking with a precise kind of desire, precise insofar as it was aimed at me. I felt it. Felt it in me. Knew someone was looking, just had to find the directional field from which the energy emanated. And each time (it happened about four times throughout the duration of the evening after we'd met to say nothing of the before) when he realized I realized he was looking at me, he'd sorta almost—faintly—smile but not really, because there was also a slight hint of embarrassment on his face, in his heart I presume as well, that he was looking at me like that in the first place. Or maybe it was in my stomach because I felt butterflies with each look and look away. Made me question what it was that prompted his search that landed in my face, in my eyes, each time, causing him to further still: search. I mean, I knew but still didn't *know*.

(Are metaphors a displacement of thought? Do they get us closer to the heart of the matter? Or are they some other kind of complication?)

I think he saw something familiar in me that he'd not ever named. It almost sounds egotistical to say it the way I'm thinking it but that's not what I mean. I wish things were much less complex but this has happened with so many dudes that it's pretty common now. His rushed girlfriendofthreeyears declaration was to make sure I knew, understood, not only that he was taken but that he was, indeed, straight-identified. So much so that I knew it was to reassure him and not about me at all. Declarations of heterosexuality are cool but then the people long for something otherwise and see and really really *sense* me, and act as if whatever that otherwise might be is somewhere hidden in me, is something familiar.

And I had this weird experience when I was a kid that was all about familiarity. We took a bus trip when I was in the fifth grade to Baltimore or some other city and the trip included everyone in the fifth grade so all the teachers, most of whom I did not know, went along. There was one teacher on the bus who, upon catching my eye in the rearview mirror the first time as she was staring at me, continued to look at me. At first I didn't pay it much attention but I would turn around to someone behind me and begin to talk and she'd walk up to me, grab my arm, tell me "Didn't I tell you to turn around?! Stop talking! And look forward!," forcing me to turn around on the bus so she could continue to look at me in the rearview mirror. She would not let me talk to others, made me face forward. She stared into my reflection in the mirror. Needless to say, I was uncomfortable.

I told my parents what happened when I got home and when I told them who it was, they said "the next time you see her, ask her if she knows us, ask her if she went to our church." So the next time I saw her I asked her if she knew my mother and when I did, she exclaimed loudly, hugging me hard, "I knew it!" Turns out, she saw my parents—daddy's mouth and lips, mother's voice (even though I was too young, fifth grade . . . but I suppose I had prepubescent hints of the voice to come, its otherwise possibility already with me, and if I learned anything from my mother, it was the insistence in voice, the conviction)—in me, on me. The point is that familiarity shows up in all sorts of weird ways. Something about—literally external to—me bespoke something in me. But that something was noise at best, incoherence, or at least, incomprehensible, ineffable audiovisuality (sorta like how cell phones used to produce all of this static whenever you'd go out of range).

Having seen me without knowing but still that noise prompted knowledge in her, a knowledge of having known, a knowledge of knowing, a knowledge of desire to know. That knowledge—the who that I was—was there, while withdrawing with each pondered "But how do I know him? But where do I know him from?" furrow of her brow. I felt abused by her force on the bus, felt ashamed and felt that she was misunderstanding my simple wish to talk to other kids. And I won't even get into the kind of erotics that sorta underpinned her staring into a mirror to figure me out. All I know is that she was trying to remember something without knowing what it was. She didn't know me, she left the church before I was born. But she could sense familiarity. That's what I'm getting at.

And so dude with the girlfriendofthreeyears, I think, also was cathected by some sorta erotic-libidinal excess, provoked by the insistence of my voice, an insistence that produced in him some desire to know more. To "get" what was so familiar. Maybe he thought he could, if he stared enough, figure out what it was for which he was longing. A few days after the event, it all became a bit clearer with a message on Facebook that would feign the flirting that was certainly implied, so vague that a claim of ignorance and misunderstanding—another sort of noise and static—could be made, though the apparentness of the interactions is no less there.

Anyway, here's his pic . . . And how have you been?

A

Dear Moth,

What if it were possible to vibrate at the same speed and velocity as our favorite music, our favorite sounds? What if we resonated the way Mahalia Jackson sorta wails and sways and sorta just breathes it out the first time she sings the word "souuul" in "How I Got Over"[1] or like a Twinkie Clark Blackpentecostal shout on the Hammond organ at the end of "Accept What God Allows"?[2] What if we could just move and tremble and quiver and quake and spin and spin and spin until equilibrium is off and we just slip into the sonic world? That'd take a kind of breathing that would be between, that would match in intensity and force what each of us were attempting together. It'd necessitate a kind of breathing that is communal and collective, something like what you get when the preacher is whooping and there is the ongoing call and ongoing response, the breathing *between* preacher and congregation as egging each other on until they're all out of breath.

I watch *The Flash* a lot—even though I have to catch up on the episodes—and the show keeps demonstrating that when Barry vibrates at the same speed as what is presumed to be "solid" and impenetrable matter, he slips in and into and through matter itself. Impenetrability then meaning a renunciation of openness, a forced enclosure against possibility. So, what if we could do the same with music, with sound? To, maybe, evaporate. Evaporation is important because it names something about air and atmosphere, and it also names transformation, change, difference, dissent. To evaporate is to be made into that which can be inhaled and exhaled, that which can be breathed. Would we perhaps then evaporate into and be united with it? What then would be our mode of existence?

What song or sound would you choose? I'd wanna choose something that resonates with a simultaneity, spin and quiver and quake and be one with you. Withdraw into you and you withdraw into me. And I know I sent you the picture of the dude but, really, I think about you. Not only, but certainly always, you. What kind of sound and vibration could be achieved that even the concept of *becoming-one* would have to be recalibrated? That's what I hear in the song you sent. It's mystical.

And I'd been meaning to ask you about mysticism because you said you went on the silent retreat and it made you think about all kinds of things, that it was this mystical experience for you. Who are some folks you'd suggest for me to read?

Moving,

A

Dear Moth,

It's been a while because I've been reading Meister Eckhart since you said I'd enjoy him.[3] Interesting dude. "Stop thinking of being alone as lonely. Think about it as a moment to reconnect with your deepest self, think about it as a chance to sit in silence and be still and to breathe and to be. If you can think of being alone as a chance to hear God, then you'll be ok. Check out this Eckhart," you said. Well, the more I read, the more I figured out why I have a sorta resistance to this shit—to silent retreats and shit like that—why it makes me feel weird. The Eckhart, and the other stuff I've been reading actually, seems to be tied to particular traditions and that unsettles me. I'm not looking for a New Age individuation, not looking to enlarge my territory or to have health, wealth, and blessings unending, theologies of conspicuous consumption and acquisition that discard the histories and practices from which certain mysticisms emerge. But I guess I have the same problem with mysticisms that I have with what I guess we could call, imprecisely of course, nonmystical traditions. (Does such a thing even exist?) Mystical traditions, at least the western ones, seem to run up against their own limit, seem to be about the production of normative function and form.

The limit, I guess, in Eckhart would be a kind of normative Christianity. And his aloneness, his negativity, his nothingness all emerge from *that* limit even if he is trying to approach something otherwise. Because for his experience to be *about* Christianity, such experience is against the very interconnectedness of all things mysticism presumes to seek. How, in other words, can I be connected to all things, how can I be integrated as a part of a whole, while remaining steadfast in a conviction about Jesus being the *only way to the Father*, for example? Some folks, some doctrines, are much more dogmatic about there being only one path whereas others even in the same traditions seem to be much more open and capacious and imaginative. I wanna be like them, I guess.

So yeah, I've been reading Eckhart and I think he's cool. But Eckhart assumes a certain theological world with a certain deity, godhead, a certain understanding of the human, a very particular understanding of immanence and transcendence. It's that particularity that is introduced that seems to produce an antagonism for other traditions, even in their mystical strains. (Also, perhaps because of the invention of the category of religion as a product of modern thought and, thus, the concept of tradition too is one that I don't know how to feel about. And I'm thinking of Talal Asad here, at least, if not others.)[4] Based on our conversations about this, it seems you think it's impossible, or only "New Age," for mysticism to be devoid of a particular religious tradition. If that's the case, that's very unsettling to me.

I'm thinking of Eckhart and also Teresa of Ávila and St. John of the Cross. And Athanasius and Cassian and *The Rule of Saint Benedict*. I'm even thinking of John of Fécamp who says, in his book *Lament over Lost Leisure and Solitude*,

It shames and horrifies me that I must appear in public assemblies, going into the city, talking to those in power, looking at women, mingling with the chattering masses and enduring so many other things that pertain to the world.[5]

He's just one example but think about it: he was an eleventh-century Benedictine monk lamenting over the fact of *lost* leisure and *lost* solitude, what was lost was the idea of a social world that monks could pretend to be unencumbered by, the social world made itself evident in the ways the monks had to alter the practice of their daily lives. For John of Fécamp, what was desired was leisure and solitude from the social world, from the noise of relationality, so much so that he lamented having to deal with the materiality of people, their funk, their voice, their breath. It's just hella Kantian before Kant because wasn't Kant, too, also worried over the material fact of beggars on the street, the fact that beggars became too numerous? And didn't Kant escape their noise because they were too much for him to engage? John of Fécamp gives a Kantian analysis of the transcendental aesthetic before Kant, or really perhaps models the sorta idea of the aesthetic to come.

What intrigues me about all these folks is their desire for a vertical relationship with god over and against all other kinds of relationships, how there is a sorta necessity to renounce sociality, how there is a retreat, how there is a movement away from noise. And so, even when monks were called upon to recite the psalms in communal prayer daily, the emphasis seemed not to be on the communal aspect but on the regimentation of following the rule, of following order, of inculcating obedience in the service of the creation of the individual, of the self, of the subject. Such an individual, a self, a subject would be rational, would be higher, than the base emotions, than the flesh. There was an assumption, a moving out from the flesh, a renunciation of the body, to produce this vertical relation.

Living alone, ridding oneself of the appetites of the flesh as much as possible, retreating from the world into the desert. I've got no problem with renunciation, retreat, or movement, it's just the direction of such that worries me. And you wanted me to read this because you thought it'd help me think about being alone, or single, or finding god. I don't know, I *am* thinking a lot but more perturbed than anything. But I'll keep thinking.

More soon,

A

Dear Moth,

I hear you, I do. I understand that you think I'm not being necessarily fair to mystics but that's not the case at all. Thanks for sending the various readings, the Hollywood, the McGinn, that help me contextualize a bit more. You're right, and I agree, there *is* something radical even though I think the ones I'm discussing do have limitations, and not just because of the times in which they lived. Limitations mean to me that we have to work with and on and against each other in the service of a liberation project, that we have to be engaged in the thicket of the social world, not retreat from it, if we are to realize freedom. Iron sharpens iron and all that.

I've been thinking about what Rebecca Chopp says:

From codes of purity to acts of Jesus' healing, the implicit theological
assumption has equated perfect bodies with wholeness of the spirit.
And, as if to ensure the quest for purity, physical afflictions become
elevated to virtuous suffering when, and only when, they can be
spoken of as trials of obedience.[6]

I guess I'm thinking about this again because I'm also thinking about Teresa and Julian and how their experiences are of physical pain and torture and how that constitutes one way to think about mystical experience. Julian *opens* her discussion about it like this:

I asked for three graces of God's gift. The first was vivid perception of
Christ's Passion, the second was bodily sickness and the third was for
God to give me three wounds.[7]

What I'm thinking about is the way perfect or perhaps normative bodies have to be the ground from which the desire for physical affliction, bodily sickness, and wounding occur. One would have to consider oneself as already whole, as in need of something sensate to occur that is nonnormative, that is queer, that is different than what so-called or so-thought normal people experience. To desire affliction in the body is an individuated thing, it does not connect to all that is but connects oneself to a greater sense of self. It seems to be about the movement of and desire for a radical, rooted individualism that is enclosed, that physical pain, that bodily sickness, that wounding, would come to do the work of making oneself complete and perfectable *as an enclosed subject.* Does that make sense?

And, I don't know, that just bothers me because I used to frequent A4A and I keep going on Grindr and Jack'd and other shit like that and keep reading people say they want "no fats, no fems." What they're asserting is that there is a body that is considered to be normal and for those that are considered to be abject, they occupy a kind of categorical distinction. And for a long time I've been thinking about how "no fats, no fems" rehearses a kind of theological-philosophical concept of the flesh, a kind of denouncing of its capacity to hold, its capacity to be exorbitant. It's like we're supposed to literally hold our breath in order to be more perfectable, to inhale and hold so that we may appear to be thinner, inhale and hold so as not to be considered out of control. And I think about walking down the street or up stairs or hills and how that makes me entirely out of breath, how walking, how movement itself, can bespeak something of breathing.

With "no fats, no fems," the individual is considered to have failed to conform to accepted and acceptable religious doctrine *and* secular rhetoric; not only are you queer and thus a kind of repository for sinfulness, but also, the appetite is considered to be out of control too. It seems to me to be the case that similar to Black Christian rhetoric and theologies, it appears that the flesh is nadir in the blackqueer masculine-desiring culture, and that particularly, but not only, for cisgender dudes. Because the flesh is the site, the ground zero, upon which religious meaning is made and transforms one into a body that has value (I'm thinking of Spillers here), it seems that blackqueer masculine-desiring people take up the flesh as a site for rupturing normativities and for creating of its own meaning. They reproduce the theological-philosophical as a kind of category, it is not removed from Christianized concepts but is a deep entrenchment of the *idea.*

"No fats, no fems" seems to be a rhetorical admission to and underscoring of the ways gender performance as well as the physical musculature of the body are ripe with social and sacred meaning. Similar to blackqueerness in a Black Christian imagination, fat and fem bodies intimate one that is out of control and given to excesses: it is a different rendering of a sinful body, yet equally engaged in discourse of pleasures, ecstasy, and behaviors of the of the nonnormative. Whereas in normative theologies of the body and sexuality, and certainly within institutional historical Black Church culture, there is much focus on the sexual appetites of the congregants; but in the purported redressive space of blackqueer culture, there is a focus on the physical appetite and how *that* affects and produces a body that can be devalued. Fat and fem bodies displace the Black Church's regulatory control of the libidinal drive and replace it with a new paradigm toward which blackqueer folks must aspire in order to be holy and acceptable: the rational and controlled physical body that has six-pack abs and performs masculinity.

All this to say, I wonder about mortification of the flesh as a means of attempting an ideal of the religious, the spiritual, the set apart, mortification in order to have an experience of god. Because what about those of us that are mortified, abject, to a normative understanding of the flesh? What of us that breathe heavy when we walk down the street? What of those of us that experience life itself as a kind of tripartite that Julian describes? What of those of us, in other words, that do not have to *become* or be initiated *into* such an experience of bodily pain but experience it as a grounding of being? This is not to say, I want to caution, that blackness or queerness is itself a painful experience. It's just to mark that the relation blackness and queerness have to the normative is through the already distanced abjection that folks like Julian desired. What if we dispensed with, discarded altogether, the normative ideal? What then would be an experience of the mystical?

I guess I'm just wondering aloud.

A

Dear Moth,

What I'm saying is we breathe, and in the fact of our breathing, we experience—not optimism per se but—the plural event of possibility as beyond exhaustion. We keep going. We fight for our lives here, now, because also there is a critique of the demands of linear time—another kind of violence of white supremacist capitalist patriarchy—that makes a demand on us. That's why CP Time is more than a joke for standup comics. It is a way to live.

And you're right, I don't mean even in *this* world but for various reasons: I think there are and always have been *worlds*, and that the white supremacist capitalist patriarchy is but one of many. One way it does violence is by a colonial process of attempting to exclude worlds, to produce itself as *the* world. I don't want to *rehearse the modern text's scientific imaging of The World as an ordered whole composed of separate parts relating through the mediation of constant units of measurement and/or a limiting violent force* as Denise Ferreira da Silva says.[8] I'm just riffing on Wynter, really: there is an overrepresentation of one genre, or kind, of world as *the only* world, and all other such worlds that are not normative in their constitution make those dwelling therein vulnerable to all kinds of violence.

So I'm totally uncomfortable with a kind of apocalypticism that seeks the destruction of *the* world because that—destroying the world, the earth—has been the project and crowning achievement of western epistemological force, of western imperial-colonial farce. That's why Jason Moore's work is so important, thinking the way capitalist production has always been the exploitation of the earth.[9] We have to figure out how to exist on the earth with a kind of buoyancy and delicateness, a way that honors the fact of our creatureliness as in relation to all that is. This lightness and vulnerability of being, this caring for the earth by inhabiting otherwise worlds—not as places but as modalities of existence—is what Black and indigenous and queer folks *beeeeeen* been doing. And this because we never submitted to the idea of a "*the* world" as a kind of individual thing, an only thing. (And in the case of indigeneity, I am heartened by the concept of refusal that Leanne Betasamosake Simpson talks about: refusal, for her, *is about refusing colonial domination, refusing heteropatriarchy, and refusing to be tamed by whiteness or the academy*; and she says that these refusals *center ourselves in generating the alternatives.*[10] I've learned a lot about refusal and think of it as also a blackqueer possibility enacted in worlds otherwise.) These worlds are tangled but the presumption of white supremacist capitalist patriarchy that there is only ever *the one world* makes me really think about Sylvia Wynter all over again, how she talks about the genre of the human, about Man and his overrepresentation. It seems to me to be the case that the concept of *the* world as the only one is a result of a kind of renunciation of the fleshliness of blackness, the renunciation of the plural event of vibration—the irreducible movement of things—in the service of the singular, in the service of *becoming-singular.*

The overrepresentation of Man is because this particular kind of human, this genre of human, is represented as the *only* way to be human and also the normative way to practice humanity. If one does not think, dress, eat, behave, relate to others in ways that this particular kind of raced, gendered, classed human does, one is not human at all according to this particular logic of what it means to be human and be Man. What is the normative race, gender, and class? In the sixteenth, seventeenth, and eighteenth centuries, it was (and still is today) white, landed gentry, which is to say, cisgender men that owned property, who claim whiteness *as* property.[11] This owning of property in the so-called New World would necessitate the violence of genocidal practices, called colonization, that is still ongoing. To be normative in terms of race, gender, and class was to *also* be normative in terms of religion, it was to *have* religion, it was to be Christian. In some ways, we might say that to be Man is to be one that wants to decide who is and is not human at all. And the one who decides what is and is not, what does and does not constitute, *the* world. It is to be the one to judge and establish value of objects. It is this version, this kind, this genre of human that Sylvia Wynter says is overrepresented.

Religion is an anthropological category because it is the study of the varieties of the human and the variance from Man, and the way it emerges in western thought is by making normative the genre of human that has been overrepresented, it has been the study and making normative the practice of the category Man; any creature that does not do what modern Man did and does would then be an aberration from the normative, a freak of nature, a necessarily exploitable resource that could also be discarded at a moment's notice. Religion as a category colluded with the making of modern Man and its overrepresentation. Anthropology is the ground from which the study of normative Man and his behaviors could be found in places like the university. Modern Man, the modern liberal subject position, is created by the relinquishing of otherwise as possible.

Otherwise possibility is not utopic—what is discovered in some otherwise possibility isn't necessarily desirous—but it *is* the elaboration of the fact that alternatives exist. And such alternatives are infinite in description, they are irreducible. This is why, for me, *there are worlds.* They are textured and tangible and sometimes ephemeral. And I keep going back over and over again to Foucault and what he says,

They have to invent, from A to Z, a relationship that is still formless, which is friendship: that is to say, the sum of everything through which they can give each other pleasure.[12]

and that,

What we must work on, it seems to me, is not so much to liberate our desires but to make ourselves infinitely more susceptible to pleasure . . .[13]

Both these are very important to me because susceptibility implies a kind of vulnerability, an openness, a belief in existence as radically undone, unhinged, unruly. And to be susceptible means a kind of porosity and that makes me think of air and breath and movements of inhalation and exhalation. One has to relax. Susceptibility and vulnerability together underscore the idea of existence as interstitial, as a circuit always waiting to be closed. This closure comes through friendship, which is another way to say sociality, another way to think vibration. The inventive impulse of friendship emerges from the fact that it is not institutionally informed or produced or protected. It's not like marriage where there are ceremonies and rituals that people perform in order to enter into it, it's not like marriage where there are institutions that give or withhold people's capacities for engaging the practice. Friendship is anti-institutional.

People entering into such a relation must be committed to figuring out what that mode of existence will be, how they will behave, what rules to establish by which to abide. Seems to me that friendship is one such thing we are constantly after as otherwise possibility, it is a mode of constituting otherwise ways of being in the world.

And I find this kind of plural possibility in Blackpentecostal performance without ever wanting to normalize this performance as a doctrine and theology toward which folks should aspire. I focus on practice because the practice doesn't belong—as private property—to the Blackpentecostals, though they do demonstrate what such practice has in terms of transformative potential, in terms of transformative critique of the idea of *the* world. It's the invention, from A to Z, of something formless in the service of liberating the flesh from its being put into strictures of thought. It's also about the capacity for pleasure and ecstasy, being beside oneself. It's also about liberation making oneself more susceptible, more vulnerable, more available to pleasure.

This, being open and vulnerable, is antithetical to western logics of the right way to be human, of modern Man, that presumes being enclosed and protected against vulnerability is the best way to be human. This is not just antithetical to how folks behave in general but also how the biological functions. Our central nervous system is open, nerve endings are discontinuous. This means that our sense experience of the world is through our openness to it, not our closure against it.

And then, Hortense Spillers talks about this:

[This writing] really started with my concern about the intramural, our relations within the community. That really has been the thrust of the discourse in Black life, what the community is doing in relation to a perceived mainstream or dominant force, and it's clear to me that we've not done enough work on internal or interior relations and so it occurred to me that there were reasons why we were avoiding the interior. One of them has to do with gender, and so I thought the way you put together some kind of protocol that you can pursue is to talk about it in psychoanalytic terms.[14]

So the intramural is the internal relation, the interior relation, the way Black folks are with one another. But the intramural as *possible* means that it could be imagined, it could be thought. If the intramural was and is possible from people that would be called Black, they would be called Black because they were open, were vulnerable, to the intramural, to this working together. They rejected what was an imposition—the violence of not being modern Man—and cultivated the rejection of that imposition as a way of life. They did not degrade the working together, the friendship that emerged, but they worked tirelessly against the occasion of the imposition itself. And the work against the imposition was *through* rejecting the imposition as an imposition. They refused to renounce the thing that was considered to be necessary.

It seems to me, the way to become Black—which is another way to say, the way to refuse the renunciation of the flesh that produces the modern liberal subject—is to make oneself vulnerable to the intramural, is to make oneself, in Foucault's language, *infinitely more susceptible* to the intramural, the inner life, the sociality of blackness. And it is to recognize there is no categorical distinction between the inner and outer life, that if there is a so-called outer life, it is suffused with the inner. And it is pleasurable. The trick of Cedric Robinson's elaboration of racial capitalism is to presume categorical distinction as possible and maintainable such that the possibility of abolishing racial hierarchies would be seen as a problem. But we must go *through* racialization to show its ruse.

They had to imagine that relation with others was possible and that cultivation of relationship with others was important. And after thinking, after imagining, materially producing such possibility. They had—not merely because of necessity and certainly not because of geneticism or biogenesis—a different episteme of operation, one that was not enclosed. They *imagined* memory, they *imagined* a people, they *imagined* possibility. The episteme of operation that produced the occasion for the indigenous land to be razed, for indigenous people to be killed, for Black people to be stolen was an episteme that shut down, that renounced, the capacity for imagination. But it did not succeed.

I've never been comfortable with Marxist accelerationist theories, that we should drive ourselves—resources, land, people—to the end of the world in order to realize some different, new, heretofore impossible reality. What would be done with what has been made, that continues to be made, otherwise? A kind of accelerationist thinking, an apocalypticism, seems like a conceit by thinking one knows what the destruction of the world would yield. It puts in the place the subject that knows, the modern liberal subject and the epistemology of its operation, as the one that necessitates such a drive, such a move, such a force toward death. This isn't me thinking that we must *reform* the state but me thinking against the concept of the state since the existence of such is predicated on the possibility of destroying the other for a colonialist expansionist project, since the state exists to produce exclusions and violences on peoples for its proliferation. The thing that's gotta be destroyed is the racialist fantasy of racial capitalism. This fantasy, this long history of racial capitalism, is an apocalyptic dream.

And I became uncomfortable with apocalypticism when I was at Open Door. Ideas of being raptured out of the world so we could worship in heaven while intense violence would be experienced on earth seemed vile to me, seemed to me to be the very antithesis of what incarnation supposedly teaches about god.

And the way I think about blackness is that it's really a way of life that is fleshly, incarnational, the renunciation of rapture, the digging down and into and dwelling with the fact of the funk, the fact of the flesh. Blackness is the non-spacetime to go, the non-spacetime to dwell, it is refuge against normative space and time. Life therein, life in blackness, desires the end of a world that considers itself as *the* and *the only* world. Life therein, life in blackness, is an opening up to and the flowering of the plurality of worlds, worlds already here, worlds that *beeeeeen* been here, worlds to come. It is a kind of particle physics experimentation wherein blackness hails us from beyond spacetime to become now what we will have already been, to become now what we will be, to be now what we are in some kind of futural orientation. Blackness is nothing from normative space and time, from normative epistemologies of operation that consider the possibility for and aspiration toward *the* and *the only* world.

And I think about wanting to be nothing because of the music in the church, because the Hammond organist is a theorizer, is a thinker, that wants to be made instrument. To empty oneself out in the service of the congregation, to empty oneself in the cause of becoming entangled with machines and technologies, this is a sort of becoming nothing that is all about elaborating the question—what does it mean to live and breathe and be nothing, and to celebrate such a concept because of a general misunderstanding of what nothing can contain? The answer is in the music, in the sound, in the breath, against the individual subject, against the fashioning of an enclosed self. It's in the clearing. There are worlds in nothing music, in the chording and padding and soft music of the Hammond organist. Listen.

I know I talked to you about him before but I keep coming back to the fact that Brother Steadfast ended his testimony at F. W. McGee's "Testifyin' Meeting" saying that he wants the saints to pray that he'd *be used as an instrument in his hand*,[15] and there's something really lovely and kind and gentle about this desire, to ask others to pray for such a desire. To be made instrument, to be made implement, to be made that which hollows oneself out in order to be filled and to be hollowed out again and again, as in breath, as in spirit, as in *ruach*, as in Black *pneuma*. To be made instrument is to be made available for use, to be made instrument is to be made implement, to be made chamber, to be made something like a through line, a connection, a point of departure and a point of convergence. To be made instrument is to be made connection, to be a meeting place, to be the clearing, to carry it in your being, to become plural or, again and again I keep saying, to recognize and accept and to dig back into the fact of plurality and meeting and gathering and clearing as the *grounds of existence*. To be made instrument is to audiovisually, choreosonically announce the renunciation of the thought-theological, thought-philosophical that would have us relinquish the fact of the flesh. Brother Steadfast wanted to be made into that which he already was, wanted to be made into that which western theology and philosophy would have us renounce.

And I.

I want to be an instrument.

For you, with you, in you.

If only.

   A

shouting³

Dear Moth,

I was driving and the random shuffle played Steve Reich's *Music for 18 Musicians* (the Nonesuch recording),[1] Movement XI, and it was the first time I heard it in a long time and it was so moving—the cello especially, when the sound comes in and how it sorta gives the movement grounding—that I listened to the entire album as if for the first time. And I've gotta say, playing the entire thing and *arriving* at Movement XI made me tear up in the car. (It was a particularly long drive.)

The entire song is about movement, about incremental change and difference, so you end up wondering how you get from the first Pulses to the last Pulses. Between here and there, between now and then, was a world, were worlds, of sonic possibility. It could have been otherwise. It's as if I slipped into a crack the size of a neutrino but, I kept falling in, I experienced expanse as the mysterious beyond of spacetime, a beyond that is not predicated on but fundamentally an alternative to Newtonian physics and the conceptual linearity of time, the conceptual smoothness of space. The piece is based on an eleven-chord cycle and each movement is a reworking of the rhythmic pulse and harmonics of this eleven-chord cycle. Limiting himself to this constraint, Reich and his ensemble produce worlds of sonic inhabitation that vibrate out and produce feeling. Limit, Nahum Chandler would say, was also possibility, impossible for it *not* to be possibility.[2]

I felt finally prepared to hear what was in Reich because I'd been thinking and talking and, really, *feeling* Blackpentecostal music so much more. Even when it doesn't emerge from Blackpentecostal churches. Like a performance of Mt. Do-Well Baptist Church and their singing of "He Set Me Free" a friend sent me from YouTube.[3]

Listen to the way the song incrementally increases in intensity and density and space, increases in tempo and velocity and haste. It moves. It's moving. But there never is a moment when it is decided that some *now* is the moment to increase in any of those things, it just happens, it just builds, it constructs itself by drawing to itself feeling. And this construction is released through a collective practice and process, they feel their way into the moment-by-moment change. It moves while it's moving, it's moving while it moves. Being held in the caress and embrace of their choreosonic, centrifugitive sounding out, their singing. It feels so good.

It's like what Mackey says about dreams, how one doesn't really know how one moves from scene to scene, one just ends up in the middle of them, sorta abruptly in the middle of two scenes at once.[4]

The two scenes are really, then, a doubling. And if double, always more than double, if doubled then a continuous unfolding of plurality. The abruptness in "He Set Me Free" is measured by how the one man stands and stomps, by how the one woman stands and claps and spins and sits—all in one sorta fluid nondivisional mood and movement—by how the other woman sorta wiggles her arms in the seat and such wiggling that seems to emerge from her arms ends up moving through and quickening all her flesh until she stands and enters into an almost choreographic battle with the other man. It, they—these abrupt moments—weren't planned but happened, weren't planned but announced an entanglement in the congregation. A different kind of shouting.

Abrupt changes through incrementalism when division between is imperceptible but happens. That's how it feels listening to Steve Reich or to Mt. Do-Well. It's a mysticism, a Black mysticism, a mysticism that requires the renunciation of the one in favor of becoming plural. Or, not really becoming but acknowledging the plurality that is the grounds of existence. Music, Reich announces, is for *eighteen* musicians, the singing at Mt. Do-Well is a collective, improvisational project. They retreat into rather than away from the social, into rather than away from the dense folds of secreted sound. It seems like an incessant, restive, ongoing refusal to be alone such that the categorical distinction between alone and lonely evaporates away. They have a feel for this thing . . .

And I've been thinking lately that trying to argue about doctrine and theology is important but the Black church is so much about feeling. How is it that a place like Mt. Do-Well can have all this good feeling but can also be a place from which emerges sexism and homophobia? And what Moya Bailey and Trudy talk about as misogynoir even?[5] How can a place that feels good also be a place that hurts our feelings? And I think we gotta talk about hurt feelings in clear and precise ways.

Doctrine and theology mark a certain epistemology but it seems blackness is one of feeling, not against thought, but feeling *as* thought. This is not an antiintellectual argument. I keep thinking about this quote from the introduction to *Sister Outsider*:

The white western patriarchal ordering of things requires that we believe there is an inherent conflict between what we feel and what we think—between poetry and theory. We are easier to control when one part of our selves is split from another, fragmented, off balance. There are other configurations, however, other ways of experiencing the world, though they are often difficult to name. We can sense them and seek their articulation.[6]

Listening to them sing, I want to stand and shout too. I want to let go, release, be free. I *feel* them, what they feel, feel it in me. But I also have a sort of anxiety about church because I also feel hella blackqueer and different and dissident and distant from the doctrines and theologies of my upbringing and, because of this, church makes me feel hella excluded. It makes me feel all kinds of things, in other words. Heartbreaking in the most robust sense. Broken open that allows for feeling and sensing and mood but also broken through melancholy and mourning a now relinquished life. And feeling lonely, feeling alone, wanting connection, feeling hurt because of the inequity produced in a place and a sound that feels so good and inviting and invitational and warm: these complex and often contradictory feelings are all about ways of existence that let feeling flourish as the grounds for experience. And being between, slipping into a crack the size of a neutrino and experiencing worlds of affective encounter is, also, about the unfolding of feeling, the flourishing of mood. Can Black Study do this sorta thing?

A

Dear Moth,

Yes, I want to know if Black Study can do this. I'm not asking if this music, this sound, this feel of withdrawal into the world, can be *studied* in terms of sociology, ethnography, religious comportment, class, racial configurations, musicology, in theology and philosophy. I'm not talking about looking at gesture and behavior, though those things are important, yes. That has been done, of course, many times over and again. The question that looms for me is this :: can—and what would be such consequence of this doing—Black Study open itself up to becoming this object that is studied in its very studying and pondering of this social field?

What would a Black Study look like that gains in momentum and pace, as they sing in Mt. Do-Well, the more and more and more one delves into the repetition of the phrase "set me free"? What would a Black Study do if it opened itself up to being so moved by its very inhabitation of the critical space of study that it cannot contain itself to propriety—sorta like what the dude does at 2′54″ when he stands and stomps three times because it got to be too good to him; or sorta like what the woman does at 4′44″ when she leaps from her seat, claps three times, and speaks the words a bit behind and before the beat? Could Black Study cry? Could it weep? Could it laugh? Can it shout? Can it produce and be produced by the choreosonic, centrifugitive force of blackness? That to ask, could it be, and does it need to be, fleshly? Does it need to be fleshly and animated by spirit? What would that even mean? How would that be realizable?

I found the notes Reich produced about m18m. One thing he says struck out at me sorta hard.

There is more harmonic movement in the first 5 minutes of *Music for 18 Musicians* than in any other complete work of mine to date. Though the movement from chord to chord is often just a re-voicing, inversion or relative minor or major of a previous chord, usually staying within the key signature of three shapes at all times, nevertheless, within these limits harmonic movement plays a more important role in this piece than in any other I have written.[7]

It's as if he were working with blackness. You know when we talked on the phone last I said to you that it sounds like what an African dance would be if it were a harmonic *and* rhythmic thing, if the polyrhythms were something like a way to sound out harmonically, melodically. And then I learned, from the research about the piece, that he used the voices of women to get at something of the breathiness of life. That breathiness is a kind of shout because it is both choreographic and sonic, it is choreosonic, it is movement and sound together. But the blackness? The blackness is in the constraint, in the way constraint becomes the occasion, literally for me at least, for tears, how restraint is the processual possibility for unfolding. Unfolding and, I'm discovering now because I keep reading about mysticism, *enfolding* too. But wait, he said more.

Rhythmically, there are two basically different kinds of time occurring simultaneously in *Music for 18 Musicians*. The first is that of a regular rhythmic pulse in the pianos and mallet instruments that continues throughout the piece. The second is the rhythm of the human breath in the voices and wind instruments. The entire opening and closing sections plus part of all sections in between contain pulses by the voice and winds. They take a full breath and sing or play pulses of particular notes for as long as their breath will comfortably sustain them. The breath is the measure of the duration of their pulsing. This combination of one breath after another gradually washing up like waves against the constant rhythm of the pianos and mallet instruments is something I have not heard before and would like to investigate further.

The structure of *Music for 18 Musicians* is based on a cycle of eleven chords played at the very beginning of the piece and repeated at the end. All the instruments and voices play or sing the pulsating notes with each chord. Instruments like the strings which do not have to breathe nevertheless follow the rise and fall of the breath by following the breathing patterns of the bass clarinet. Each chord is held for the duration of two breaths, and the next chord is gradually introduced, and so on, until all eleven are played and the ensemble returns to the first chord. The first pulsing chord is then maintained by two pianos and two marimbas. While this pulsing chord is held for about five minutes a small piece is constructed on it. When this piece is completed there is a sudden change to the second chord, and a second small piece or section is constructed. This means that each chord that might have taken fifteen or twenty seconds to play in the opening section is then stretched out as the basic pulsing melody for a five minute piece very much as a single note in a cantus firmus, or chant melody of a 12th century Organum by Perotin might be stretched out for several minutes as the harmonic centre for a section of the Organum. The opening eleven chord cycle of *Music for 18 Musicians* is a kind of pulsing cantus for the entire piece.[8]

Listen, again, to Movement XI. It sounds like there's a question and there's an answer, repetitious, compelling, daring. Movement. Movement. Movement. The entire performance is like an apophatic prayer, the saying and unsaying and saying and unsaying all in the service of deep and abiding and impossible connection. It stirs me, hard. I still am about to cry yet again. And I think it's because of the breath, because breath means life means vitality means transfer means performance means blackness. All this movement built alongside and next to and within the sound, it's a kind of choreographic movement through an eleven-chord constraint. And the breath, the breathing, the use of the cello, the cycles of the eleven chords, this all makes me want to praise, I want to shout, I want to dance as if I were in church.

Blackness is the making of tradition in constraint, small and elongated breaths, like Harriet Jacobs in the loophole of retreat.[9] Shallow but still breathing but still living. This, the *but* in the declaration *but still breathing but still living* should not be considered to be insouciant or glib or a theory and abstraction of superficiality. It's the fact of her breath, the fact of the *but still breathing but still living* that made possible her testimony. It is not an acceptance of the conditions of inequity and violence, an acceptance of systems of domination that produce violence. The scene could not fully contain her, she exceeded its possibility each and every breath she took. Each breath she took is praiseworthy, leads me to a kind of worshipful posture. And the kind of praise I want needs breath, it's the shout, the dance, the choreosonic, centrifugitive movement. Jacobs stretched the possible in order to enact care and concern, in order to produce fugitive flight and escape. Cramped space became an occasion for expansive imagination. Not a sort of colonizing expansion but a movement inward, a movement into the exterior, she made herself plural—or, really and again, accepted the fact of plurality as that from which life and breath and shouting emerges—like the music.

And to learn that Reich thought, in 1973 before he began composing the piece such that this was definitely on his mind when he did, that "non-Western music is presently the single most important source of new ideas for Western composers and musicians," and, thus, his interest in African drumming in Ghana and his study of Gamelan music from Bali. Morrison was always right but we can radicalize through extending her.[10] There is an Africanist presence of western thought itself, a presence some would acknowledge, others leave dormant in shadows, others merely exploit as raw material. But the western intellectual tradition, it seems to me, is the elaboration of a fundamental aversion to the very darkness, blackness, that makes it possible. It is a practice of renunciation of darkness, blackness, the social.

Reich's creativity through constraint is a minimalism, a minimalism that is incredibly capacious and expansive and incredibly full to the point of overflow and excess. It's a different kind of scale and modality, a different kind of axis around which this sorta meditative sounding out spins, a non-centered, anti-centered movement. It's a kind of minimalism that reminds me of Baldwin,

There is always a beat beneath the beat, another music beneath the
music, and beyond.[11]

Is there a chance of getting at the thing beneath, the thing underneath, the thing beyond? And this is another way to ask about the unfolding of possibility, of joy, of gods and the human, of love as ceaseless pulse and noise. What the beat, what the music, reveal are the things that remain, the things that exceed capture by the thing called beat, the thing called music. And I wonder if, too, if the thing called love, the thing called god, are the remains of that which exceeds capture similarly, of that which exceeds capture likewise?

Asking questions ever still,

A

Dear Moth,

I get it now. *Music for 18 Musicians* is a sermon, a preached word. My Blackpentecostal heritage would say it's a *rhema* word, on time, appropriate to the moment, contextual, full of feeling. I get the sermonic feel for the piece, for the song, by the way it moves, by the way it grows then decreases in intensity, how it sorta tarries in seeming stillness only to explode into a sorta praise, a sorta shout after a whoop, explodes into a dance and then a sorta quietude, a nothing music that's there but almost sparse, almost bare.

It's most pronounced in Movement IX, Movement X, and Movement XI.

Listen to them, against this: For Movement IX, I think about the end of Bishop Iona Locke preaching "Let's Get It On," her whooping.[12] For Movement X, I think about Twinkie on the Hammond, her playing shout music at the end of "Accept What God Allows."[13] And for Movement XI, I think of the soft-chording Bishop Keith Darnell Goudy-Johnson (RIP) after playing a song to open up the service.[14] It's abandonment heard in Movement XI. It didn't hit me until I heard this praise break, how the organ comes in at 1'45",[15] how that movement on the organ is the meeting of loud with soft, of intensity and force with softness and vulnerability. And all this happens after Movement VIII, the lushness, the softness, the quietude, sounding out almost like a lullaby. There is a gentleness that infuses Movement VIII, reminds me of nothing music before the church service begins, or during the offering, or while someone is just talking.

I listened to all these movements again yesterday and began to cry. And it made me think about being held and abandoned. I began to wonder if there is a link between legitimate fear of being left abandoned on the one hand and having had an experience of intensity and openness—to and by spirit, to and by love—left undone, unsettled, vulnerable on the other. Similar to the move from Movement X to XI, I was literally moved to tears listening to this particular praise break, the space of sonic transition at around 2'10", from the minor, augmented, and suspended chording of the organist, loud and raucous, to soft padding, the nothing music, the lingering in and over chords, soft transitioning and the hearing of tongues. I cried a lot . . . and I don't cry often. There was something of the sound in transition, something of the organ, that recalled history and memory that is quite personal for me. But I was not led away alone: the transition from high to low, from loud to soft, carried me, held me without allowing my withering away.

I think about aversion, first and foremost, because I am a product of its edge and an insistent need to refuse it. When I went to seminary and said to a friend that I "wouldn't think about Pentecostalism anymore," it was particularly in response to hurt and melancholy I felt produced in that space. Repudiation of certain homophobic, transphobic, sexist theology turned into aversion for the entire space itself. But such an aversion would also be a turn inward too, a sorta asceticism in order to produce a stable and coherent self that would not be vulnerable and open to being moved by the sound, by the music, by the sociality of blackness. I sought escape. But listening to this music, to these sounds, I had a choice :: either to regulate myself as a means of protecting the borders of my individuality, my desire for a particular kind of academic subject, or I could yield to what I felt and let it move through me, my body, make me cry, throw my hands up, shout.

So my attempts at theorizing aversion are kindasorta really trying to figure out how one can engage particular modes of social life, not discounting or dismissing that which is problematic, but not going so far as to claim that there is nothing there otherwise than value, worth. And because I have been attempting to theorize aversion and how it operates, manifests, in (and as) Black literary studies and cultural theory, these sounds and songs make me think about Edmund Burke's valorization of and recoil from—which is to say, aversion for— noisiness and enfleshment:[16] so maybe a literary and studies tradition itself is animated by a social field of (things like) Blackpentecostalism that it knows is there but cannot think this field without it thinking (theorizing, judging, undoing) us, a social field we cannot claim without it making a counterclaim on us.

I'm not trying to make everything Blackpentecostal either. I guess I'm just noticing the relations between, the relays, the resonance that Blackpentecostal force has with all kinds of ideas and ways of life and performances. And by resonance, I mean the way Blackpentecostalism is evoked or suggested in decidedly non-Blackpentecostal spaces and places and practices. Such that the idea that Blackpentecostalism could be evoked or suggested means that it is a force, a kind of quality, that perhaps western logics have attempted to train us out of, have attempted to have us renounce in order to be considered a good and proper human.

Blackpentecostalism is the abandonment, the reckless abandon, of the idea of the stable and coherent logic of the individual subject, abandonment and recklessness as having priority, as that which comes before western logics of the human, of modern Man, of the coloniality of being. And in such an abandonment, one is carried with and along and on the flows of the sociality of blackness, the radical abundance of excess and overflow and outpour and the unfolding of plentitude. It's a kind of plentitude heard in the transition Reich's ensemble makes from Movement VIII to IX to X to XI, from the luxuriant and soft to the raucous and loud and frazzled and, maybe W. E. B. Du Bois would call, the frenzied, to a sorta warmth and vibrational stillness and gentleness and air. And air. And air. It, Movement XI after all that piano clanging and banging, sounds like air.

But, what do you think?

A

Dear Moth,

It's been some time, I know. It took me a while but I was looking over things I'd written in my sent box and figured I should tell you that I started painting—or really, attempting to make art—again.

Remember when I showed you the paintings I'd make when I was just a kid, maybe twelve or thirteen years old when I had dreams of becoming the Black Bob Ross, afro and all? And remember how I told you my father had a couple of the paintings in his office when I was young and you said that you wanted them too? I really just thought you were being kind, and him too really, to offer such a thing. I don't think much of what I painted then but I'm back into it now.

I still remember it being so sweet to want to bring them home with you so that you could, you'd said, constantly be reminded that I was someone's child, that I belonged to my parents, that I was at one time in a high chair needing to be fed, and struggling on floors attempting to tie shoes, and a child who cried a lot. It was this toddler that'd become a child that attempted to paint, to make a world he'd never seen except on *The Joy of Painting.* You said, then, that the paintings reminded you of the fact that we all come from some place, that we all have dreams and ideas and goals, even when we are young, even when they don't necessarily turn out the way we thought. And I definitely could not have anticipated the life I have now then . . .

Anyway, I started this art-making process, though it's not good at all; been recording the entire process, actually, with my computer and sometimes my phone. I've been using my apartment, getting paint all over the place, but it makes me feel alive, to get all this color on the walls and on the floor and have to scrub myself with various kinds of soap to remove oil paint and acrylic ink and watercolors. It's been fun.

Explorations in color and movement, they're abstract. But when I told my friend Sofia about the process and showed her some of the work and said it's not about landscapes, she disagreed:

i don't agree i think your painting is totally about landscapes! yes it's abstract but it's all about space and moving through space and so it IS about landscape, just it's not about the property owner's gaze and observing the landscape within the laws of perspective, ok, it's absolutely not about the western tradition of landscape painting, but it is still about landscape because it's about inhabiting a space—the space of your apartment where you paint—it's landscape painting from the inside. this makes me think about marronage and the relationship to land. not looking at landscape as "what can i do with this land i own" but rather "can i shelter there, can i get in there, can i stay there for a while."

She got what I was attempting to do so I wanted to share with you. It's the first time I've attempted this since I was a kid, so it's been an interesting process. But Sofia was so precise to name it, that I'm attempting a way to shelter, to find refuge, in the practice, to escape into the social world I left behind as it left *me* excluded.

I was inspired by this one video Desiree sent me of a little girl making art in her home. She was covered in paint, had it all over this large room—splattered on her dress and tights, in her hair, on the floor and walls. It was mosaic. Her parents must have all kinds of financial resources because one of the reasons I stopped painting as a kid was because it was too expensive. It's one thing to buy a ten-color kit of paint and a couple of brushes. It's another thing altogether to run through that in less than two weeks and ask your parents to buy more. And more. And more. It was too much, I had to slow down, had to try a different creative outlet. And I think about Alice Walker, searching for gardens, and wonder what kind of art practice folks have created without access to tools and materials, but also what was squandered because they couldn't get them.

Anyway, the comments on YouTube were full of people saying things like *my kid could do that too!* or *this isn't really art! she's a child!* which is just sad. I was moved by her intentionality. And sure, she's a child, but aren't we all? And sure, she's young but does that mean she can't make choices about color and placement and mood? So much of what happens in the normative world is because of the idea that only certain people have the mental capacity to think and conceive of the beautiful, that only certain people have the mental capacity to think and conceive of aesthetic choice. Or that the *beautiful* is even a thing that we can attain, aspire toward, be. It all needs to be interrogated. My nephew hates peas and pineapple and milk, he refuses to eat or drink those things and the very sight of them makes him have a fit. And yeah, he's only five, but he knows what he likes—broccoli, for example—and what he doesn't. He makes choices all of the time. So why can't this little girl?

Desiree sent the video not hours after I'd been sitting in my office, having another one of those moments of deep nostalgia, crying while listening to "praise breaks" I found on YouTube yet again. Something in the music, in the clapping and stomping and in the shouts and orations, something in those sounds made me sit weakened, almost no energy, so the tears just flowed. So I was already vulnerable, already open. Then she sent me a video of a little girl making art and it was in the middle of that video when she had all this blue paint on her hands and she was bent over and began to clap them, lightly, and blue splattered all over the canvas spread on the floor.[17]

I don't know if I can convey how much that very simple, nuanced, barely there movement hit me with so much force, but it did. It felt like the heavens opened and I heard the cello bass notes and a choir of breathy sopranos and altos singing, like Movement VIII of M18M all over again. I was stunned but also deeply moved. Clapping. Who knew it could make something alongside and otherwise than sound? I wanted to run around the apartment as if I were in church—I definitely was getting happy, as the saints would say—but, instead, I hopped on the computer and began ordering paint, brushes, canvases, paper. I had the inkling of an idea and needed to get moving as quickly as possible. The supplies I ordered arrived a couple of days later. Bottles of blue, purple, green, yellow, and red acrylic paint, muted colors, inks and oil paint too, old socks I never wear anymore and my laptop in hand, I placed the canvas on the floor, plugged up the laptop and began to play all these testimony service songs and shouting music.

Then I stopped. It was moving too quickly. I needed to see something first, needed to start with something much less drastic, much less involved. So I experimented. Like the little girl, I wanted to see what it would look like to clap

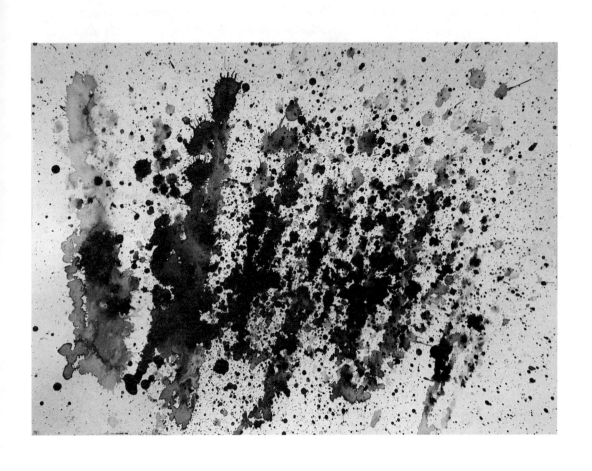

my hands with paint on them, to see what the paint would do when it fell on the surface.

I took a big brush, dipped it in water and whipped the brush over the paper and let the water fly over the surface at random intervals. I wanted the water to approach something like the creation of its own path. What I was really after was to think the fleshliness of the practice of clapping, how it—in Blackpentecostal praise, at least—can get sweaty, how the flesh heats and attempts to cool itself. So the random arrays of water lines and passages allowed me to think about and approach something like the wetness and moisture of sweat. I then took muted green and Black acrylic ink, poured it in my hands, and began to clap lightly. I wanted to see what the color would do once it found its meeting with the water. I wanted the paint to be carried in the air to the water. And it made all these patterns and splotches. Seeing the splotches, the black and green and how it sorta fades out toward the edges, how the color becomes less opaque and more transparent toward the corners, how color deepens in the foreground, I took the next couple of days to make several handclapping pieces.

Paint got all over the place, not just on the paper, as you can see, but also on the walls, on the wooden floor, on my gray kitchen cabinets, on the refrigerator. It was a lovely, delightful mess; I couldn't be happier. Eventually, I felt prepared to challenge myself with shouting. My wood floors just had to adjust to being messy because there was no way around making everything soiled with paint color. With the first two shouting experiments, I dipped one foot in red paint, another in blue and began to shout on the surface after wetting the surface with water like I did with the hand clapping experiment. I almost slipped, almost— my mother would've said if I were a kid—*broke my neck*. The slipperiness of the wet surface with the slipperiness of the paint on my feet made me slip quickly. But I got my bearings and began to shout, kinda delicately, kinda politely, I just wanted to see what'd happen with the color. I was too cognizant of the whole ordeal, so wrapped up mentally in it, couldn't release myself into a full praise because the music was too low and I was too self-conscious.

I took a couple of days off. In that time, I created a playlist of songs that would allow me to clap my hands, stomp my feet and shout rather quickly, up-tempo songs that would make me break a sweat if I were really into it. Keep in mind that I haven't seriously done this in a long while so it took a minute

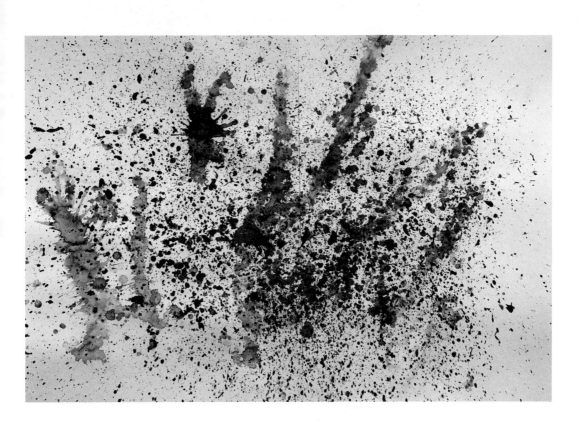

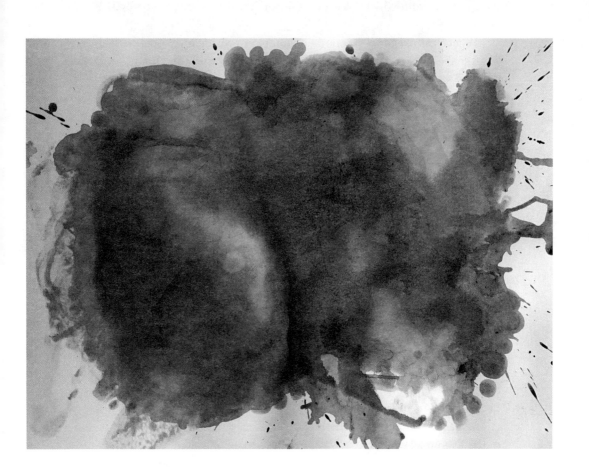

to get my de-composure; that is, I was way too serious—instead of playful and jubilant—about it at first. I was too conscious of not wanting to look or feel or be silly. But I also didn't want for what I was doing to not be sacred, to not honor the tradition from which I learned this kinda choreosonic, centrifugitive way of life.

When I returned to do another shouting experiment, as luck would have it, after the 4′08″ rendition of "There's a Storm Out on the Ocean"—a rather mildly paced "fast" song; nothing too strenuous—some shout music that I'd downloaded from YouTube came on. A church in Baltimore, a clip of Bishop Robert Evans talking about "dancing in one spot," and it really made me think about the sorta refusal of tightness-as-constraint in the Black Radical Tradition, a kinda mysticism of movement that takes constraint as impure possibility, constraint as occasion, constraint as expanse.[18]

In the clip, voices of small yelps and hollers with the pronounced sound of the Hammond and the drums let me imagine kids laughing and jumping up and down because their mothers were shouting and not paying much attention to them, where the men would say *hooooo* loudly. He talked about storefront churches as places where praise happened but because of the tight compression of flesh in not-large spaces, people had to find a spot on the rug or the wooden floor and just go at it. Dancing in one spot is a kind of expansion of compression through praise, through the movement of the flesh.

So I poured paint on the canvas-floor and began to dance, began to shout, as if I were in church with them; eyes were closed now, mouth was frowned now, lips were flattened out now; I was moving to the rhythm *one-two-three-dip, one-two-three-dip*. It was the loudness that allowed me to get lost in the sound, in their posture and posing.

It was the loudness of the music that broke me out of my thinking-too-much-about-it just momentarily enough to open out into something else. I kinda put my head down, smiled to myself. But after I smiled, I closed my eyes and listened to the people praising, to the drums, to the B-3 creating sonic distance between the bass and the use of the notes in the highest register, all drawbars pulled out. And then it happened. Some some*thing* happened. And when things got too sticky, I got more paint and poured it in a tray, stepped in it, then recommenced shouting.

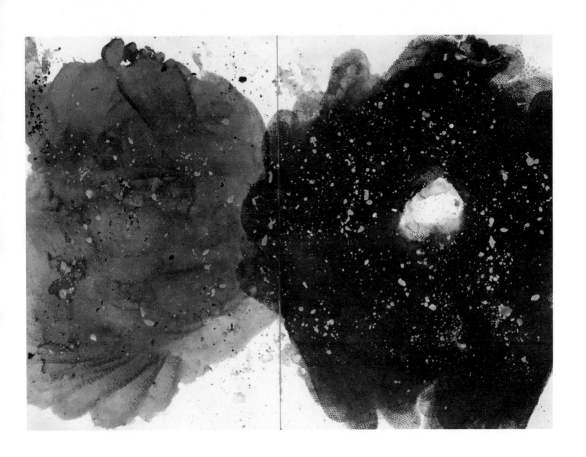

After I opened my eyes, I saw blues, reds, and the breakthrough of purples in various intensities, depending upon how hard and where I danced, how much I mixed and, quite literally, scratched the canvas with old-new colors. I opened my eyes, tired and sweaty, feeling as if I'd touched some otherwise, as if I'd worshipped even while maintaining disbelief as to why—and what—people often say they worship in the first place. I discovered something in the movement itself, something that could not be contained by a confessional faith, something that is not merely transcendent but that is, most fundamentally, constitutive. Upon opening my eyes, the canvas had a few splotches of color here and there, a few strings of paint every now and then.

But it was still far too empty. One person simply can't do the kind of spiritual-material thing alone. (And I use the word *thing* here intentionally; it's etymology, meaning *the place of gathering to discuss matters of concern*—though I'm sure "discuss" could also easily index a desire to work out, a desire to perform, a desire to think—is important to what I'm envisioning for the soon to come.) So though I've been practicing by myself a lot lately—with all sorts of paint—I'm hoping to invite others to play along, to re-create a church service where the residue of such sociality will be the colors we leave behind.

Residue. That's the word for it. A kind of remainder, an excess that cannot be explained. Or explained away. Residue kinda names an excess that is experienced or gained at the moment when the mode of shouting and clapping is sorta *unconscious*, maybe *aconscious*. Weird thing is, if consciousness were all just a thing our brains manufactured and it was experienced differently for each of us, if our realities were all a dream that was ephemeral and would wither away at a moment's notice, that still would not answer the question of why it exists, how it came to be. What would ephemera or a dream mean in such a case? If it were manufactured, we still wouldn't understand the sensations created. If a dream, why we have it.

If we had "scientific" explanations for life, that still would not explain why it is we feel love and joy and heartache and sadness. What, to explanation, is happiness experienced, butterflies endured, elation given and withheld as so many breaths? Even if we could explain all, we would not know what it means. There is something in the gift of life that exceeds the enclosures of logic, of science, of explanation, of analytics. And that—that excess, that residue—is a gift.

It is a gift that doesn't seek to explain as much as it seeks to experience, it's not so much about the product—though I do hope the series created, the series waiting to be created—will be considered beautiful and moving. The fundamental force of it is the experience, the movement, the verve, the fact that it happened, it happens, it will happen.

I've said all that to say: the little girl quickened in me the notion that even clapping, even shouting—any movement, or hairsbreadth nuance of breathing, of dilation—contains within it the *potentia* for the thing we call art. Such movement simply needs the work energy to convert. Her clapped hands with blue made me want to see what it would look like, what the sorta Blackpentecostal praise I love would splatter on the ground and upon walls; I wanted to *see* what praise looks like after the flesh—the material force of such creation—left the building, after flesh escaped. Would I be able to look at the canvases and papers or whatever other surfaces chosen and see something of such gathering, of such moving of spirit, by spirit, for spirit? I chuckle a bit after I am done with the experiments because it brings me a kind of unconscious, *a*conscious joy, but I'm also becoming much more adept with color mixture and I'm getting my good breathing back too, which means I've convinced myself that there might be something to this experimentation, in color, in song, after all.

Let me know what you think.

A

Dear Moth,

I bought a tambourine. I wanted to add to the percussiveness of the handclaps, wanted to add to the visual noise of Blackpentecostal dance, play, force. So I bought a tambourine and tried it out. The first thing I did when I pulled it out the box was begin to lightly beat it on my left hand—into a fist balled up—sorta held my breath a bit, created a kinda up-tempo rhythm and pat my foot too. The thing I'd forgotten about tambourines is how loud they are. And you know my apartment has these high ceilings, so it was very, very, very loud.

As with the first experiments, I poured paint on the surface of the tambourine and began to beat it to the rhythm of various songs and sounds. It included shouting music—more praise breaks I found on YouTube but also Movement VIII of *Music for 18 Musicians* and even a bit of *Become Ocean*; they're all meditative in various kinds of ways. And let the paint splatter. I'd go from hand clapping to tambourine beating and back again. One thing I realized, after having not done this in the context of church, is how much praise requires of the flesh in its varied manifestations.

It's been good to do this, to experience this, to think my relation to praise and worship differently than the sounds and grounds of my spiritual emergence. It's been a process of profanation, of, riffing on and off Agamben, restoring the *anaesthetic* practices of Blackpentecostalism to their common use.[19]

That's what the visuality of the sound is about, it's an attempt to think the broad implications of the sonic made manifest—made flesh—in the color through how they emerge in their particularities. It's also to think the audio and visual together, to make apparent the fact of the movement of air and space displacement through paint, through the line of flight any particular drop of paint takes before it reaches its destination. This is the choreosonic, the ongoing vibration of the refused categorical distinction between choreography and sonicity. My friend Emma said it best, that it's about "the way this one calls attention to what the instrument does as an instrument between flesh and trace." In some sense, the air—the breath; the Black *pneuma* because it is freed from restriction, because it is fleshly and celebratory—*carried* the color to whatever surface destina-

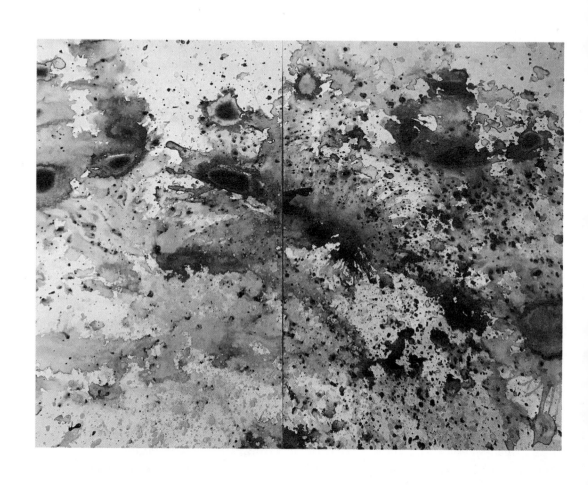

tion to which it arrived. The air, the Blackpentecostal breath, carries, it holds, it embraces color for its eventual delivery. And I'm thinking about this passage:

The mass movement is taking place every day in town, we're here, all caught up in it. So it's not like now, when one would have to sit down and make a conscious decision to say, "I'm going to do this." Rather, you were carried by a movement something like that in America in the sixties, the Black and other movements which had begun earlier with the bus boycotts, in Montgomery, Alabama.[20]

Sylvia Wynter offered that about her time in Jamaica in the forties, how one was not necessarily intentionally a part of movement but was carried by its currents. I think of Blackpentecostal performance practice like that, the noise and the joy, the fervor and fury, somehow it carries those near it, in it, and it spreads. I wanted, and still want, the practice of artmaking to match in intensity and force this kinda desire for, this movement of, being *carried*. I think so much of what's wrong with the misrepresentation of the Black Radical Tradition these days is because of a fear of being carried. Because, let's be honest, one can be carried and carried away.

But the Blackpentecostal church services I miss are the ones driven by joy, the kind when walking in the service, you say "I love this kinda carrying on . . . ," the noise, the praise, the exuberance. It's an exuberance that isn't embarrassed about the noise, the fleshliness, the excess. We called that kinda carrying on "getting happy" and it's just such a simple but wonderful concept, that one can get happy, seize hold of it, because they *give* or outpour or release praise. It's not a seizing or holding that is about a claim for private property but a seizing and holding that only is when it is relinquished, released. And so one must open oneself up to being carried, carried away, carried away to get happy in the way Wynter describes it. This is what I want the artmaking to invoke, to convoke.

And it makes me miss things, miss church, miss the sociality of it all. Maybe things entangle that we cannot yet detect. Maybe entanglement announces relation that is not yet fully grasped or comprehended because it is a kind of relation that goes and runs against the limits of knowledge, or a western way of thinking relation.

To miss the one you do not know but feel. Entanglement. The fact of unbroken claim to connection that cannot be detected by normative sense experience, entanglement announcing relation that cannot be fully comprehended or grasped. Though not comprehended, ungraspable by the finite senses already discovered, relation still is no less real. It happened, it happens, it will happen. Searching for something, reaching for something, like what N says of the falsetto voice, to critique the insidious falseness of the normative world, seeking new words, new worlds.[21] But not new, otherwise. I guess what I mean to say is, the spiritual does not belong to and is not the private property of the things we call the religious and there are epistemologies that do not assume such, especially given the fact of religion being constituted as a modern way to think, and think against, relation.

The spiritual has been sequestered to the religious because of the modern epistemological desire for categorical distinction and coherence, a desire for enclosure against spilling and spillage, another way to say excess and vulnerability and openness as a way of life. And so I feel a spiritual connection to these various things but I need not be a believer in a religious tradition in order to have such a connection. It's like the momentary key change the Hammond organist does when following along a singer that is performing an arrhythmic song and just talking, the kinda key change that causes the saints to go *whooooo* and scream and throw up their hands without being conscious of it, it's the accessing of another reality, a Black dimensionality, otherwise possibility. Black dimensionality opening up to that which has been sequestered.

That's what I've been attempting to discover in this practice, in these performances: how to release the spiritual from its being sequestered into the zone of the religious while taking account of and never degrading the spiritual or the religious which has carried—as air—the content of the practice with such intensity, with such precision, with such love. Maybe the spiritual needs to be released from having been sequestered in the zone of the religious. Maybe that's love. Maybe that's desire. Maybe that's entanglement.

Maybe worship,

A

Dear Moth,

Worship, even in the context of congregational gatherings, is a deeply intimate practice. The clapping of hands, the shouting, these are all grounded in the fact of the flesh. They're a sort of publicly intimate practice, communal but deeply stylistic for the individual, they unmake the desired subject of western thought through a releasement into practice, through a relinquishment of the hoped-for individual. This is what the series is attempting to announce. I call it *There is no center of the universe* . . . and this because I'm against the concept of centering.

Centering assumes a certain spatial logic, that a center can be approached and maintained, but—as far as human knowledge has been able to discover—a center of a universe doesn't exist.

In a conventional explosion, material expands out from a central point. A short moment after the explosion starts, the centre will be the hottest point. Later there will be a spherical shell of material expanding away from the centre until gravity brings it back down to Earth. The Big Bang—as far as we understand it—was not an explosion like that at all. It was an explosion of space, not an explosion in space. According to the standard models there was no space and time before the Big Bang. There was not even a "before" to speak of. So, the Big Bang was very different from any explosion we are accustomed to and it does not need to have a central point.[22]

This has really stuck with me, the explosion *of* rather than *in* space, the way spacetime is a gathering of an otherwise relation to knowledge production. A prepositional problem, again, kinda like Bishop Mason talking about shouting, *of, to, for.* What does it mean that there is no center of the universe? It means that there is no center at all, that to desire centering would only ever be a momentary interruption of the flow of the universe. It means that the axis on which the earth spins is a gifting of a particular temporality but cannot account for the whole. That space between, that rupture, is where life is.

| SHOUTING |

Lambert stared at them a moment, then began by saying that all the talk of being "more centered" was just that, talk, and had long ago become too easy to throw around anymore. He then asked what, or where, was this "center" and how would anyone know it if it were there. He went on, tilting his chair back on its hind legs, folding his arms across his chest and saying that he wasn't sure anyone had anything more than the mere word "center," that it didn't simply name something one doesn't have and thus disguises a swarm of untested assumptions about. Then he shifted his argument a bit, saying that if our music does have a center, as he could argue it indeed does, how would someone who admits being "somewhat uninformed" recognize it, that maybe the fellow from the radio station wasn't saying anything more than that our music churns out of a center other than his, one he's unfamiliar with.[23]

What can be made in absence of the center, the concept of centering? What can be produced, what kind of relations can flower and flourish in such a case? If there is no center of the universe, what does this mean for how we can relate to the physical world, the material world? Whiteness is dependent on centering as its logic and ground of operation. To emerge from a way of life that is antagonistic to whiteness, to thought-theological, thought-philosophical as racial hierarchizing, is to consider the ways the tradition of emergence precedes the concept of centering. Isn't this what Cedric Robinson was getting at by talking about the terms of order for the Black Radical Tradition not being an alternative *of* political economy of racial capitalism but an alternative *to* its line and root?[24] There is no center of the universe because, like the prepositional proposition Robinson introduced with *of* and *to*, the universe likewise is a prepositional conundrum, the explosion *of* and not *in* space. We gotta think relationally differently.

Well, it's like, I don't go to church anymore but I will never deny the transformative impact growing up like that has had on me. I wanted to figure out a way to honor the tradition, to take it seriously but also to say the practices can be deployed otherwise. And I wanted to also really think about how the practices of social dance, of breathing with a kind of intention—like whooping—

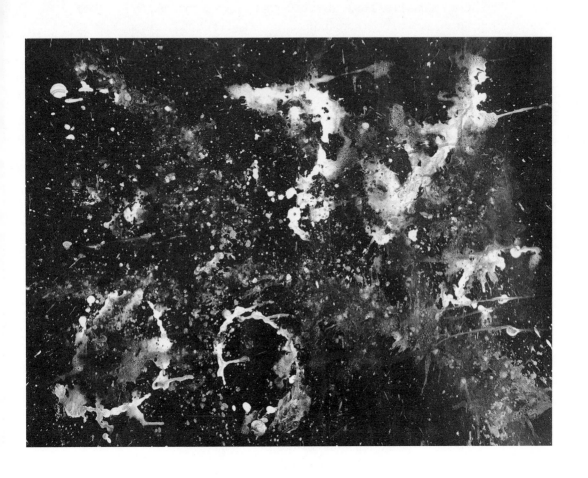

how praise noise and glossolalia have been sequestered into the religious and how they need a certain kind of release, they are practices that call for the flesh unbound, flesh liberated.

You asked me how it feels to produce these, to perform them. I'm still figuring it out. So far, I've been both intimately present but also kinda ecstatic, kinda beside myself, attempting to outpour myself, get myself out of and release myself into the sociality of blackness that Blackpentecostalism has carried with a kind of love and exuberance and joy. It's not been exactly how it was when I was a member of, say, Open Door, but the clapping and the shouting are attempts in the direction of that intensity. How does it feel? It feels good, nostalgic, sacred. But a different kind of sacred, a sacred that doesn't presume a separation between the natural and supernatural, between the visible and invisible worlds. It makes me long for more, more practice, more breath, more exhaustion, more connection and joy.

One time I posted a praise break on Facebook and Rocky said that there was a "noise underneath the noise" and this is why I've been playing a lot with texture too, what the visuality is trying to approach, a way to map and color and make visual that underneath, that underside, that underground, that undercommon noise, noise that makes possible the emergence of noise *and* music. And I've been using pigment powder instead of and in addition to acrylic paint to add to the texture and percussiveness of the shouting experiments.

I'm hoping to create in such a way that having gone to church isn't a prerequisite for engaging the work even though having gone does give a certain kinda insight. Can it be familiar without it being "known" . . . ? Can there be some kind of noisiness in the work that reaches out, that hails towards something like familiarity in others? This is kind of *knowing at the limits of justice* that Denise Ferreira da Silva talks about, I think.[25]

I wonder if there's something that called and hailed me from against and otherwise than the spacetime of linear thought that compelled me to be in relation to a sorta Black Radical *Mystical* Tradition, a tradition that seems to be against genre as a certain kind of delimitation, a certain kinda enclosure, on thought. I think about W. E. B. Du Bois, how he was a sociologist, a historian, but also a novelist and an artist too. Something about the precision of his craft that is moving to me.

And I think about Zora Neale Hurston, how she was an anthropologist, a novelist, and—also—a singer and playwright. Or Sylvia Wynter, a philosopher, a novelist, a playwright. I don't know, it just seems to me to be a pattern to which we should attend. It seems to me, when contending with the force and verve and import and movement of Black life, they couldn't confine themselves to a certain form, had to escape form itself in order to present in various, multiple ways. They had to be textured, layered, in their exploration and elaboration of the textures and layers of Black sociality. It's so reminiscent of what Wynter says about the genre of the human that is overrepresented, Man, how it is produced by a kind of categorical distinction of this genre over and against all other genres. A categorical distinction that would at the same time be a flatness, a flattening. I wonder lots about a Black mysticism as an antidote to such distinctions and flatness and the *genre of human that thinks pure distinction possible*. And I wonder about how these practitioners perform a resistance to the genre of human by performing a resistance to genre in their creative work. And I'm trying to let that inform my art practice, my thinking, my writing.

Let me know, though . . .

A

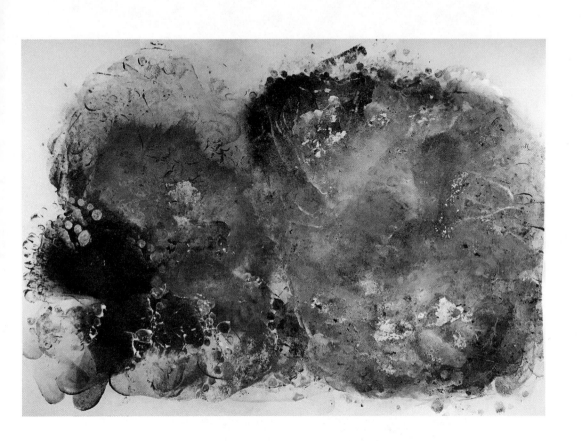

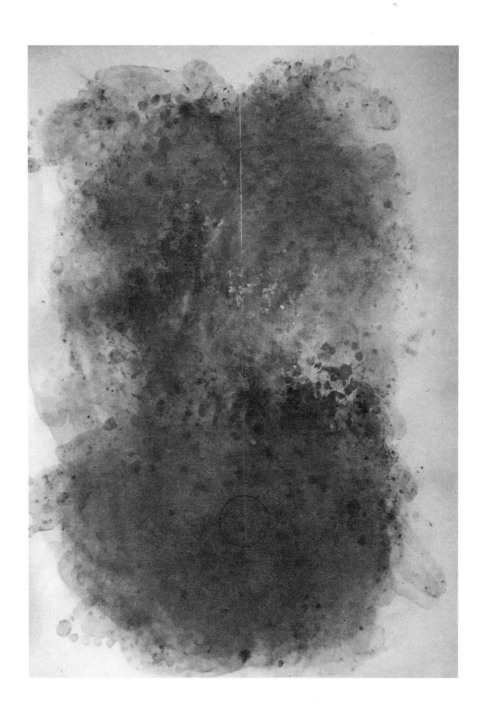

Dear Moth,

Black performance is about making oneself acutely and precisely aware of the fact of their flesh, it is the privileging—not of a loss of feeling or paralysis—of an alternative to feeling being an individuated, individual thing. I keep thinking of astonishment, astonishment as an *anaesthetic* encounter, something like what anesthesia does. Black performance is the encounter of the *anaesthetic* that produces not an individual but a public, a social, a gathering of waters, of matters, of ephemera. Black performance is against the process of subjectivity and the making of the possessive individual. I'd read something Sylviane Diouf wrote about maroons in the United States and it resonated for me.

Borderlands were spaces of freedom that provided what enslaved people were denied elsewhere: autonomy, mobility, enterprise, a sense of physical security, freedom from scrutiny, control over their time and movement, and access to varied foods. . . . They stood at the intersection of three worlds.[26]

And if three, then, not only ever but always more than three. If three, then an exorbitance of worlds. Black performance is at the border, of the between, in the break. Marronage is the practice of being ever and always between. Borderlands are between and, as between, mark relation. Being between worlds is where worlds were made. We can consider this *between*, then, as the enactment of otherwise possibility in the flesh, in the refusal of civil society, in the making otherwise at the border. The border marking limit and possibility for its dissolution. Such a making wasn't about or predicated on notions of home, dwelling, as produced by possessive individualism and the acquisition of property as private. This was an otherwise politics, otherwise social, what Cedric Robinson, in his various elaborations of Black life and the radical tradition of blackness, would consider to be not an alternative *of* political economy of racial capitalism but an alternative *to* such a political economy and its terms of order. And I'm thinking about maroons and blackness because I keep returning to the music, to Reich and Mt. Do-Well and all the random shit I find on YouTube.

Hammond B-3 organists in Blackpentecostal churches are some of my favorite folks to listen to, to engage and think with, because I think they do the thing maroons did, they carry the insistence of Black performance. These organists call the space between choruses and verses *passing chords* or, sometimes, *turn around* chords. The passing chord or turn around is whatever occurs between the singing, sorta. So, in a way, these chords are also spaces that mark *betweenness*, spaces wherein radical thought of improvisation occurs, where improvisation as a means to comment upon that which has come before and that which will come after, happens.

Technically, at least according to Wikipedia, the passing chord is a "nondiatonic chord that connects, or passes between, the notes of two diatonic chords." It's another way to think about progression, movement, verve. To consider the passing chord, the turn around, is to think sonically about the borderland, the space between, the relation. So all the *nothing music* that we love and talk about, the talk music, the sounds heard before and after service and while someone is giving announcements, just that sorta music backgrounded but always heard during the church service, I want to think about as a series of passes, as chords constantly playing the in between, chords diggin in, gettin down, in the borderland of musical possibility.

So, like, watch this clip, particularly after the singing finishes.[27]

He doesn't want to stay in any place resting but wants to continue playing, wants to continue to dig deep, to go underneath, to explore the between, the pass. I asked a friend of mine to examine the chords, he's getting a degree in music theory, and this is what he said:

This dude's harmonic vocabulary is wicked . . . It's impossible to put a name on it because he literally does everything you name—suspended harmony over a secondary dominant; augments another chord to create a #11 chord; he does a diminished arpeggio in that same area. You could mention either of those things, but I wonder if simply saying something like "he uses an intensified chromatic palate to create even more biting dissonances" would suffice?

My reply:

It doesn't seem to be about theory at all, it's so murky and playful and inventive that it sorta resists being named. And that's one of the things I've been trying to theorize lately. And this, the way you talk about it, underscores that sorta drive in Black gospel musicianship I dig so much.

It's not even not *not* about theory or theorizing but it does not take western musicology and its logics for harmony as its root and source. Like marronage, the sound is about the practice, the preparation, not about home, not about settling, not about property or ownership. It's the refusal and renunciation of individuation in cause of becoming part of the unbroken circle of sonic possibility. This sonic possibility in black, is a way to say love.

And I'm still thinking about Reich and his music with relation to Blackpentecostal music, to the Hammond organ. I know I've said something like this before but repetition is my thing, feels like I need to say it again differently. Movement VIII is like pushing in the drawbars on the Hammond, sorta like playing talk music, nothing music, accompanying through a sorta nonchalance, sorta like what the Hammond organist did when they finished singing. Movement IX is like the preacher tuning up, whooping, you feel the intensification moment by moment and then you're sorta on the edge, waiting, waiting, listening to the Hammond back her up as she preaches. Movement X is like the shout, the frantic pace, the energy, the possibility of getting lost in the music, it is so spirited and repetitive such that the repetition allows one to imagine relation differently. And Movement XI is after the break, some other thing renewed, revised, refreshed. It's like listening to expanse and contraction and expanse again, the sound of apophatic possibility that isn't an unsaying but a search.

I know you think I'm reaching but the thing is, Steve Reich knows about Blackpentecostalism, so what I'm thinking isn't so far off. He says,

Black Pentecostal preaching hovers between speaking and singing.[28]

If he knows something about the speaking and singing in between which the preaching is, he understands something about the sound generally. He understands that the music and sound in the Blackpentecostal world are about layering, are about repetition, are about finding in the most cramped of spaces some otherwise possibility as inexhaustible. And this I keep hearing in the Hammond organist too. I was an adequate musician at best, but these other organists I keep finding on YouTube are the ones that really show what I'm thinking about here. The organist is a sculptor, is an organizer of sound, by virtue of the machine itself but also by virtue of the way the musician must become a conduit. I've before called it a *holy nonchalance*, but maybe it'd be more precise to say a meditative nonchalance, a mysticism of the nonchalant, a detachment that attaches itself to the social away from the self, the citizen, the subject.

Reading about maroons again and such reading always gives me a kinda emphatic and intense hope and charges my imagination to keep going and believing that otherwise is not only possible—and that otherwise is not utopic in any sorta futural sense that is grounded in western metaphysics of Newtonian space and time—but that otherwise possibility has been enacted in the world as a critique of the normative world. What I mean is they carried in them a different epistemology and that epistemology *interrupted* western metaphysics, western theological and philosophical logics, western concepts of man and human and such difference they carried was *material* in them insofar as they used that epistemological difference as a means to literally run away, to settle in woods and borderlands and to keep going going going and running running running all in the cause of justice. The *thinking* of this otherwise way of life was not confined to thought but the imaginative capacity of another epistemology occasioned escape itself. It was the *potentia* turned *kinesthesia* of otherwise possibility, unfolding into the normative world *against* the normative world. It was the enfolding of the otherwise world, the freedom world, into the normative world. It took the limit and used it as possibility. The construction of a kind of life that could realize otherwise epistemologies.

What I most enjoy—really, enjoyed, since it's been a while—about playing the B-3, especially during testimony service, is how the song would come together and break apart. The height of the song, that moment when everyone seemed most into it, in the spirit, singing loudly, praising and clapping and even the unison voices sound somewhat harmonic (because everyone's sorta both on and off key a bit, wandering, some talk-singing through it), but that moment is when the song is most fully together, intense with centripetal and centrifugal, centrifugitive force. But before the mother sings or the deacon stands is the potential for all that sonic stuff to happen. The flesh is there, the drums are there, the organ is there. And you figure out that Blackpentecostal song ain't nothin but a dispersal of sounds that Black flesh produces, sometimes from violent necessity. The organ scream, the percussiveness of the snare and bass drum and hi-hat, the rhythm of syncopated clapped hands, stomped feet, the breathiness of song through swell and decrescendo. All of that is like a decomposed meal, the breaking of song into its component parts, the practice of construction.

And Black life is construction, it is putting things together and breaking them apart as a repetition. I guess what I'm saying is Black life—marronage— is quantum life is queer life is indigenous life. And we all have access to such life. And it is life that is a construction also of memory. So the sound of the Hammond organ can become the conduit from which to think and imagine and spatialize and to organize the sensual ensemble, the nondivisionality of sense experience. So Black life sounds like horns, sounds like chicken and fish, sounds like the sting of clapped hands, sounds like us in our queerness, in our love, in our entanglement. So many examples.

A

Dear Moth,

There are two types of churches: ones with low ceilings and others with high. Think about it. Aren't those the only types you've ever attended? This is to say nothing of how big the church is or how many people it can seat. But rather, the space between floor and ceiling creates some amazing room for the sound to bounce around, from what I've experienced.

Low ceilings, of course, mean everything will sound out with a bit of a muffle on it: think of a trumpet mute. Or maybe something akin to the antithesis of a noise filter, where all this stuff stands between your ears and the "pure" or true sound itself. It doesn't matter how loud the sound is in the church, the low ceiling will compress that sound, make it less angular and things will sound—accordingly—more insular, will sound more pressing. Imagine listening through something like Harriet Jacobs's crawl space, if you will.

Growing up, one bishop's church building we often visited might be the very definition of low ceiling. It was an old supermarket, a converted A&P or Pathmark or ShopRite, now for church services, with the purpose of the up-building of the kingdom. And the sound of that church was so very different from the sound of other churches and I suspect it is because when sound would ring out—from the Leslie speaker to the tambourines to the hand clapping to the preacher in the microphones—that sound would only be able to go up but so high until being dispersed. The sound had to travel horizontally much more than vertically so stuff happening in the front of the church didn't reach the back until maybe a beat or two later, so much so that if you sat in the back of the church, you were already behind the move of spirit that took place in the front (the two Leslie speakers, of course, were in the front of the church and not the back). This is why, I think, most of the people who sat in the back were more spectatorial in their engagement with the church. Not because they didn't want to feel anything but, because of the sound, their arrival was always late a bit.

But then there is, then and of course, that other type of church building, one where the ceiling is high and the sounds have to travel vertically as much as horizontally, so sound circulates differently, it sounds like it *circulates* in a literal sense, creates a circle by its centripetal and centrifugal—centrifugitive—force turning turning turning around and around and around, sound going under over and above you (though I know physics doesn't confirm my intuition; sound circulates in the low ceiling building too but . . . stay with me). In this high-ceiling church, sound "rings" a lot more, it remains in the air and is heard thereafter, it seems like sound strikes everyone much more at almost about the same time (but, still, a ruse, really), it sounds "bright." If the low ceiling muffles, the high ceiling releases and sounds tremble with treble. Everything seems clear in those types of environments.

If you had ever paid attention at all, you would have noticed in the low-ceiling church the organist playing in the high register a lot more (at least an octave above middle C) to invoke the spirit and in the high-ceiling church, this same organist might very likely muddy the waters by playing dark bass notes. I think, in both instances, the musician would feel the difference created by the architecture, by the acoustic environment, made possible by the height of the ceilings. Without knowing it but certainly feeling it, they'd play in ways to create as much balance as possible in the space.

Would you be surprised to know that my first time really, really touching D was in a high-ceiling church? It was the second week in August right before I was to leave for college, so I was eighteen years old and we were having convocation in one of those churches. This church, of course, was a converted synagogue made possible by white flight from inner cities years and years ago (and I think there might be a relationship between Blackpentecostal sound, white flight, and synagogues: think Detroit—Bailey Cathedral, a former synagogue, is pretty famous for its sound—there are, of course, too many examples; there are others, of course). In any regard, this synagogue-turned-cathedral became the home to many Blackpentecostal services where the power of the Lord came down. But—and this is true for lots of synagogues-turned-churches—when services weren't big, or there just weren't enough people or not enough money to pay the electric company to light the full sanctuary, services would occur in the basements of these large tabernacles, cathedrals, temples of the Most High. And those basements are the perfect mix between the high and low ceiling, at least in terms of sound. Thus, the organist has the best possibility of balanced sound and, subsequently, moving the congregation.

And it was then in August. It was a Monday night so not a lot of people planned to be at the service anyway but D and I both sang with the convocation choir and he had just directed some song and winked at me ever so faintly, bravely, sinfully and erotically while directing and nobody saw it but me and I was astonished and shocked and scared shitless because the Lord was certain to strike us down at any moment, given his display. But nobody saw it and we had never had sex, only'd lay in the bed next to each other and touch ever so slightly but I already told you about that. It was in August after we sang that I first noticed the grace of his body when he was shouting.

And you know when someone is gonna shout. Vanessa was playing the organ—can I tell you how much I love a girl organist? Nineteen years old, killing the bass and the drive and the changes. Augment, suspend, seventh, minor: go! She did it all. She was playing as we marched back to our seats. The basement was full of metal folding chairs, so you know the sound just bounced off everything and sounded so good. The song was an up-tempo tune where we sang about climbing mountains or knowing what prayer can do or some other song where the only thing that really mattered in the song was the vamp—or the drive, or to be really throwback, the *special*—and once we were done and back in our seats and Mother Jackson was encouraging the saints to *praise the Lord, church!*, Vanessa began playing ever so faster and ever so faster and ever so faster and *eversofaster* until it was at full shout speed. Brooklyn pace. So you know it was quick.

And it was in that Monday in August when I noticed D's grace. So he was gonna shout and I knew it. At first, he was seated (he was tired from directing). But then as the music swelled and sped, he stood and began to clap a bit hesitantly . . . elegantly, looking about him and smiling at the saints dancing but— you could almost hear the commentary in his head—not himself dancing. Then, he put his right hand in front of him on the metal chair. Then, he put his head down. And, you know what happens when the hand is gripping the chair or pew in front of you and the head is down? He had his program in the left hand and he began to dance *playfully*, eyes still open, head down but looking around a bit. But then Vanessa hit the chords that everyone was waiting for, some chording that Twinkie's been doing since at least 1979 before I was born—*dun dun dun dun dun, dun dun dun dun dun, dun dun dun dun dun-dun dun dun dun!*—And he let out a little yelp and by then, his feet were moving and he threw the program down and he moved from out of the row into the aisle and had both his arms bent at the elbow but tight next to him and his head was down and his eyes were closed and his feet did some hopscotch shit.

The pit of my stomach dropped because Vanessa did it again and this time more people were screaming and the sound was a bit more clear and more people were dancing and I knew that if someone as young and beautiful as D could dance in public—I didn't do such things very often, I always felt the display too public and I never wanted people to look at me—*dun dun dun dun dun!*—and I ran up next to D and it was the spirit moving me, I promise, I had no idea what was occurring—and grabbed his left hand and we shouted together. My stomach always dropped right at the borderland and line of playful dance and full out shout. It was indeed holy terror, I suppose. Our feet did not cross, we did not step on each other's toes. And he didn't fight me but—and I don't know how I knew this—he knew it was me, though his eyes were shut tightly.

We were sweaty after it all. The preacher got up and because we were still a bit young and people would not ogle us leaving the basement sanctuary for some air—or to pee—after such a display, we went to the bathroom. Vanessa was backing up the preacher who, I'm sure, wasn't making much sense but used the high energy from the high-low-ceiling sound to animate his sermon. He was, if anything, smart. Folks were already praising so he just kept a spirited engagement with the congregation so, in the bathroom, we heard a combination of *Yes! Thank the Lord! Praise Him! Bless me! Fix me! Do it Lord!*

Anyway, we both peed. In separate stalls. Went up to the sinks to wash our hands—*shhhhhhhh*—the water said and then we turned off our faucets. I was drying my hands. He was drying his. We'd said nothing. He was so graceful and that was all I could think about. We were both sweating. He took his brown paper towel—the rough ones that, when you fold them, have rough edges and corners and aren't too soothing—he took that paper towel and brushed it over my brow. I said *thanks*. I took mine, smirked a bit, and brushed it over his brow. He said nothing. He took his paper towel—he was standing to my right—placed it in his right hand and put his left arm at the small of my back and I sorta knew to turn to him. He brushed it against my brow again but my right arm was caught and could not move between our bodies and his left arm; and my left arm was

| SHOUTING |

caught between his upheld hand brushing my brow. I turned around. Someone could have walked in. I was terrified. Terrified. Simply terrified.

The sound from the basement sanctuary of that former synagogue forced its way through the door but was muffled. We—in the bathroom—said nothing. We were barely breathing. And. But. Breathing heavily too. Heaving. He dropped the towel and took my right hand and took me to the handicapped stall. Undid my pants. Undid his. We stood there, shirts on, pants and underwear at our ankles. He kissed me. We rubbed against each other for nothing more than a minute. We said nothing. We pulled up our pants, washed our hands again and sat apart from each other in the sanctuary. He would not, of course, take my phone calls for weeks after that, not until I left for college. Maybe the music caused us to act out of ourselves, or to be more fully who were already were. Or wanted to be. Or had always been from some otherwise temporality. It, of course, felt good. But it, between us, would never happen again.

The building, the praise, it all made possible that moment of imaginative rupture, imaginative disruption. Right there in the church. The constraint became an occasion.

A

noise^3

Dear Moth,

One hundred trillion neutrinos pass through each square inch of matter every second, though it is presumed to be the case that human flesh cannot feel them with sensual registers already discovered. Quantum physics verifies what we have always known, what Black folks and indigenous folks and queer folks have known for such a long time: there are things that happen in the world, in the universe, that are not easily perceptible to human flesh. We cannot see on the quantum scale, eyes cannot detect atoms, electrons, neutrons, photons. We simply feel the effects of such material, how these tiny particles come together forming the building blocks of, while moving through, matter. Neutrinos are part of what quantum physicists call "dark matter," teeny, tiny particles unaffected by light, uninhibited by gravity.

I keep thinking about these two quotes:

Quantum particles have no intrinsic properties that neatly correspond to position and velocity, and that measurement forces a quantum system to cough up values for these quantities in a way that depends on how the measurement is done.[1]

And,

For [Niels] Bohr, what is at issue is not that we cannot know both the position and momentum of a particle simultaneously (as Heisenberg initially argued), but rather that particles do not have determinate values of position and momentum simultaneously. . . . What he is doing is calling into question an entire tradition in the history of Western metaphysics.[2]

So what would *knowing at the limits of justice* mean—have you yet read the da Silva essay I sent you?[3]—if knowing itself is in need of interrogation. I guess what I'm trying to say is, what if otherwise possibility doesn't simply name a different epistemology, what if it attempts to name what is literally unknowable because it is a zone and inhabitation that does not *have* intrinsic properties that correspond neatly to what we call the good, the merciful, the just, the equitable—it does not and cannot have intrinsic properties of the possible and the just—until there is a forced measurement of sorts, until there is the simultaneity of events that causes a necessity? What I'm trying to say is maybe these values emerge because the normative world in which they are given or withheld based on categorical distinctions of identity markers is what makes these values possible. What I'm after, by thinking about otherwise possibility, are worlds where this is not even possible because food and shelter and healthcare and joy and love cannot be given or withheld, only practiced as a social fact of breath. These worlds exist, I think, because I can sense the noise they emit, I sense them deep within me.

Sorta like what I said last time on the phone, that because western man, the citizen, the human, doesn't account for what da Silva called the "others of Europe,"[4] then how can we measure or make attempts to understand actions and behaviors, how can we think about the ethical for those that are not considered to be human? If being ethical and having a commitment to ethics are dependent on modern man and *his* capacity but Black folks and indigenous and queer and *and and* are outside such possibility, maybe what is enacted and is actionable is the *anethical*, a sorta way to measure and think relations of the good, the merciful, the equitable for those that don't fit in modern epistemologies of identity and difference. And this *anethical* possibility would also be a critique of ethics, ethics as a normative concept that necessitates ethical being, being that emerges through the coloniality of being/power/truth/freedom.[5] And then perhaps maybe the *anethical* would also mark the relation to and be the decolonial, not as a corresponding direct response to coloniality but the fact of the noise of its existence previous to colonial possibility. It seems to me to be the case that the tradition of western metaphysics Karen Barad attempts to critique because of the way knowledge is presumed in such a tradition also influences the way we think knowledge of the possible and knowledge of justice simultaneously.

One example is found with how Werner Heisenberg begins his book *Physics and Philosophy* with the following:

When one speaks today of modern physics, the first thought is of atomic weapons. Everybody realizes the enormous influence of these weapons on the political structure of our present world and is willing to admit that the influence of physics on the general situation is greater than it ever has been before.[6]

And he's just doing the thing that I think is kind of terrible, he assumes thought itself as totalized, as universal. And this totalizing and universalizing thought is assumed to exist previous to thought itself even being possible. If I could, I'd ask him why atomic weapons are considered to be the *first* thought? What is the order of things such that atomic weaponry is assumed to be the first thought? (I've been reading Cedric Robinson a lot lately, so he's on my mind too.)[7]

What we think a person is is based on myth, is based on narratives that are told about the possibility of being human. So the first thought of atomic weapons Heisenberg assumes is because of a mythic being that anchors such thinking. What is the myth of personhood, of racial and class distinction, that produces an occasion such that Heisenberg thinks the first thought of "modern physics" is weaponization and annihilation, the first thought for him is cataclysm and chaos? And what is assumed about modern man such that the mere mention of modern physics has within it this *first* operation, this *first* thinking with regard to warfare and destruction? Wouldn't this first thought be the renunciation of the flesh, the renouncing of noise? Wouldn't this first thought, in other words, dissimulate the fact that that first thought is limit, is the renunciation of possibility, that first thought would have been produced through refusing to think other possibilities as able to rise to the occasion of thought *as* thought? I guess I mean the concept of the "first thought" is a misnomer of terribly large proportions, it's only first insofar as it is the renunciation of the world, of the materiality, from which thought occurs.

And doesn't Heisenberg's purported *first thought* not assume modern man and all *his* intellectual capacity? Isn't this a universalizing impulse that grounds the way he thinks thought itself? A universalizing impulse that proclaims itself to be a first operation that cannot deal with the irreducible plurality from which thought is nominated? In other words, the first thought ain't first, it's a choice, a decision, a desire, and such a choice, decision, and desire is produced by the way one thinks relation to self, others, earth. This first thought is the thought of European man, the colonizer, the citizen, the human, the subject. Not that it's intentional or conscious, it's just a first thought insofar as it announces the epistemic world, its horizon and thrust that makes such a thought possible.

And what for those of us that hear about modern physics but do not take atomic weapons as a first thought, even if that thought does perhaps occur? Would those that do not think atomic weapons as a first operation be marginalized as having improper thought? Such impropriety would be queer. It just seems that this illustrates the way thought has been hierarchized, how it has been assumed, how it appears to be totalizing and producing modernity itself. Perhaps what is needed is a way to think, to cognize, to have knowledge of possibility and justice that only emerges through the simultaneity of measurement, a simultaneity beyond the limit, beyond the horizon, in the zone of darkness, a sorta *an*ethical thrust or drive or critique. Maybe that's what Black performance is. This zone might be the secret place of marronage.

More soon but I gotta get going. Anyway, I miss you.

A

Dear Moth,

Here's a quote from this great essay about Ralph Ellison, Albert Einstein, and George Jackson written by Lindsey Andrews:

I was lonely and I found these three lonely men. Oh, Ellison: "To paraphrase myself, I love you, write me, I'm lonely." Dearest Einstein, his "lonely ways." And Jackson, "alone in the most hostile jungle on earth." The fundamental condition of writing, of study, is enforced solitude, loneliness. I've been thinking of Michael Cobb who writes of the queerness of loneliness, of being alone. And through him I think the queerness of this binding, these men bound together by me is queer in me, through me. And here, too, all the women who are communing with each other, and with these men, as ghosts and at the same time materially real and so far from one another. . . . Lonely, we have come to study together, to write each other.[8]

I'm into this, writing and study and loneliness, about aloneness. But, I guess, I'm also bothered by it. It is perhaps why I have been writing you letters, why I have been reading letters—James Baldwin to his nephew, Celie to God and Nettie, N to Angel of Dust, M. NourbeSe Philip to the dead who are yet with us. I have been thinking about a theory of the letter and how it is a search for what N calls "a 'broken' claim to connection,"[9] where what is sought after, what is desired, is relationship, what is sought after, what is desired, is that which exceeds the broken claim *for* and *in the service toward establishing* connection. And I guess I've been thinking about blackness and mysticism because there's something about the practice of noise making that Blackpentecostals perform that is so mystical to me, that announces a fundamental and deep and moving and abiding connection with one another and the creaturely world, an immaterial drive that is suffused with and deeply material.

In such a world, nothing is inanimate, everything moves and vibrates. But western mysticism seems to be so much about renunciation—of the flesh, of the social—before the possibility of discovery of the divine, of the intangible but perhaps felt world. One has to leave the flesh, the social, as a first move in order to hear more precisely, to feel more properly, before reentry into the social in this sorta mystical tradition. We keep thinking that mystics talk about leaving the noise of the world to hear more clearly but what would the noise have been in the medieval era? Certainly not the same noise as one hears in the world today with electricity and cars. It worries me. What was bothering John of Fécamp so much, in other words, that he had to lament? What did he lose other than the ruse of solitude?

I've been reading lots of Cedric Robinson and have been moved to tears because what he establishes is connection by a reorientation to direction, by just giving up on linearity though he goes through linear history to show its ruse, its uselessness for thinking the Black Radical Tradition. So don't think I'm picking on Eckhart or Teresa of Ávila or St. John of the Cross or John of Fécamp. I'm worried over the epistemic, not particular actors in and of it. We all have to be interrogated because it affects us all.

Robinson and the way he talks about the limits of Marxism helps me think about the radicalism internal to the mysticism even of European traditions but also the delimitation that they cannot get beyond though they move in the path of such an approach. For example, Eckhart believed in the differentiation between the divine and creaturely worlds, that there is a fundamental separation that can perhaps be bridged. There is a difference immeasurable for the divine and the creaturely. But this immeasurable difference emerges from a way to think worlds that presumes difference that is categorical, that such difference could be maintained. So with western mysticism, perhaps similar to what we find in Robinson's *Black Marxism*,[10] is the beginning of racial thought and categorization. All right there in European mystical thinking. This immeasurable difference as being possible, as being possibly maintained, as being possibly maintained and thus pure and categorical, would come to mark racialization to come, precedes and functions alongside racialization internal to European thought.

Robinson:

It is still fair to say that at base, that is at its epistemological substratum, Marxism is a Western construction—a conceptualization of human affairs and historical development that is emergent from the historical experiences of European peoples mediated, in turn, through their civilization, their social orders, and their cultures. Certainly its philosophical origins are indisputably Western. But the same must be said of its analytical presumptions, its historical perspectives, its points of view. This most natural consequence though has assumed a rather ominous significance since European Marxists have presumed more frequently than not that their project is identical with world-historical development. . . . Racism, I maintain, was not simply a convention for ordering the relations of European to non-European peoples but has its genesis in the "internal" relations of European peoples. As part of the inventory of Western civilization it would reverberate within and without, transferring its toll from the past to the present.[11]

The point for me is to think about the "epistemological substratum," to interrogate analytical presumptions, historical perspectives, and points of view that are what we might consider to be, after Wynter, an *ethnocentrism* (because she talks about particular kinds of being human as related to ways particular peoples think their relation to the cosmos that map onto the way they think about the earth, calling these ethnoastronomies and ethnogeographies)[12] that comes to overrepresent itself and, as such, produce violence through that overrepresentation. I don't want to simply replace what Robinson said about Marxism with the word *mysticism* though I don't think it would be too off or imprecise to do so. I want to argue, and his work helps me make the case, that the epistemological substratum that produces Marxism is the same epistemological substratum that produces mysticism as a narratively possible construction, it is a western mode of thinking the internal relations of European peoples previous to encounter with non-European peoples.

Bernard McGinn:

The basic pattern of withdrawal-purgation-transformation was the structure that gave shape and purpose to the other values and practices of the first monastics. Flight from the world to the solitary and silent life of the inhospitable desert remained the foundation.[13]

And,

The force that really transformed Western Christianity, however, was the monasticism that spread westward in the second half of the fourth century. Ascetical tendencies had been present throughout early Christianity, and the West doubtless had "free-form" monastics of its own before it received the impulse toward classic forms of monasticism. . . . From the outset, however, Western monasticism was not just a carbon copy of what was found in the East. For one thing, the eremitical life was more difficult to lead in the West (given a generally harsher climate and other dangers) and was considered less of a practical reality, especially for beginners. The solitary hermit remained the ideal, but the cenobite, or monk living in community, was the standard form. This fit well with the other major characteristics of Western monasticism— its tendency toward an urban and often a clerical setting and its close connection with aristocratic and episcopal sponsorship. The monasticism of the West that became evident ca. 370 sprang not from the movement of peasants and village dwellers out into the desert, as in the East, but from the efforts of bishops and literate upper-class Christians to encourage higher forms of life for themselves and especially for their clergy.[14]

What McGinn demonstrates is a kind of ethnoastronomy and ethnogeography of early monasticism, a Christian choreographic-sonic, choreosonic vibration, that would make meaning out of space and time, how they'd think the relation of inhabiting the earth and its hills, valleys, and accesses to waterways, as the possibility for realizing the divine. This pattern of withdrawal-purgation-transformation was at the base of what would become European mysticism, a triple movement that I think is also at the base of racial capitalism. And this withdrawal-purgation-transformation had a particularly sonic register, the sensing of and dispensing with noise, whether racial capitalism or European mysticism. Maybe they are shades of the same force because they are of the same epistemological substratum. And Robinson helps me to get there.

The philosophical and theological origins of mysticism are deeply western because of the varied assumptions about the categorical distinctions of worlds, of hierarchies of people, of the necessity for assumption and movement out from the social into higher ideals. So I'm not attacking particular people within the European mystical tradition so much as I'm thinking about the epistemological formation that made possible the cognition of a thing called mysticism. But I'm also thinking that Robinson kept talking about maroons and that perhaps he's pointing to something that I've been ruminating on over and over again.[15] Maybe marronage is a mysticism to which we can attend, a Black mysticism, a mysticism of afrodiasporic, indigenous possibility. Maybe I'm after a way to think a mysticism that is about renunciation of the singular, the renouncing of individual-divisible being, the retreat *into* rather than away from the social, the retreat into rather than away from noise, the retreat into the social as the centrifugitive movement away from the subject.

I never wanted to possess you,
I wanted to be with you,
make the fact of our entanglement audible,
felt,
make the fact of our being co-constituted in otherwise spacetime
    known.

A marronage,
with you,
in and as you and I as otherwise than separable.
Could it be?

It, the sorta practice of marronage I'm thinking, is against John Locke's concept of possessive individualism. And it's because I've seen *Moonlight* and have been thinking a lot about intimacy and the failure of western epistemologies to capture excess.[16] This, of course, is the gift of excess.

I never told you about the dude I went to undergrad with that was, almost twenty years later this year, flirty as hell with me but also straight(-identified), so wouldn't own his affections or desires but he kept projecting everything on me. One day after our conversing, I purchased a copy of Baldwin's *The Price of the Ticket*—he said he was a Baldwin fan but never had the occasion to read it, so I had it mailed to him. He read a part of it and called me on the phone excitedly—and we'd never talked on the phone once in our lives—just to talk about the book and other things. He told me how he couldn't stop thinking about this one essay, "Here Be Dragons," how he kept talking about it to every-one he was encountering, so of course I wanted to talk more about it to him. After talking that one time for about forty-five minutes late at night, a week later I sent him a message joking with him that he disappeared after that phone convo and he replied that he was "running out of politeness" with me. I haven't spoken to him since because I refuse to be disrespected because he can't deal with his emotions and desires.

Well, I woke up thinking about him last night because, I don't know, that shit hurt my feelings. And I think about it every now and then. I liked him, sure, but I wasn't making things up. I know it—whatever those brief moments of in-tensity and interaction were—was reciprocal and likely overwhelming for him but I was never *never never* intense or even too flirty. I guess it was my writing in the book something like "to my new friend" and closing with "xoxo" but why are straight(-identified) men so afraid of shit *they* start but don't have the will to finish?

Then it hit me after watching *Moonlight*: it was the intimacy that bothered him. What's been so astonishing to me about intimacy and about the way folks talk about *Moonlight* as supposedly "emasculating the Black man," and the idea that intimacies between Black men are cause for lament and terror *and*, be-cause of these things, intimacy between men should be shunned, is this: inti-macy means connection is possible, that sexuality isn't something that can be explained away with biogenic conceptualizations of the human, of evolutionary development. Intimacy means that there is something ephemeral and immate-rial that is sought after, desired, that cannot be put into charts, metrics, that cannot be measurable in some sorta "scientific" way. What is science to a held hand that causes goosebumps, or a voice that causes butterflies in the pit of one's stomach? What is science to desire that cannot be named with precision but is no less there, dark desire, like dark matter? And this, it seems, is the problem, specifically in a world that presumes that science can answer all, a world predicated upon disciplinary knowledge, predicated upon the coloniality of being/power/truth/freedom.

I'm just trying to say: we exist in a world that'd much rather have a scientific explanation for sexuality but intimacy is such that it resists such easy analytics. And this, intimacy, is a gift. It is the gift of resistance. It is the gift of being resistant to being incorporable into western knowledge regimes.

And, truth is, I enjoyed talking to him because I'd been feeling alone and lonely, especially a lot lately. Though you and I have been talking more, it's still not the thing we had or could have and so loneliness seems to creep up on me in ways I'm not in favor of. And this isn't to say that I don't enjoy my friends, that their relationships are not sustenance for me; they are integral to how I've been able to live. But there still is something different that I seek though I still cannot fully grasp what that difference is.

I enjoyed talking to him because my feelings of loneliness often feel like a dispossession or a displacement of sorts. And with him I'd felt a measure of being placed, of being possessed in a noncoercive giving of myself away, letting myself go. And I've been exploring mysticism because I don't want to be lonely and I was intrigued by the call, the almost forced inhabitation, of loneliness. That's why I've been thinking about Eckhart and John of Fécamp and all those others, to be honest. But then there's intimacy and it seems to me to be against the kind of forced solitude I've been reading in terms of mysticism.

Tell me if I'm wrong, I guess, but maybe intimacy is also about entanglement:

Quantum entanglement is a physical phenomenon that occurs when pairs or groups of particles are generated or interact in ways such that the quantum state of each particle cannot be described independently of the others, even when the particles are separated by a large distance—instead, a quantum state must be described for the system as a whole.[17]

Though quantum entanglement can be measured, what I'm into about it is the way entanglement means that divisibility and separability emerge from within certain epistemic assumptions about the world and its behavior, a particular—to use Robinson's language—epistemological substratum. Such a world and the assumptive logic are normative. But what of the nonnormative? Quantum particles literally queer insofar as they defamiliarize the so-thought familiar through otherwise relationality, they behave differently from what is considered to be normative interaction. Little, Chiron, and Black all entangled to and with and in Kevin, all three stages and phases were irreducible to and in Kevin, though he was also a sort of grounding for him, for them.

It's about connection and I write a lot about possibility because I've been so disappointed in the world, in both big world-historical ways but mostly on the level of the personal. How much is one supposed to endure, is something I think about a lot. It isn't easy talking about the things I write about because they emerge from so much disappointment. Everything said, everything written, is in search of a connection.

But, admittedly, I'm still learning.

A

Dear Moth,

I guess you could say quantum theory and mysticism and loneliness are all about, for me at least, explorations into the possibilities for deep and capacious and abiding interconnection. Loneliness isn't about that connection but about trying to figure out the shit that gets in the way of such possibility. One thing I loved about *Moonlight* is that the film never resolves exactly why the character Terrell antagonized Chiron so much, it never attempts to psychologize or analyze him. Some think he was maybe a closet gay or maybe jealous of Chiron's relationship with Kevin or maybe he was just a terrible person.

I appreciate the film not resolving or really even exploring this because it simply didn't matter; what mattered was the impact such antagonism had on Little, then Chiron. What mattered is that Chiron was continually berated and belittled and made to feel that he didn't belong in the world by someone. When we rush to psychologize, which really pathologizes, *why* someone behaves the way they do rather than lingering with the impact such behavior has on the targets, we end up making central what they've done, we find ways to explain it away. And I sorta wanna remain with the impact a lot more.

I'm feeling this particularly because I'm sensitive to how you're saying dude could've been lonely as a reason he both drew near to and withdrew from me, that he may or may not feel sadness because of the church and that perhaps his homophobic rant, his desire for distance, is because he's confused, that he is perhaps experiencing loneliness and that is a reason why he would say such things.

But listen. I've been lonely. Sometimes, very much, still today. And you know this. I came out the closet thinking it would make available to me the possibility for relationship and dating, though that simply has not been the case. I've failed, utterly, with an erotic life. In all my years alive—and you *know* this— except for with you, I've been single. And much of what we had was undefined— and I know that's my fault mostly—so I don't even consider that.

I've dated here and there but I'm just alone right now. No relationship life to speak of, really. And I ain't saying this to be mean, what we had, what we have, whatever it is, is beautiful. But first I kept fighting you and the pull you had on me and now you keep fighting it and the pull I have on you, so it doesn't make sense to even say that it's been successful, you and I. It has been so much frustration for me because there's so much I want to give, and give to you, and be with and for you, but you have these ideas about how you want to occupy the world, you're doing the very thing I think is a problem, escaping from the social to be alone. And I don't wanna relegate whatever it is we have and say it's unimportant, that friendship is of no consequence. I'm a victim of patriarchy too, I keep saying I need "more" when really, I don't. I'm not sure. I try to fight my own impulses of relationship as ownership and as property relations. It's so difficult, though, to relinquish the hold and grip on that idea because then I'd have even less. Or that's what I presume. I'm trying to figure things out and I really am lonely.

What I *do* know is that it's not an erotic life, an intimate relational life, that has sustained my ability to remain, to have joy, to have peace of mind[Or, really, the intimacy that has sustained me isn't normative at all, it's a queer intimacy, the intimacy of close sitting and held breath, of sharing thoughts and ideas and laughter.]There has been loneliness and sadness on both sides of the closet, on both sides of attempting to speak more precisely about who I am without fear or shame or loathing. Loneliness, then, cannot be a reason that I accept for folks to say shit that is violent and dangerous.

I'd been lonely as a kid and teenager just trying to figure out my relation to church and life and love. I knew I was attracted to men but also felt deeply that I needed to connect with god, that I needed to change, that I was vile and sinful and terrible. I prayed and cried and searched and read scripture looking for connection to all that was holy even when I felt the most connected to what I thought god to be. What I mean is, even when I was supposedly saved, I felt distance from god and things holy. No amount of churchgoing changed the loneliness. I went to church, you know, all of the time. Remember when I took you to my parents' house and showed you that gray tape recorder? That's the one I took with me as a teenager to churches for services and musicals. People called me the "boy with the gray tape recorder," if they didn't know my name. And they did this because I was always there, always praying, always fasting, always attempting a deep relationship with god.

But I have not been altogether honest. You are not the only one that has

tried asceticism, that has tried to renounce the world and the flesh for something higher and different and other. For a very long time, I thought I was to
be celibate, thought my life was some sorta sacrificial example of how to move
through the world without wanting, without desiring. Or, not really *not* wanting nor desiring but channeling want and desire into the direction of something
bigger and higher than myself because I really did believe that I was a fallen
creature, that my existence itself was as fallenness. I tried to quiet the disquieting noise of queerness I felt reverberating in me, a kind of queerness that made
me open and vulnerable and feminine and not-boyish, a kind of noise of the
nonnormative. And the attempts to quiet this noise put me on a pursuit for god,
yes. You know that I wanted to be a preacher but you do not know that I seriously considered Catholic priesthood because of celibacy as a way of life. I'm
older than you . . . by the time I was in college and considering seminary as a
next step, you were—what?—just entering middle school?

I don't talk about that time of my life much because it is so difficult to recount. I was very conservative, would tell folks that they were hellbound for being queer, would tell myself most intensely of all. I remember when the college
choir was asked to sing at an event for the yearly LGBTQ celebration week and I
said to the choir's executive board—since I was the director—under no circum-
stances would we sing for them. "We" don't want to give "them" the impres-
sion that "we" are ok with "their" "sinfulness" is what I said. I was serious. The
executive board argued with me, yes, but in the end, I persuaded them and we
didn't sing. If I try to recount now the kinda faces they made at me it was likely
because they were thinking, *this gay ass muthafucka* or something similar . . .
but, though contradictory—I'd go home and get on AOL and chat or call the party
line and have someone come over late at night—I was still convicted that queer
shit was sin shit. And I was convinced, above all, of my own need to reform lest
I be hellbound.

So maybe I was all into telling other folks about hell as an end because I was
hoping to prove to god that I could be serious about my purported calling, that
I could really be true and honest and pure, that I was serious about sacrificing
all the shit I felt in order to be saved. And it seemed like Catholic priests—even
though I knew so little of Catholicism—had done so much to control their flesh
and I knew I needed a way too. (And I have a much more thorough understand-

ing of Catholicism today, so I'm not casting aspersions on this tradition; I'm just telling you how I thought about things then.) So I started attending St. Martin de Porres Church on Lehigh Avenue, would go there every Sunday for Mass and I'd leave there and go to Open Door. I'd arrive to Open Door late, of course, but because the service went from 11:30 until about 2:00 or sometimes 3:00, it didn't matter much. I sat in the balcony at Open Door anyway, wanted to be anonymous as possible. They were very different kinds of churches in many ways but very Black in similar ways too. One Black Catholic, the other Black-pentecostal; one male priest, the other Black female pastor.

Anyway, I went to Open Door because it connected me to what I knew but St. Martin de Porres I attended because I was seeking, seriously, another path and direction. I began talking to the priest there, going to confession and everything, hoping to get rid of what I kept feeling and desiring against desire, what I kept dreaming for even though they were like nightmares. I tried to escape, was serious about the priesthood, so no, you're not the only one that's doing the thing you're doing now. I read scripture daily, prayed the stations, lamented and praised, cried and wailed. I tried to perform what it'd mean to do this sorta serious thing that ascetics did. I wanted to retreat into my personal desert, retreat into my own catacomb. Maybe then, alone and in solitude, I'd find god and love him and do what was required and would be sheltered from my longing and desire for men. And I thought I'd be, finally, united with someone—with god— and that would let me feel better about the world.

And then, years later, I met you. And then, sometime later, that smile.

Anyway, I guess I'm figuring out all over again that my search for connection with god didn't dissipate the loneliness, that the aloneness I felt was a kind of isolation from the world, from worlds, that that isolation made me desire connection that always felt, and still today feels, thwarted. I suppose there are differences—between loneliness, aloneness, and isolation—that I'm still attempting to figure out. Isolation seems to be about physical remove and removal, an exclusion and severance, and I suppose loneliness is the affective register of that physical, material reality. Aloneness perhaps names something like a physical but not necessarily affective distance and differentiation. What do you think?

What I do know is that I didn't have to go into deserts or retreat from the world. I'd prayed alone and cried there so much, alone, for a change to come, for relief, for reprieve. And it wasn't until I met you that I felt what I came to later read about and consider entanglement to be.

So my life, the way I have attempted to live it, has meant choosing black-queerness even if that, at the same time, has meant choosing loneliness over and over again. And I mean loneliness precisely in terms of an affective register of a physical, material reality of being excluded. But it's not the kind that operates from an epistemological substratum of European thought . . . I hope. It's really a variation on a theme because I was alone with god and then, again, away from it. And the loneliness didn't go away when I chose blackqueerness. It only seemed to dissipate when I felt that quickening in my heart and butterflies that time, that first time you smiled at me, for you. And I felt it dissipate again with Dan—dude with *girlfriendofthreeyears*—we hung out once or twice because they're in an open relationship and the first time we hung out, they wore a skirt and it kind of made me question a lot of things but Dan's openness to gender-queerness really made me quiver.

But you're right, I guess I always try with intimacy because I always try with my parents, with the church. And my friend Sofia kinda put a name to it, said that it's about a kind of forgiveness. We've been talking, still a lot, about the art practice and there's this one thing she said recently that I really dug:

What you wrote to me about the project—really, they are projects, connected but also deeply attempting to do different registers—made me think about tarrying and being together and it made me want to ask you about forgiveness. I feel like forgiveness is pulsing so much about in the work you do . . . forgiveness as healing and the coming-into-being of community . . . but sometimes it's just not there, and you say it too, that you know the church isn't utopia, it participates in sexism, classism, homophobia, transphobia. And yet you write, "something is there, in the aesthetic practices," that is working for us, all of us. No matter what, the music is on our side.

I'm reading a lot of Mennonite missionary stories these days . . . stories of my family, kind of . . . you know my mom was a missionary in Somalia, and that's how she met my dad. And reading what you were saying about the Sufi tradition made me think of how the missionaries

viewed, and maybe still view, Somali Sufism. There's this idea that sufism is less violent and extremist than other forms of Islam, and that for this reason, it's a good entry point for Christian missionaries, like you can get close to a Sufi mosque, get people to talk to you, get inside. I really can't help seeing this as imperialist! So it's painful, you know? And it's like—how do you tarry together with that—how to live along? I keep thinking of Jacob and the angel: "I will not let thee go unless thou bless me." That struggle, that wrestling, that tarrying, active waiting. And what if the blessing never comes? Can we—
I wonder, after reading about the kind of thing you're attempting in the show—can we see the wrestling itself as a reconciliation? Or an analogue to reconciliation, anyway, a tarrying despite everything, a sharing of the breath. This, it seems to me, would bust the whole notion of forgiveness out of time, and maybe return it to itself. To refuse to move on, to always be in a mode of tarrying, ceaseless movement, living and wrestling along. Wrestling along, breathing along through racism, imperialism, homophobia, holding to the music. I don't know, there are ways I don't expect the church to bless me in this life and I don't expect to let go either.

She made me cry. She made me cry because each instance of attempting relation, I know now—I feel now—has been a certain kind of forgiveness, a way to reach for connection after its having been severed, after its having been broken, a reach and desire for a different way to exist in the world. And one of the things that moves me about Sufism, I was telling her, is that there is a search for something that is connected to the search in Black Christianity, a search that I hear and smell and touch in Blackpentecostalism, a search that is deep and true in Catholicism too, a connection that is not *about* those traditions, though it is found in those many theres. And I've been thinking that bringing folks together, bringing them in contact, is what I'm attempting with the art project, a way to do something like *forgiveness out of time*, forgiveness against normative time. Maybe wrestling itself is the tradition, wrestling as refusal, wrestling as resistance, wrestling as being discontent with the normative world, a refusal to be done with or satisfied by it. I'm trying to get at something I sense in the noise that we're told to quiet, the noise we are told is disquieting, something that the noise can teach us about life. That noise helps me wrestle, whether the noise of sensing desire for love and sex and pleasure or the noise of sensing joy and praise and worship.

And though I do want to say I wrestle with you in this kind of way, I don't wanna normalize wrestling when a lot of times what people engage is really just abusive behavior, is refusing to let go of someone that doesn't want us and so we become violent. That's not what I mean here, by us, at all. I just felt we were together in some spiritual and mystical way. And I don't even know, really, what mystical and spiritual mean because I'm not really a believer anymore. I just know I feel you. (I talk about the noncoercive a lot because I think we have to keep raising it as a necessity. Patriarchy indoctrinated us, and we have to un-settle it continually.)

Anyway, dude doesn't get a pass, even if he is lonely and his weirdness, his rudeness, his distance is grounded in disbelief that something beautiful could come from thinking more intentionally about me. And so I want to hold out the space to say that my choosing loneliness because of the lack of erotic relation-ship doesn't seem to be the same as choosing a sorta mystical experience of the individual, of individuation, of the subject or something. And maybe I need to say I haven't chosen loneliness at all but the possibility for an alternative to com-munity, so many folks I've met and love and cherish because of choosing the sociality of queer folks. You, of course, included.

But I'm rambling,

A

Dear Moth,

There was no church scene. There were no tambourines or drums, no preachers loudly proclaiming Leviticus 20:13, Romans 1, and 1 Corinthians 6:9. There were no flamboyant choir directors, teenagers named Arthur or Crunch or bluesmen named Jimmy; no John or Gabriel Grimes; no Elishas.

Yet *Moonlight* could've been James Baldwin's, could've been his fictional narrative. And this is because *Moonlight*, like Baldwin's work, is all about feeling. And in that way, like Baldwin's work, it's also, then, about blackness, religion, and the failure to find sanctuary in the most ordinary, everyday, supposedly safe spaces.

I don't even remember his name. I sorta remember his picture from AOL—a chat room, but which one, I don't remember, either—but I remember how I felt. I was experimenting, a high school senior with a college sophomore. I remember I didn't like him much, that who he was, what he said in his profile and his picture didn't match the person who showed up at my door later. But I wanted to try because I'd felt so alone that I let him in anyway. I remember thinking that I'd go to hell as soon as he left my parents' house. It was around 3:50 p.m. and I walked him to my bedroom, up the creaky stairs that made too much noise. I had an hour and maybe ten minutes. He'd have to get in and get out before my parents got home. His breath stank. His Afro was asymmetrical. We barely did anything at all. I have not seen him since that first and, thus, last day. I let dude in my house because I wanted to be touched and wanted to feel . . . wanted. I let him in my house because I was seeking connection.

I'm thinking about this, and so many other random encounters, because what *Moonlight* highlights so well is a kind of loneliness and desire that can lead to all kinds of random encounters. Random encounters that are grounded in touch. Random encounters of intense feeling include Juan reaching out and extending care to a little boy he didn't know but felt a kinship with, an affinity to. He touched Little, held him gently in water, baptized him to life as possible.

Random encounters of intense feeling include Paula and her addiction to crack, how she went from moods of intense love to explicit and harsh rejection of her son. She was touched, too, by Black as tears streamed down her face. Everything in the film, this masterpiece, was a reach for connection.

Little, then Chiron, then Black, at each stage of *Moonlight*, felt the touch of Kevin. In such touch was sanctuary and refuge, in such touch was gentleness and quiet. A kind of quiet that was softly vibrational. For Black, in act 3 of *Moonlight*, it is revealed that he'd not been touched since Kevin in high school. Was it just the teenage experimentation on the beach, head held in hand, hand gripping sand, he meant? Or did he also mean the violent touch on high school property, the confrontation with Kevin?

The intimacy, discomfort, touch, and feeling produced a confrontation with viewers. Would you dismiss it as a gay tale that is sinful because of what the Bible says? Would you discredit it as lacking a plot altogether because a bildungsroman of a Black boy is much too much askance for you to consider it real? Or is watching the intimacy between men the occasion for memory and remembrance? The film compels visceral response to it by capturing the visceral quality of Chiron's lives.

It's about discomfort that emerges in dreams that allow you to consider that other ways of existence might not only be possible, but also pleasurable; that they might bring joy against sorrow, joy unspeakable. Such unspeakable joy becomes imaginable through the discomfort of watching Little, then Chiron, then Black, with Kevin.

It's about intimacy, touch, feeling.

It's about the search for something so wildly and radically free that he would wait to be touched like that again.

The film also confronts viewers with a fundamental truth: Homophobia in Black is not worse than its performance in other shades. The film does not allow audiences to decry the nature of blackness as the zone in which homophobia is produced. There was Juan. There was Teresa. There were the three Kevins. Each provided a space of reprieve and sanctuary; each provided refuge without judgment, without shaming.

What's that song that, when you hear it, makes you remember? That smell wafting from the kitchen that reminds you of Mama's cooking? That color seen that dredges up what happened that day in school so many moons ago?

Kevin hears a song and it forces him to recall Chiron. The sound of the song is memory for him and produces the occasion to reach out, to call, to seek reconnection, to seek touch. *Moonlight* is a sensual film because it uses various sense experiences—taste, touch, smell, sight, hearing—to be not just the path toward memory, but memory itself. In being about sense experiences, it is about how one feels—and Black religiosity, its history and tradition in the so-called new world, is all about feeling.

At its best, when not colluding with white supremacist capitalist patriarchy, Black religiosity allows us to learn how to love our flesh, and love it hard, in a world that does not deem blackness as loving or lovable. The characters typically would be considered sinners according to a lot of religious logics. So we have to think about how religion is unmarked in *Moonlight*, creating the opportunity to critique the way spaces of so-called sanctuary can become spaces of violence.

This is the genius of *Moonlight*. The film wages battle at the level of feeling. Such feeling is often the taboo of dreams or sometimes nightmares, never to be spoken aloud, never to be admitted. You dreamed of her but are not into women. You think of him, how he sometimes hugs you on the court quickly, but in that minuscule moment your heart heats, chest heaves, but he's just a basketball buddy. It's the feeling that emerges in night terrors that makes you smile and open your heart to capaciousness, to expansiveness, to possibility.

The film gathers and depicts the quiet brush of soft intimacy between friends. It is an intimacy learned and produced by gesture, by deep looks, sustained grasped hands. Grabbed sand, chopped onions, slow stares, held head. But then, I guess it's also about fear, about the fear that such a connection—once established—could be sustained. So, for many of us, we just reject the possibility altogether, reject the possibility as desirous, dismiss the possibility as ridiculous. But if we remain with the film, if we open ourselves up to its visceral nature, its touch and rub, its hush and hum, it has the capacity to transform what we think imaginable. And it produces the excitement of imagination through the most ordinary and everyday of encounters, the most simple and gentle ways of existence.

Moonlight is not a frivolous film. It is a film of its time, rooted in the 305, in the blackness of the Liberty Square housing project, in the complexity of character and life and love in Miami, in the freedom dreams that emerge from within the struggle with living, with touch, with desire. *Moonlight* is a touching film, illustrating the healing and generative force of touch between characters. And in such exchange between characters is the capacity for healing and a generative force for viewers. *Moonlight* reminds me that Black life is about a life touched and held, and that there is joy therein, that the touch I have sought and still seek is one that many of us desire, and that such desire is worthy of its pursuit.

And *Moonlight* reminds me that we should seek out and find delight in Black life, and that this joy and delight can be found in the general spaces, the regular places. That we can desire and find touch that frees; touch that makes us remember and makes us forget; touch that holds us close until we lovingly and intentionally embrace those parts of ourselves that we dared not speak into existence.

I want to have a life, a Black life, a resistant life of joy and peace and journeying into worlds otherwise, with you. Maybe that's just another way to say ongoing friendship and the joy of this way of life.

    A

Dear Moth,

Yes. Single. I've been single and the shit bothers me. And I know you wanna spiritualize it and say that I need to wait and be patient but I think, coming from you of all people, that it hurts to read you say that. It hurts when you say it on the phone. And you know it does because I hear your voice and you hear mine and you still talk to me and remain engaged and you know how I feel. And I know how *you* feel.

You never believe me when I say you're beautiful, though I suppose I said it after a bit too late. I know you think priesthood is what you desire and I'm not here to stop you, never have been, but I think and have thought you were and are beautiful since the first time I saw you, since the first time you opened your gap-toothed smile up to me, hesitant, speculative, hopeful. The way I felt when I first met you? Astonishment might be the closest thing to it, the best way to describe what I felt. Astonishment as a kind of intensity of sense experience that is, at the same time, a rupture into spacetime, making time and space otherwise than Newton.

Look at this article. It says that particles' "current" behaviors are based on their "future" states:

Quantum laws tend to contradict common sense. At that level, one thing can be two different things simultaneously and be at two different places at the same time. Two particles can be entangled and, when one changes its state, the other will also do so immediately, even if they are at opposite ends of the universe—seemingly acting faster than the speed of light.

Particles can also tunnel through solid objects, which should normally be impenetrable barriers, like a ghost passing through a wall. And now scientists have proven that, what is happening to a particle now, isn't governed by what has happened to it in the past, but by what state it is in the future—effectively meaning that, at a subatomic level, time can go backwards.

To bamboozle you further, this should all be going on right now in the subatomic particles which make up your body.[18]

Your smile? Astonished me, opened me, made me feel some future, some moment to come, as if it'd already happened. Your smile? It's as if the gap caused me to fall into a Black hole, a space of opportunity, your smile made me quiver. Your smile? It illustrated what I think science only wishes to approach, that when I saw it, I *knew* you, knew you before I knew your name, knew you and knew us as *us*, as *together*, as *entangled* from some hallucinatory effect from something bearing down on me from outside me. Your smile? Ecstatic force, that which was outside myself caused me to withdraw into it and, by withdrawing into it, made a different relation to spacetime not only possible but plausible, not only possible but desirous.

It's been years, yes, but it feels like yesterday. It wasn't so much that I thought you the most beautiful thing in the world—I did—and it wasn't that I thought our conversation was so wonderful—it was—that did it for me.

It was this: that first time we talked at the diner, I mentioned ever so briefly that *Just Above My Head* is my favorite novel, and that I'd been meaning to buy an original copy of it because the one I had was so marked up but never had the opportunity to purchase and, of course, I'd want an original printing of the book. Then we moved on to another topic but you took that information and lodged it in some *somewhere* far away in the recesses of your mind, only letting that knowledge flourish once again when months later—we were arguing, at that same diner, that night, after having spent so much time together that day and evening and the argument, of course, was not an argument at all but our closeness warming to each other—you allowed that knowledge to come back to the surface when I said to you,

You never listen or pay attention to me! I already told you that!

Did I know that you would go home that very evening, go online, find a copy of the original printing, purchase it for me? And then your scribbled handwriting in the front:

To prove that I both listen and pay attention to you . . .
—Moth

It was that that did it. That attention given to things that I did not even attend to as acutely as you did scared the shit outta me. What was I supposed to make of someone who could detect in me the traces and remnants of hurt and pain that I did not even realize I enunciated? I did not know that I had spoken to you so freely, after all. Of course, now that I think about it, I said nothing different than I'd normally say or do when spending time with someone who I was interested in. It was that you had an inclined ear toward those things, you not only heard the surface but into and around. It was the pauses and breaths I took that, I think, let you hear into the silence that was pulsating with meaning. But, of course, you heard the contours, heard the melody. It's like you opened up what was in the statement, like pulling out the drawbars of the Hammond B-3.

You see, *Just Above My Head* was recommended to me by someone who took notice of me when I was still in high school and he a senior in college and my mother—she was a secretary at the university—invited him to our house to eat on several occasions because he was far from home—New Orleans—and he said her kindasorta southern accent reminded him of everything he missed from home. That, and the piece of fried chicken she gave him when he smelled it wafting from the microwave as she heated it up when on break at work that day. He told her of how much he missed home and my mother was always inviting someone from the school down to the house and even though we didn't have much, she shared with everybody. So I was used to seeing all sorts of folks. Until I saw him. He was not what I was expecting. Sorta short, sorta fat, sorta nerdy, glasses, sorta high tenor voice, sort of a drawl whenever he spoke. And, well, I was into skinny boys who loved Jesus so that we could pray together for our sinning after we laid in the bed together.

He came to our house more than once and I was taken by his ability to tell me what to do:

Can I have some cold drink; can I have a napkin; may I borrow a fork

He'd ask all the time in the most polite way possible so much so that I knew I had to comply to that insistence, those painful but loving and shy requests. Painful, of course, because he did not want to ask for anything, he felt it a slight and imposition. He was the embodiment of sweet. Anyway, somewhere in the middle of the year of his visiting our home, probably in December now that I think about it, he went back to New Orleans for the holidays and I was expecting him that Sunday because he always came to our house every Sunday after church but not that Sunday.

Momma, is he coming over?

and

No, he's home for the holidays.

So I sat in my bedroom, held my teddy bear and began to cry. I still don't *know* why. I'd only watched him from the corner of my eye when he visited. I'd give him the things he'd ask for and retreat to my part of the table, not talking much, though he'd try and coax me into conversation often. Sorta amused contempt with this dude that would come to my house every Sunday as if he belonged. I resisted him for reasons I still do not comprehend because he was nothing if not kind to me. So there I was, in the bedroom, fourteen or fifteen or sixteen years old sobbing quite quietly because I did not want my mother or father to hear me.

Then the phone rang but it never rang for me so I didn't give it much attention. My mother knocked on the door and told me to pick up the phone and it was him on the other line,

I know you miss me just kidding but no I'm not I'm playin so I wanted to call and say hello I just wanted to wish you a happy holiday because I know I've been bothering you by stealing your mother every week and now you have to deal with me taking some of your food and my bad but I just wanted to thank you because you're a cool dude and you should know that and one day . . .

I did not, of course, know what to make of that run-on sentence but his voice washed over and under and through me like the spirit so I just rejoiced and was happy in the fact that I did not need to speak because my voice would have cracked anyway because I was crying.

That day began a new phase of our, I guess we could call it, friendship. And that same day, he told me how he had been reading *Just Above My Head* but how it was too much for me because I was still a sophomore, so too young to get it. He told me he would buy it for me when I was older but of course, he graduated, and I guess forgot about me, though I've never forgotten about him.

So yes, I mentioned *Just Above My Head* to you but only because I needed a new copy and wanted the original printing if possible. Your buying it for me was a closure of sorts and it also made me know that you would be attentive to me in ways that would both delight and annoy me. Isn't it the case that we want someone to fawn over us until they do and then we think it to be the case that perhaps something is wrong with that person to give so much attention to us in the first place? That, perhaps, that attentiveness will mean that they will also detect that which we want to remain hidden away?

At that moment you were more beautiful to me than beauty itself, than the concept of the beautiful. And, shit, it scared me. It was the book. It was the scribbling inside. It was that you knew how to make me overjoyed. But if that was joy then surely lurking around the corner was disappointment, or so I convinced myself.

Astonishment is like that. You are confronted with something awe-inspiring and -inducing. You are taken up in and assumed by that confrontation, dwelling therein, listening to it like music from some world otherwise—like a chord that keeps expanding and changing and inspiring through its progression—abiding and loving and existing in some otherwise temporality, some otherwise zone where *time is not* but what is given is and is *as* something constantly being taken away. Of course, what was being taken away in that infinitesimal encounter and confrontation was the idea that loneliness and brokenheartedness are perpetual and unending. Meeting you? I knew that shit was a farce and that happiness existed. Right in front of me. Smiling, gap-toothed, always. That smile? Maybe that's the moment of entanglement, the moment of being taken and joined with another. It's a sort of pairing that cannot be produced by laws and churches but only by intimacies, intimacies that emerge from the soon to come that determine the past nows.

But, of course, that's only one side of astonishment's encounter. You can't stay there forever, can you? Who knows? I'm pretty sure none of us stays long enough to find out if you can actually remain there so then we're released to the other side and we run far away from that which prompted such feeling in the first place. (And don't judge me for having many *in the first place* phrases; they are all anoriginal, in a way, they are all rooted in the same tradition of fear.)

By the time I figured out that kind of experience was possible and that it could be ongoing—how long had we lived together, sung and fucked together, and me not trust you still?—you were gone and talking about becoming a priest again. Again, as if for the first time. You know I still look at your copy of *Just Above My Head* almost daily, it's still on the bookshelf underneath the television. Do you know that I often pick it up off the shelf, thumb through it so as to act as if there is nothing written on the front flap such that every time I open the front flap I feign surprise? Or, not feign really, because I am and always am surprised by your knowledge of who I was (and am? and would be? who knows?) demonstrated by your scribbled writing, but be astonished, still?

It's because Baldwin says this:

Arthur realizes, for the first time, consciously, that Crunch listens to him, responds to him, takes him seriously—takes him seriously, even though he always makes fun of him.

And this:

You think, just because I'm bigger than you that I can't be in love?

And this:

Peanut and Red were happy simply because Crunch and Arthur were happy.

And this:

There is always a beat beneath the beat, another music beneath the music, and beyond.

And this:

The song does not belong to the singer. The singer is found by the song. Ain't no singer, anywhere, ever made up a song—that is not possible. He hears something. I really believe, at the bottom of my balls, baby, that something hears him, something says, come here! And jumps on him just exactly like you jump on a piano or sax or a violin or a drum and you make it sing the song you hear: and you love it, and you take care of it, better than you take care of yourself, can you dig it? But you don't have no mercy on it. You can't have mercy! That sound you hear, that sound you try to pitch with the utmost precision— and did you hear me? Wow!—is the sound of millions and millions and, who knows, now, listening, where life is, where is death?

And this:

Thirty [years old]. And I was alone, had been for a while, and might be for a while, but it no longer frightened me the way it had. I was discovering something terrifyingly simple: there is absolutely nothing I could do about it. I was discovering this in the way, I suppose, that everybody does, but having tried, endlessly, to do something about it. You attach yourself to someone, or you allow someone to attach themselves to you. This person is not for you, and you, really, are not for that person—and that's it, son. But you try, you both try. The only result of all your trying is to make absolutely real the unconquerable distance between you: to dramatize, in a million ways, the absolutely unalterable truth of this distance. Side by side, and hand in hand, your sunsets, nevertheless, are not occurring in the same universe. It is not merely that the rain falls differently on each of you, for that can be a wonder and a joy: it is that what is rain for the one is not rain for the other.[19]

Baldwin named an experience I sorta knew was available and possible in a vague sense but gave it flesh and bone, he didn't romanticize it nor make it heroic, he just made my imagination sense and feel and sorta hear and touch and taste and smell that there could be something if I opened my clenched fist of conservative theology, my clenched fist of dogmatism, and breathe and breathe and breathe and be, and hope eternal that perhaps I could find some kinda love if I stopped valuing solitude and loneliness and aloneness as the only possible habitation of divine call and encounter. I felt something echoing in me, a kind of noise for and of and about and in the service of freedom that I did not create, a noise that echoed that I had to have a fine attuned sense for. Baldwin heard and felt and sensed it too. He didn't romanticize nor make heroic the pursuit of blackqueer life, just elaborated as if it were one in many, one in infinite, ways that one could live life. And there's a devastating precision with which he writes.

Whatever we hear in music is after the fact of its having been sounded out before its being played. Music is always after the vibration, it is delayed. And if what the song sings is different than the song, then the singing is always an attempt, a failed attempt, to get at the song. And if the song doesn't belong to the singer but the singer is *for* the song (but, it seems important to note that Baldwin did not simply flip the statement but replaced *belong* with *for*), what it seems Baldwin is doing is also considering song and relation to it as necessarily a decolonial practice, a practice against possessive individualism, a practice that is about unfolding and outpouring and always having a posture of opening and yielding and giving.

There is a sorta clarity, a kind of refusal for the ornamental if the ornamental and the flourish meant dispensing with material and textured ways of life. The ornamental and flourish, for Baldwin, emerge through expanding upon the mundane and quotidian and ordinariness of love and heartbreak, of friends and family all. It's why the novel, every time I read it, still moves me.

I recently reread *Just Above My Head* again, as if it were the first time, and was struck by the chords of what always struck me, how—this time reading it—it's like Baldwin talked about love and song as a sorta laminated analysis of quantum entanglement. What I'm trying to say is, what I've been saying to and about you, about us is not novel at all, it's something that I can only write to you because of folks like Baldwin, because Baldwin gave me a kind of language and spacetime in which to dwell, his elaborations of Arthur and Crunch, of Arthur and Jimmy, of Arthur and his love for Hall.

Come over. Come see me. Please. Soon.

A

Dear Moth,

You're right. I don't think of the flesh and body as the same thing. I think of them as marking different sorta ideas about living in the world. Yes, thinking this way emerges from my having read Hortense Spillers.[20] But also, Toni Morrison. It almost feels trite quoting Baby Suggs to you because you know this shit better than I do but I think what she says, through Toni's pen, is what I mean by flesh.

In this here place, we flesh; flesh that weeps, laughs; flesh that dances on bare feet in grass. Love it. Love it hard. Yonder they do not love your flesh. They despise it. They don't love your eyes; they'd just as soon pick em out. No more do they love the skin on your back. Yonder they flay it. And O my people they do not love your hands. Those they only use, tie, bind, chop off and leave empty. Love your hands! Love them. Raise them up and kiss them. Touch others with them, pat them together, stroke them on your face 'cause they don't love that either. You got to love it, you! And no, they ain't in love with your mouth. Yonder, out there, they will see it broken and break it again. What you say out of it they will not heed. What you scream from it they do not hear. What you put into it to nourish your body they will snatch away and give you leavins instead. No, they don't love your mouth. You got to love it. This is flesh I'm talking about here. Flesh that needs to be loved. Feet that need to rest and to dance; backs that need sup-port; shoulders that need arms, strong arms I'm telling you. And O my people, out yonder, hear me, they do not love your neck unnoosed and straight. So love your neck; put a hand on it, grace it, stroke it and hold it up. And all your inside parts that they'd just as soon slop for hogs, you got to love them. The dark, dark liver—love it, love it and the beat and beating heart, love that too. More than eyes or feet. More than lungs that have yet to draw free air. More than your life-holding womb and your life-giving private parts, hear me now, love your heart. For this is the prize.[21]

And I keep thinking about what Adrian Piper does in her performance piece *Untitled in Max's Kansas City*, or not what she does as much as what she says she wanted the performance to do. She says:

Max's was an Art Environment, replete with Art Consciousness and Self-Consciousness about Art Consciousness. To even walk into Max's was to be absorbed into the collective Art Consciousness, either as object or as collaborator. I didn't want to be absorbed as a collaborator, because that would mean having my own consciousness be influenced by their perceptions of art, and exposing my perceptions of art to their consciousness, and I didn't want that. I have always had a very strong individualistic streak. My solution was to privatize my own consciousness as much as possible, by depriving it of sensory input from that environment; to isolate it from all tactile, aural, and visual feedback. In doing so, I presented myself as a silent, secret, passive object, seemingly ready to be absorbed into their consciousness as an object. But I learned that complete absorption was impossible, because my voluntary objectlike passivity implied aggressive activity and choice, an independent presence confronting the Art-Conscious environment with its autonomy. My objecthood became my subjecthood.[22]

It is the doing away of the distinction of object and subject that seems to approach what Baby Suggs discusses as the loving of flesh, that Adrian Piper's performance was already prefigured by Baby Suggs (and yes, I know that Baby Suggs was written *about* after Piper's performance but what I mean is that the withdrawal into the clearing is one that has been performed, time and again, a practice of marronage, Black mysticism in the flesh). Piper is talking about a particular world, the artworld, as producing a certain set of relations to objects. Baby Suggs, too, is talking about a particular world, let's call it the *yonderworld*, and how it too produces relation to objects.

The way yonderworld produces relations to blackness-as-object is by the renunciation of what is done *here in this place*, by renouncing anoriginal flesh, anoriginal laughter, weeping, dancing. What Baby Suggs allowed folks to withdraw into was a world that was not replete with Art Consciousness and Self-Consciousness about Art Consciousness, she allowed them to linger in a world that was not predicated upon the knowledge, and thus the philosophical and theological epistemological substratum, of European consciousness.

Of Piper, Fred Moten says,

This is what objection is, what performance is—an internal complication of the object that is, at the same time, her withdrawal into the external world. Such a withdrawal makes possible communication between seemingly unbridgeable spaces, times, and persons.[23]

So I'm thinking about Baby Suggs and Adrian Piper because I think of marronage as a tradition of Black mysticism that is, like Eckhart, Teresa, and St. John, about renunciation, retreat, and movement, but these things are done in the direction of the social, of the noise, of openness against the knowledge of western civil society.

Marronage, in a word, is a *withdrawal into the external world* that attempts a similar kind of refused absorption by operating at lower and otherwise frequencies and vibrational patterns, which is to say otherwise epistemologies, as a means to move into the outside, into the clearing, into the secret place of open space. It is a kind of knowledge that is antithetical to epistemological Consciousness of western thought. And we discover the internal differentiation, the fundamental and radical plurality, of the object as being otherwise than simple, simplistic, passive. Because, like Piper discovered, even the sense deprivation was a kind of statement of radical exorbitance, exceeding the desired deprivation and passivity, her entering the space with the announcement and enunciation of will and volition of the purportedly unwilled and unvolitional object. We typically think passivity the antithesis of will and volition, but she opens us up to other possibilities, that perhaps vulnerability is aggressivity too, that we need not give up or relinquish passivity as a means to becoming normal, as a means to cohering with a normative epistemology of passivity and aggression.

Marronage is the practice of what Audre Lorde calls the erotic, it is an otherwise spacetime density and field and zone in which deep longing and poetry as a way of life, a coming together of knowledge as performance of otherwise possibility, dances and plays and settles in love and joy. She says,

In the same way, we have attempted to separate the spiritual and the erotic, thereby reducing the spiritual to a world of flattened affect, a world of the ascetic who aspires to feel nothing. But nothing is farther from the truth. For the ascetic position is one of the highest fear, the gravest immobility. The severe abstinence of the ascetic becomes the ruling obsession. And it is one not of self-discipline but of self-abnegation.[24]

What Adrian Piper attempted was a performance of asceticism in the service of refusing collaboration with the external world, she attempted to protect herself against it appropriating her into its project of enlightenment thought. And what Baby Suggs did was attempt to preach the love of the flesh as a response to the violence of the external world, another sorta protection against being appropriated by the knowledge regime of coloniality. But rather than refusing withdrawal, Baby Suggs creates another world altogether, or really, allows us to sense the way yonderworld and hereinthisplaceworld are carried and renounced wherever one goes. Audre Lorde got this, that what blackness is a calling of, a sending to, is a movement to the world, for the world, as otherwise possibility.

Piper wanted to resist collaboration and I understand because she was resisting a specific world, the *Art Conscious* world, a world predicated upon individuation, predicated upon possessive individualism, predicated upon the exclusion of blackqueer, Blackpentecostal social life. But I want to think about entanglement as a consent to be in ongoing collaboration, the collaboration fundamental to alternate modalities of existence. What would it mean to withdraw into one another as the condition for how we live and survive the brutality of an antiqueer, antiblack world?

I keep thinking about particles and their current behavior being something that is anything but current, how the very concepts of past, present, and future need to be rethought given the way particles only determine what they are *now* based on what they will be. What they will have been, what they will be to come, determines what they are now. And there's something very lovely and loving about that sorta collaborative possibility, that entanglement, that literally goes against linearity of time and space. What particles show me, I think, is that

love is here because it is coming,
because it will come soon,
because it made a way soon to come for it to be now.

    This is the clearing, right? This is what withdrawal into the *external* world would mean. Baby Suggs knew that there was something to come that established the possibility of her momentary *now* of the clearing. That the clearing could be available, would be available, *now* meant that something, some affective mood or movement, some ancestor-ly protection and plea from outside spacetime, against the linearity—which is also the coloniality—of spacetime and its subject and subjectivity, made a way "ahead" of time, against time, before the *now* time, that something soon to come made the way to preach the love of the flesh. This is not, though it can be thought alongside, the Christian concept of already/not yet. And the reason I don't think it is the same thing as Christian theology of the already/not yet is because that is Kingdom theology, a theology of sovereignty under Satan and sovereignty under God. What remains, what is left uninterrogated, in such a theological proposition is the conceptual place of and for sovereignty, that a deity or deities or their opposites and oppositions are ultimately in control, and that sovereignty is not itself a problem against the flourishing of life. And, also, that the *kingdom* exists already but awaits its fullness is, to me as well, a problem. Not just the fact that it awaits fullness as a kind of perfectibility but also that it is a *kingdom* or what some have opted to call a *kindom*. In either instance, it marks a relation to the divine that is about a being that is ultimate, absolute, in control. And I'm not with that. What I'm after is a way to think the practice of something to come not in linear or causal relation to now at all. It'd be something more like—but imprecisely so because our language is undermined by being organized around the coloniality of and as linearity—now/because to-come.

It would have been this way
But it would have also been
Otherwise

Otherwise announcing that something could have been this or that, the soon-to-come possibility as bearing down on the now. What is time, what is space, in such a set of potentialities? Some entangled reality, some entangled materiality, across and against and beyond spacetime determined the possibility of a *now* love, of a preaching *now about* love, to preach and compel such love in order to get the prize, a prize that'd been determined already won. *This is the prize.*

I don't know. It's beautiful. And I think, maybe, astonishing too. Maybe that smile of yours was sent from outside that time and space too. You know, Muslims got a belief that gap toothed smiles are sacred, that the Prophet—peace be upon him—had a gap in his front teeth, right? You're so holy to me, it's like a move into a different mood and dimension.

A

Dear Moth,

I had another one of those dreams again last night, and, as with each time, I was able to feel just a bit more last night which, it turns out, made me even more upset with you. It's like this thing I read recently written by Sam Delany:

The process as we move our eyes from word to word is corrective and revisionary rather than progressive. Each new word revises the complex picture we had a moment before.[25]

But maybe not even *corrective* because if life is something like a thing that unfolds, revision would be without correcting because what would correct be if there weren't the assumption of normativity toward which one aspires, or breaks? And perhaps not just a sentence but maybe also a song?

Or a dream.

I keep having that recurring dream but last night, it was revised again with another scene. And you were in it, so of course, providence would have me write you again. I swore to myself the last time I wrote that it would be the last time but the declaration to myself of a last time is always a ruse unless the last time is really the last time and I thought it was the last time but indeed it was not the last time just the first time my saying it would be the last time in a long time.

It was that same dream I'd have as a kid about me being some sort of Black Superman—no doubt because of the sheets my mother had for the twin bed, the sheets that were a shade too thin because they were a bit too old and faded, and had been hand-me-downs from some other boy who would have slept on them. But she cared about making me feel good and the sheets were the stuff of dreams for boys.

The sheets were full of repetitious images of a white Superman—I suppose, the *real* Superman—with all of his musculature twisting, and the word *zzap!* written on them. Three different images of this Superman: one with him in a white cloud in some would-be attack pose, as if in hiding, waiting for the right time to surprise the enemy, no doubt Lex Luthor; another with his body twisted, mid-action as if he were about to be hit with something, right arm over his head, left arm as if he were trying to push some *something* away; and the third with him flying directly out of the sheets, looking at me, smiling a bit, almost erotically. I'm sure the latter was my own libidinous bullshit or whatever. (I googled. And checked. The sheets do exist. I didn't just dream them up.) The point is that I slept on these sheets all of the time.

And so from an early age, sleeping on those sheets, I would have faux race-conscious dreams where I, the Black Superman and real hero, would fight the evil one on my sheets. We'd twist and wrestle with and against each other. Things, of course, are a bit fuzzy and my recall of these dreams is not that great. Not because I didn't have the same one last night but because they've always had some noise speckled in during the fight scene.

Somehow, I'd end up:

at,
at a,
at a white,
at a white house,
at a white house with,
at a white house with a,
at a white house with a picket,
at a white house with a picket fence.

Stutter. Slurred speech. Dazed dream. You get it.

Each time I have the dream, I arrive to one of these new concepts, each one accruing on the other—at its margin and edge—until, finally, I realized that I was fighting white Superman over some living space. But last night, the newest scene, and of course, you. It was much more prolonged, maybe because of longing. I was fighting him . . . for you. Imagine my surprise when I finally opened the door to the house—with my keys—walked in, and the kids—our kids—ran up to my knees and screamed "Daddy! Daddy's home!" as if I'd been away far too long, and you came out of the bedroom with your glasses on, eyes a bit fatigued because you were reading in the office, or typing or some *something*, and the

faintest hint of a smile dashed across your face because—even in the dream—
you realized that it was me who you were waiting for . . . and not Superman.

What does it mean to go from the first dream—knowing I was *at*, that is, I
was somewhere but didn't know where that somewhere was—to this latest episode where not only did I know where that somewhere was—*with* you—but that
I knew who all the hoopla was about—*over* you? I still don't know where this
where was—Chicago? San Francisco? New Orleans? who knows? who cares?—
but I know that *where* only means something *with* you.

We left the kids—our kids, what a thought—left them in their beds with
their Superman sheets, the same ones my mother cared for, and we went into
the bedroom. And no need to tell you what happened there but I never knew
you had a birthmark on your inner thigh until last night. And I know you don't
but in the dream you did. Dreams are so cool because they open up a space for
perpetual discovery.

What to make of this dream, this discovery of *with* and *over* that is bound up
with you, this discovery of birthmarks and new ways to make love? A message
of—or would it be *from*—provenance? I guess I don't need to tell you how we
had a good time in that bedroom either. But what I do need to tell you is this:
I did not want it to end. I wanted to stay there because somehow, in the faint
smile you gave me that was real, I knew that it was a dream.

And I should tell you that I carried you—I am not strong, and you were not
heavy, but still, a feat to be noted—I carried you around the bedroom, over the
threshold into the bed and scooped you up again and then put you back down.
I wanted to carry you out of the dream and I awoke while you were still in my
arms.

I have been reading Baldwin again and he had all these great things to say
about being astonished when white people were astonished because he actually
likes his mother. Two astonishments meet. Like us? You were astonished that
you could meet who you thought you wanted and knew you felt until you felt it
and retreated because it felt too true? And I was astonished to meet someone I
could carry over thresholds—mental, emotional—because I had always wanted
to and you were large enough and small enough and great enough and humble
enough and loving enough and selfish enough to let me do it?

| NOISE |

The dream was revised—right before I picked you up a final time and I awoke with you in my arms—when I went to the armoire, opened a drawer that you had not yet seen with all of the letters I'd written to you and never sent when we were *before* dating. I just wrote, hoping to one day collect the letters and put them in a book and give to you on an anniversary or some other occasion when you needed to be reminded how much you were thought of and appreciated even when you couldn't conceive of this as an idea. And you cried and I'd never seen such happy tears. But the thing about the entire dream? The entire episode from white and Black Supermans to thresholds and drawers and carryings? There was absolutely no sound. Nothing at all. Not even a hum or buzz in the background. I—we?—felt things, intense things, great things, scary things, longing things, hard things, tight things, round things, rough things, intimate things, lovely things. But there was no sound between us, or from the universe into which we were living and through which we acted. That silence, of course, said *something* to us about us and for us.

But who is to know what exactly?

A

Dear Moth,

Ever heard of the movie *La Petite Vendeuse de Soleil*? It's this excellent film I stumbled on while reading through blogs about foreign movies. The blog linked to this review:

Senegalese avant-gardist Djibril Diop Mambety's La Petite Vendeuse de Soleil is the second in a trilogy of shorter films, called Tales of Ordinary People (the first was 1995's Le Franc). The film is an 'homage' by the director to street children. Sili is a little girl between ten and thirteen years old. She lives on the street and moves with crutches. Her legs cannot support her since she had polio. She tries to get close to the boys who sell newspapers, but they push her and make her fall. She gets irritated and decides to take her destiny in her own hands. Instead of begging, she will sell newspapers like the boys. Equal rights for both sexes. Although the world of the newspaper boys is cruel and merciless, along with pain, she also finds friendship. The film was shot on the street with the participation of the street children. La Petite Vendeuse de Soleil was screened as part of the International Forum of New Cinema section of the 49th Berlin Film Festival, 1999.—Gönül Dönmez-Colin, All Movie Guide.[26]

Funny thing is, quite literally, the day after I'd had my dream about Black and white Supermans, about our children and about carrying you over thresholds, I found the blog and then read the review for the film. So anyway, I was sold, found the movie at the library and took it to a friend's house so we could watch together but I wasn't prepared for the film or what it made me feel.

The film is about a little girl—named Sili—living in Dakar, Senegal, with her grandmother and because money was needed, she decided to sell newspapers—*Le Soleil*. Her grandmother was blind and, let's say, a highway beggar (kinda like Albertina Walker singing about Bartimaeus in the song "Spread the Word"), one who needed the support of others (and no, this is not a moral judgment against needing others; I've been trying to think lately about if *needing others* is the condition that makes us people, actually, if our vulnerability that is common and shared should be something that we celebrate and cultivate in the cause of justice). Of course, this created tension in the film because Sili was twelve years old and was competing with a group of young boys around her age who also sold the same (and other) periodicals. It wouldn't be that interesting except folded into the story is the notion of *carrying* as well as *giving*, which of course reminded me of you (I'd almost say that finding out about the film the day after writing to you about carrying you *carried* some mystical, spiritual quality, content, or substance and maybe I should just wait . . . for you . . . for me to carry you).

In the film, Sili is paraplegic and uses crutches to get around, which would—to normative eyes—make the selling of *Le Soleil* most difficult. But she doesn't allow what is deemed by some to be normative inhabitation of the flesh to hinder her desire to assist her grandmother. The boys who were her competitors used her abilities against her. They'd quite literally knock her down and steal her crutches. Intriguingly, her first day on the job, a businessman purchased all thirteen newspapers from her and gave her more to compensate for her industry, thrift, and hard work. With the profit she made from the sales, she took the money and purchased an umbrella that would cover her grandmother from the sun, giving the shade necessary for her to sit throughout the day and pray, beg, talk, socialize. Her fortune was immediately shared with others not just in the way of giving money to others, which she did, and not just by buying her friends clothes and throwing them a party—which she also did—but also by her giving care as cooling in the heat, practicing protection for and with the one who would so protect her.

But all these details don't mean much. It's the final scene that is most powerful to me: the rival boys knocked Sili on the ground, then stole her crutches and newspapers. Again.

Her friend who sold newspapers as well but who helped her and did not consider himself a rival extended his hand to Sili, lifted her off the ground, placed her on his back, and carried her so they could proceed along the journey. After having placed her on his back, he questioned, *What's next?*

Her reply: *We continue.*

This was, of course, better than the dream I had because it showed me that ones who do so much work to cover and carry others also, at various times and places, need to be carried and covered. The film was a constant display of *a shed*, of musicians playing together, filling in spaces through improvisation and creativity, who use skill, care, thoughtfulness, and rigor to create new out of seeming necessity. Sheds don't have time limits, they are determined by coming together to make music.

My previous dream ended rather abruptly with me carrying you and things going fuzzy thereafter. But this film gave me the two words *we continue* with the gesture of carrying.

The point?

In my insistence to carry, I did not realize that carrying may well be letting go, or, to sound hella cheesy, holding you in my heart or some shit. Anyway. In my insistence to carry, I did not realize that I, too, was formed in patriarchy, and you too, that we both have to work on a way to be and to be together that undoes the systems of inequity that keep us bound, even when that bounding and binding is being unkind to each other, or not being fully present to the desires and wishes of each other, consent as a necessary gate through which we must both enter together, a mutuality of enjoyment and pleasure and struggle. They, Sili and her friend, continued because they were together through it all. If my dream indicates anything, it is for noncoercive desire but it is also for friendship. So it will be what it must be in order to continue to learn and grow and make music.

(Even if by withdrawing, by letting go,) we continue,

A

Dear Moth,

There are worlds. And the fact of our experiencing them is because we are impossibly vulnerable, open, as a way of life. The central nervous system isn't enclosed in the borders of the so-called body. But it's out there, in worlds; that which is central is kind of an ecstatic force, ecstatic being, existence beside or otherwise than, the self. Such that the idea of an outside and inside needs to be thought against. Maybe entangled. Maybe a system. That's why I talk about flesh instead of a body because, for me at least, flesh names this kind of openness, this necessary vulnerability.

It's been a while since I've heard from you. You sent that text when you returned home that you shouldn't have come over, that you're sorry you cried, that you love me but can't. And then all this talk, mostly, about god. And it's taken me some time to think about what you wrote to me about god. I had to think about it, had to think about what you think god is.

So here . . .

What quantum physics is discovering is a redefinition of spacetime as not linear nor separable. If this is the case and god is, as you say, an unfolding, then this god would be the unfolding of all that is and is not detectual (able to be detected) by sensual capacities. This would mean that there is some something "behind" or that withdraws from even this quantum understanding of spacetime, some otherwise sorta relation, some sorta unity and convergence that would undo even the concepts of unity, convergence, together, sociality, unfolding, enfolding, undoing, doing, action, reaction. Does this make sense?

And that would then mean love too, right? Because don't we think of love as the unfolding of possibility in time and space, or following quantum mechanics, in spacetime, love as approaching a kinda sociality of experience? But then maybe also love would be that which necessarily withdraws, through approach, the very possibility of "possibility." Because what does it mean for something or nothing to be *of*—from or marking relation to—"possibility" if "it" recedes from sense experience? Love as the sense experience beyond sensuality, beyond or withdrawing from or below or sharing some other kinda relation to experience? It's like when Fred Moten says to Wu Tsang in conversation,

The first time I heard the sound of your voice it filled me with a sense of the future perfect. The friendship I will have had. Getting to know you. Sounding without thinking. Walking. Just walking and heart beating. Out of synch, but in time.[27]

To be *filled with a sense* and for that sense to be of the *future perfect* means that the voice was a point of departure for excess, it exceeded the very possibility of delimitation, was its own enactment of otherwise, a rip in spacetime linearity. And that's how it was with you, too. We exist in and as excess, as that which cannot be contained or engulfed or enclosed by *anything*, negation and exclusion included.

It's as if we are the flesh of what quantum mechanics is discovering.

And flesh vibrates, flesh—like matter in general—is antithetical to settlement, to settler logics, to being settled. And I won't settle. And I will continue to pursue what at times feels at most like a hunch or a vague sense of possibility or perhaps even like a pulling toward, something sorta like a dream trying to be pieced together after having awoken abruptly and having felt deeply but losing such feeling second by second though you know, though you intuit, that though you have not attained, pressing in such a direction will fulfill a promise to come. And I will continue precisely because my now moment is dictated by some moment to come sensed as verve and visitation from outside the possibility of spacetime. And I won't settle because it happened, because it happens, because it is happening, because it will happen.

What I'm trying to say, imprecisely, is this: I think I love you? I watch *An Oversimplification of Her Beauty*, as you know, a lot.[28] And I get why she sent the text she did, why it was a question that was also a statement, how it was tentative but also very sure.

I think I love you?

I finally understand because you, Moth, make me feel what I've just been afraid to say but I know to be true: I have never felt this way about anyone—*anyone*—in my life before. And that sounds like a platitude.

But this is what I mean: You are, and my feeling for you is, Black noise, is static, is sorta the background against which everything I do occurs. I don't consciously think about you all of the time, no. But I feel you. When I sleep, when I wake, when I cook, when I sing, as I breathe, as I breathe, as I breathe, it's you. A sorta quiet omnipresence, a soft enclosement, you are the noise, almost chant-like, I hear sorta far off in the deep recesses and furthest reaches of my flesh. And yet, you feel more than near, closer than anything I've ever known. I do not think *about* you as much as I think: you. It's as if you are bound to each thought—whatever that thought might be—I think. It's as if you are the ground of all that is for me. I don't mean this in a way pathological or that I cannot exist without you, that I have some sorta weird codependence that is more about ego and narcissism than about your well-being or mine. I mean that I desire you, and I feel we are one.

It's like what I said to you in that text message not soon after meeting you, it's as if in and with you I'd found the voice in my head to which I was constantly searching, the voice in my head to which I was always replying, as if meeting you confirmed that *we* already *were*, that *we* already *was*, as if meeting you were the promise and the fulfillment of the promise, a breakdown of simultaneity through a spacetime rip or tear or break.

I understand David and Jonathan and being knit together.

Unlike weaving, knitting does not require a loom or other large equipment, making it a valuable technique for nomadic and non-agrarian peoples.[29]

They were knit together and were movers, nomadic. Nomads are wanderers and I'm thinking about David's psalm, talking about walking through the valley of the shadow of death but not fearing, wandering in death's shadow but still feeling assured. And though this twenty-third is about the Lord, I wonder if it's also about what had been backgrounded, David's being knotted up and tangled with Jonathan.

And what I mean is this: I think I love you. No question mark.

And what I mean is this: I have not stopped telling everyone about you, the joy you have brought and continue to bring me.

And what I mean is this: there is not only you in the world but you are my paraclete, and I, yours.

And what I mean is this: I want a consensuality with you, a continued consent to be together, a way of life that will always have friendship as the first and always plural operation.

And what I mean is this: entanglement might be the best way to approach what I feel, that once joined together, we are a system. We maintain our uniqueness regardless of the nearness or farness, regardless of spacetime separation, we are indivisible, we renounce the individual for the social, for and with and in each other.

And what I mean is this: it's as if dreamworlds were hallucinating otherwise universes as possible, and my and your dreamworlds outpoured toward each other, enfolded into and collapsed within each other.

And what I mean is this: it's kinda beautiful, and mostly scary, because I don't know what this means and haven't since I first met you and am unsure what to do. I do not want to control you. Your consent is more necessary than my desire.

And what I mean, finally, is this: I don't want you to go to seminary if it means you will not, and cannot, be with me. I want to support you but why the priesthood when they require celibacy? My stomach churns at the thought of us not being together, I literally get sick at the thought. Your t-shirt that you left here when you were last here, I have not yet washed because the smell of sweat and Polo cologne and you and you and you linger on, in it. Don't do this. Please. I hate to even ask such a thing. Don't not go for me. But please don't go. I know St. Sabina was formative for you, that you chose that space of care and were so compelled, you were able to get your parents to join too. I know you want to continue in the tradition of the folks there, that you too think the University of St. Mary of the Lake is the place to which you are called to study for a master's degree and all but, but . . . please. Do you think this will make you happy? Can you do the justice work and the preaching work in another tradition? I need you too.

I am not just speaking metaphorically, I want to be touched by and to touch you continually. I'm not talking about some abstract kind of affection but a real feeling of and with and in you. And reciprocally. Love is a material thing, it breaks open imagination and makes possible other ways of conceiving what we can think and do and be.

Until the spacetime beyond whenwhere I no longer feel you, which will never be,

A

Dear Moth,

You said it was beautiful, that you believed me, but didn't say much else. You ignored my texts and haven't returned my calls. It's been two months and there's not been a word from you. I've given you the space you didn't even ask for but I intuited you desired, you needed. But, if the shit I said was so beautiful and moving to you, why the intensity of silence? Is the beauty also on the edge of grotesque, too much, too weighty for you? How is it that the thing you called beautiful is also that which made you recoil and retreat not into but away from me? It makes me feel you don't value me. And I don't know, shit is terrible.

I know before I said that I wanted you without it being a weird codependence but that was imprecise. There's nothing wrong with depending on another; my friends Tina and Amalle reminded me that it's sorta the condition of our lives, to need one another. Why demonize or pathologize need or desire or want? It's just, I wanna be able to depend on you to reply to me, to tell me what you feel, how you feel, when you feel it. I want to be able to depend on you without being parasitic. And I talked about consent so much because if you do not desire what I do, I cannot and do not want to compel you to do so. What you desire is just as important as what I do.

Can we figure out a way, a method, to be together, to practice intimacy and friendship, that is mutual and sustaining and joyful and, yes, consensual? I am not trying to convince you, I am asking what you desire. And if that changes, then we have to figure out *an*ethical ways to revisit, to revise, to improvise. But we haven't had the occasion to have modeled for us the kind of blackqueer relationality we desire. Joseph Beam told us that Black men loving Black men is the revolutionary act, but how can we inflect that to account for genderqueerness, for gender nonconformity, for trans identity? I think what Beam was attempting to get us to consider is how love from a blackqueer spacetime disrupts what we consider to be the normative and that that itself is revolutionary. How can we think about blackqueer feminist, womanist, fem(me) life as a model for how *we* can practice friendship and intimacy? Audre Lorde's work is a model, I think. But also, Alice Walker's.

I've been thinking a lot lately about the idea in *The Color Purple* that we piss the gods off when we walk by splendor and do not pause to take it in. Something as normal and quotidian and ordinary as the color purple should stop us and make us think about the joys of everyday living, how so much beauty is in and all around us at every moment. And I've been thinking about Celie's "I'm here," her declaration that the fact of her breath, the fact of her flesh, means we must contend with and care for and love her. Her "I'm here" is so holy to me, this blackqueer woman, in love with life, her sister, and Shug.

And I have been thinking a lot about Walker's essay, "In Search of Our Mothers' Gardens," and how she talks about what our mothers have made but also what has been disallowed because of the lack of material resource.[30] What she sharpens for me is that one pernicious aspect of white supremacist, capitalist, heteropatriarchal violence is the way in which access to resources brings to fruition what people imagine. But the garden is also where we turn to detect what is materially practiced by the imagination. What we lack is a real attunement to folks like Cheryl Clarke—to live life as lesbian—to reimagine what it would mean for cisgender, genderqueer, and trans men to reimagine queer relationships with and between ourselves and the worlds in which we find ourselves. All that to say what I desire with and in you has to be figured out differently, maybe "The Combahee River Collective Statement" can be a guide? Maybe *The Color Purple* or *Sister Outsider* and that combined with *In the Life*?

You misunderstand me when you think I say there are worlds and that I am only talking about love, or when I say that I am entangled with you and your smile, that it did something to me. You misunderstand me because I think we are an example, minuscule of course, of things otherwise. I'm thinking of blackness as the marking of alternatives. I'm thinking of indigeneity, too, as that marking. And queerness. And I'm thinking of these as mutually constitutive categories, as nondivisional, not in order to liquidate and evaporate difference but in order to say that western logics of thinking relation have been imposed on us.

Anyway, what I mean is, blackness would have to also be against linear time. And indigeneity. And queerness too. These would not be additive but a different relation. This different relation isn't created by western epistemologies but is the resistance to that categorical coherence. These would not then be identities, no matter how hard we try to turn them into property, but the resistance to identity. They would be, instead, ways of life, ways to live, ways to relate to one another *against* the imposition of identification as that which would sever and divide us.

What I mean is, blackness and indigeneity and queerness mark an otherwise spacetime. This spacetime would not be linear in its trajectory or force. And I'm thinking, what if the encounter with Black being, with indigenous being, with queer being, is also a confrontation with a kind of refused refusal of entanglement, an encounter with the confrontation of the fact of entanglement, the fact of an encounter of a different and very much material—because imagined and produced—disruptive epistemology? So what would we be if we consented to figuring out alternative modes and forms for operation? What would it mean for you to say you're straight if straightness is an operation of the western regime of epistemological problems? What blackqueerness hallucinates for us is a way to disrupt this normativity.

And that shit is scary, I know. But what else are we supposed to do?

A

Dear Moth,

You broke something open in me that had been vaulted away, deserted, renounced, for such a long time. It was in you that I found that I was seeking
something without knowing it. So thank you, thank you for all that you are,
for all that you have been. I no longer want to control you, not even the kinda
control that is attempted by a sorta counterfactual appearance of release. I have
to release you only to hope and mutuality, to a desire—noncoercive. You taught
me that, taught me the importance of that. Love is the impossible extension of
an ordered time; the desire of impossible non-spacetime where the joy of music plays consistently eternal; the raptured rupture produced in sounds of bass,
handclaps, foot stomps, melismas, and falsettos. Love is seeking a world otherwise *wherewhen* one can linger.

    May that which makes us one be always with you,

     A

Dear Moth,

Blackness is an *an*aesthetic encounter. What I mean is this: it's the performance of the refused divisionality of sense experience produced as an epistemological possibility in western thought. Blackness is anaesthetic insofar as it displaces western sense divisionality for an enfleshed, fundamental, and foundational unitary mode, an anoriginal nondivisionality. Blackness is the force of the en-counter of such an experience.

W. E. B. Du Bois in his well-known but under-read *Black Reconstruction* makes an argument that was, previous to his writing, curious and, immediately after, dismissed as impossible. The thrust of his argument was that enslaved peoples did not wait for Honest Abe to free them, that they were not simply laboring fields and in home until the day of the lord should come. He argued that these pieces of property, these supposed beasts of burden, these purport-edly socially dead bodies liberated themselves. And he makes such an assertion by discussing how, during the gestating moments of what would become the American Civil War, the enslaved began massive work stops, how they enacted work strikes, how they performed and moved beyond Marx's concept of the gen-eral strike. But because they were not comprehended by what Denise Ferreira da Silva calls "juridic universality nor self-determination," such action, such enactment, went misrecognized, such action, such enactment, was considered to be nothing at all.[31]

Following the work of Cedric Robinson, we might say that the incapacity to be comprehended because of the lack of juridic universality and self-determination produces a directional problem because of the presumption of linear time and space that is the grounds for thinking in the west. (For example, Marx's theory of alienation anticipates but cannot understand the concept; he establishes but cannot elaborate the theory because of the theory's directional assumption, and thus, problem.) Robinson argues that Marxism is a radicalism that emerges from within and thus cannot fully contend against European thought because Marx cannot account for racial categorization and distinction as a problem of

European thought that colors how he thinks the possibility for labor, exploitation, and the possibility for a strike. Forgotten labor.

In *On the Way to Language*, Martin Heidegger discusses a poem written by Stefan George that ends:

So I renounced and sadly see:
Where word breaks off no thing may be.[32]

I want to think about what George thinks of as the break and thus the no thing, the nothing, that can be, that can happen, that can occur. And it is because of this: the Black Radical Tradition has been misrecognized because its lineaments and sinews, another way to say its fleshliness, emerges from and performs what Cedric Robinson thinks of as not an alternative *of* the social order of western thought but an alternative *to* the social ordering complete with how it hierarchizes knowledge production and, with such hierarchizing, how it forces knowledge to produce and be produced by racial capitalism as its logic and structure. The word, for Stefan George, breaks off but we that are not comprehended because we lack juridic universality and self-determination participate in the tradition of nothingness in all its manifold witness, its plentitude, its fleshliness of otherwise possibility.

Du Bois figured out in his work that a general strike that Marx anticipated and desired was germane to the US emancipatory project that Black folks were producing through collective, improvisational, intellectual labor of work stoppage. And this in order to liberate themselves. Robinson extends Du Bois to say that resistance showed up emphatically and constantly as the practice of marronage, of secreting away, of revolutionary struggle. But such things showed up as no thing, as nothing, because from western thought's gaze, from its ocularcentric comportment, nothing can be where the word breaks. Yet, even the breaking is not the end of but opens the path to otherwise possibility. This is why Nathaniel Mackey could write *From a Broken Bottle Traces of Perfume Still Emanate*. Brokenness becomes the occasion for the emergence of alternative strategies for engagement. And so, like what Du Bois discovered, perhaps we need to move in the direction of, to be on the way to, a general strike.

What all this means is that the sensual register in which life *in the veil* happens, in which Black life is lived, is by way of a different genre of sensed possibility, the underrepresentation, the refused representation, of sense experience, the undoing of the overrepresentation of Man. It means that the sense register of blackness is by a mystical renunciation, a mystical retreat, away from all that we are taught to want, that we are taught we must want.

There is a blackqueer thrust in thingliness. We say, *chile, look at that thing!*, or point when the good-looking one walks down the street, *that is a thiiiiiing!*, and sometimes even double it, *that is a thing thing!* . . . Such an assertion is about withdrawal and attraction, about lack and desire.

Fred Moten:

The Marxian tendency to demystify the interiority of the thing becomes problematic, if you think about persons as things. You might want to demystify the interiority of this book, this notebook, but it is harder to feel justified in demystifying the interiority of a person. On the other hand, that tendency to mystify the thing, to imagine that the thing has the capacity of or capacity for, is problematic because of the way Heidegger envisions thinking about the thing as structured foremost around its fundamental emptiness. In other words, the thing is important insofar as it can bear content, but the reason it can bear content is because it is empty, fillable, manipulable, subject to external motive force.

I am trying to think about things in a different way. But it's tough because the discourse on slavery that recognizes the juridical and economic identity of persons and things in Afro-American history is structured by a simultaneously righteous and self-righteous moralism that both wants and has to be pissed off at the moment when persons are understood to be or to have been reduced (and the moralism is embedded in the word "reduced") to things . . . [T]he attempt to distance personhood from thingliness is the philosophical condition of possibility of the brutality we imprecisely characterize as the reduction of personhood to things.[33]

What if we accepted the fact of our being things, things among other things? What if we resisted the desire for assumption, for being raised out from and into the zone of subjectivity, the zone of being, the zone of the citizen, the human, modern man? What if we resisted this desire because such desire only emerges through a violent political economy that informs such an aspiration as desirous, as that which would produce the possibility for not being violated? It's the relay between assumption and exaltation that Fred Moten talks about, and these words both have very distinctly theological resonances, they are both about a certain kind of positionality and being valued in the normative world of western thought and action. But what if we go mystical, what if we mystify the refusal of the distinction between the interior and exterior, what if we relish in the life of thingliness as a blackqueer kinda celebration of walking down the street?

This is what I mean: I'd sit on the stoop, once I finally found my way out the closet, and talk with other blackqueer friends. And a good-looking boy—sometimes cishet, sometimes genderqueer, sometimes trans, who knows?—would walk down the street and one of us would be like, *you see that thing?!* or, *looooook at that thing!*, or, even, the doubled, *thaaaat is a thing thing!* This was not a degradation of the person, not a degradation of the flesh, but a celebration of it, a desire for deep connection even if only evident initially at the surface.

Recognizing the thing, aspiring for a connection with things, this was a sorta blackqueer force of possibility without ever foreclosing thingliness as celebratory. And it wasn't about assumption in a sorta Mary-the-mother-of-Jesus sense, it wasn't about exaltation, it was about the flesh, the funk, commingling possibility of it all. Maybe the content of the thing is only ever relational, maybe the thing is never empty but always wandering, always on the way, always walking down the street waiting for connection, for infilling, for indwelling.

A

tongues³

Dear Moth,

Why do I think about joy so much?

It's the moment when in the dance club, the DJ—through beatmatching and crossfading—mixes between two songs, the mixing announcing the fact that the beat, the rhythm, can be otherwise purposed. I've been listening to a lot of '90s house music, so the DJ as a kind of figure of intellectual practice has been on my mind, how this figure gathers and disperses sound by attempting to announce relation. It's sorta the same thing in Blackpentecostal singing wherein songs do not end so much as blend together.

It's about touch, right? Think about Jesus and him saying his virtue went outta him, after having been touched, by the woman with the issue of blood. It's like a kind of friendship where things rub up against each other, they rub up and touch, and touching is so much how I'd describe my relation to you. Once touched by you, both physically and emotionally, virtue left me and entangled me with you. I mean this: I want to beatmatch and crossfade, that's what I think love and blackness and mysticism all are, the openness to a vulnerability that would have such match and fade possibly imagined and performed.

Jean-Luc Nancy is thought to have said, "in order to touch, there must first be space to do so,"¹ and I wanna recognize the space in order to care for it, tend to it, cultivate it, move within it, to discover what can be felt by attending to the space between. But I do feel a lot of shame and embarrassment for wanting you because you are not available. And I don't want to resent you like I resent the ones that have, for various reasons, let me get away. I think the reason Tamar's narrative is one to which I return continually is because her question—*where could I carry my shame?*—is one that struck me as so precisely how I've felt for such a long duration, embarrassingly so. I don't know where to carry the desire I have for you. If I can find another, as you keep suggesting, what would that mean about our engagement, our entanglement?

Excessus mentis translates to "fiery prayer" and was an experience John Cassian had in the fifth century, it was *an intense and often short-lived experience of ecstasy or rapture in prayer.*[2] *Excessus* and *excessive* share a kind of homophonic connection, a homophonic kinship, if you will. When first reading about *excessus mentis*, I immediately began to think all over again about excess, the excessive, the way blackness is that which resists delimitation, how it is excess and the performance and enfleshment of excess. Excessus has the meaning of departure, demise, digression, deviation . . . so it's about being out, and outside. But how does one depart, demise, digress, deviate except by taking leave? And in so taking leave, in such practice as a way of life, how are excessus and the excessive about a sorta relationship of having to have as its ground departure, demise, digression, deviation? This is another way to announce, through breath I guess, through choreosonic verve and force and lilt, plurality as the basis of existence in black.

What I mean to say is that excessus and excessive have this homophonic relation because of the breath, because of the enunciation of breath into and out of the flesh. Such that the breath must also take leave, it must also yield to departure, demise, digression, deviation, it must also then, we might say, be a critique of western thought, the tangled bullshit of western theology and philosophy and anthropology and sociology. And taking leave, it is sounded out through the tongue, through tongues. Modern man and the way he thinks is critiqued by the experience of *excessus mentis*, fiery prayer, and such would be a way of life. But what does fiery prayer have to do with blackness?

I keep thinking and thinking and thinking about Harriet in that loophole and how she had to breathe shallow air, how that shallowness is what kept her alive, how each breath was the possibility for otherwise enacted as a disruption of the normative world, and in such a disruption, the interruption of the concept of there being only one world. She was somewhere else, in that breathing, she was breathing a strange utterance of babel, speaking in tongues—glossolalia, not xenolalia—of a fiery prayer that was and is and is to come, the way and work of blackness, an unfolding that is simultaneously an enfolding.

As ecstatic, then it's also about being beside oneself but what if blackness is the practice and living of ecstasy, of being beside oneself such that the ground of existence all up in and through here is being-beside. It's about Black language, I guess, it's about the way we use multiple prepositions to sorta explode meaning altogether. Perhaps we have been trained away from, we have been taught to give up, the possibility for mystical experience. Which is to say perhaps we have been trained, have been taught, to give up the possibility for touch, for touching feeling, for touching friendship, for touching relationship, unless under very strict control, by the state for example, mediated by a god or a state or an institution that says it's ok.

The cell, in this view, was the place where the monk was to seek and find God in the long and arduous askesis of silence and solitude. Dwelling, staying put, and entering into the space of the cell were means to go deeper in the monastic quest for God. Consequently, one finds frequent warnings against departure from the cell or monastery in early monastic literature.[3]

I told you I have this hunch about the relation between what in our times is called mysticism—at least the western Christian variety—and modern man, modern ways to think the category of the human. And it seems here that the way a monk was supposed to sequester oneself is through carceral logics. And, listen, I just don't wanna escape and be in solitude that much, not with you out in the world, not with blackness out in the world, doing its thing, living, breathing, speaking in tongues. I'd be happier holding your hand forever and ever, feeling the way our palms would get clammy a bit, how they'd feel a bit too much like heat and so we'd have to separate them. There's something mystical about that, about having a coke with you, or a coffee, or a vodka soda, or really anything. As long as it's with you.

Anyway, joy. I write about joy and think about it and want to live it. Yes, I do. And I write about joy, Black joy, a lot. Writing about and thinking with joy is what sustains me, daily. It nourishes me. I do not write about joy primarily because I always have it. I write about joy, Black joy, because I want to generate it, I want it to emerge, I want to participate in its constant unfolding. I write about joy, Black joy, because it is a promise, not because it is already obtained. I write about joy, Black joy, because it is something toward which I press daily, it is the prize, it is the high calling. I write and think about and attempt to perform joy, Black joy, because Du Bois said: *as long as you live, believe in life.*[4] I write about joy, Black joy, because Fannie Lou Hamer was sick and tired of the quotidian, ordinary nature of gendered, racialized violence and terror.

And I've been painting. Joy.

I think about joy, Black joy, because Baby Suggs encouraged us to love our flesh, to love it hard, because loving Black flesh is the prize. I perform joy, Black joy, because in its ongoing practice, I discover it as the resource, the well, from which to draw energy, strength. I write about joy, Black joy, because we are not supposed to have it, because the incessant nature of antiblack racism is supposed to interdict and inhibit the very possibility for it. I write about and think with Black joy because it pisses folks off that want to produce racist, classist, gendered violence against us.

Black joy is the context of my, of our, emergence. We enflesh the freedom of our foreparents (thus and then also, we are the realization—against spacetime linearity—of the freedom *they* practiced, their practiced and performed freedom against the juridical, freedom against the status and position of enslavement; the consent to enslavement they could not give they could, still, withhold; which means that they have the capacity to hold, to unfold, to outpour; which means they had and have it, that their practice was against the possibility of a totalizing logic and achievement; which means we have to attend to the pernicious violence of the system of enslavement without romanticizing it while also attending to what it was not able to short-circuit; we must be mindful of *the epistemological elaboration of a storyline . . . which is nevertheless made to appear, in commonsense terms, as being naturally determined. This commonsense naturalized story is cast as the only possible realization of the way the world must be, and is,* Katherine McKittrick offers[5]; we are not so much their freedom dreams as much as we are the practice their nonliberal, nonmodern, nonbourgeois freedom manifested).

I write about joy, Black joy, to honor the traditions that made me possible. And I want the work, whatever the work is, to meet a kinda Blackpentecostal force, not unlike what Wynter says about Aretha Franklin's voice.

Yes, I think, I WOULD LIKE TO FEEL THAT EVERYTHING I SAID HAD A LIBERATING AND EMANCIPATORY DIMENSION. That's what [Aretha Franklin] has. Black singing, at its best, it has this—like Gospel. That I wanted. But also I was always aware that it wasn't that I was thinking anything linearly. It never came linearly. It tends to come the way a flower blooms. It comes unexpectedly; and it has nothing to do with "genius." It has to do with this beginning to question your own "consciousness." It's the idea of *poesis*, again; there is also *a poesis of thought; a new poesis of being human*. These concepts don't come in a linear fashion. They build up. They build up, you know? So as you're talking they build up and they build up the way music builds up and up and up until you get that sudden . . .[6]

And this is what I paint, what I shout, what I clap, what I beat on the tambourine skin. I want that joy, I perform it, *not as though I have already attained but this one thing I do*, I move my flesh to the rhythm and arrhythmia of Blackpentecostal music and noise in order to *get* happy, to inculcate within me a joyous disposition. And to live such disposition as a way of life. I want to leave, to escape, to scurry myself away into the social zone of Black life and its pulsing, pulsating exuberance.

That's all.

A

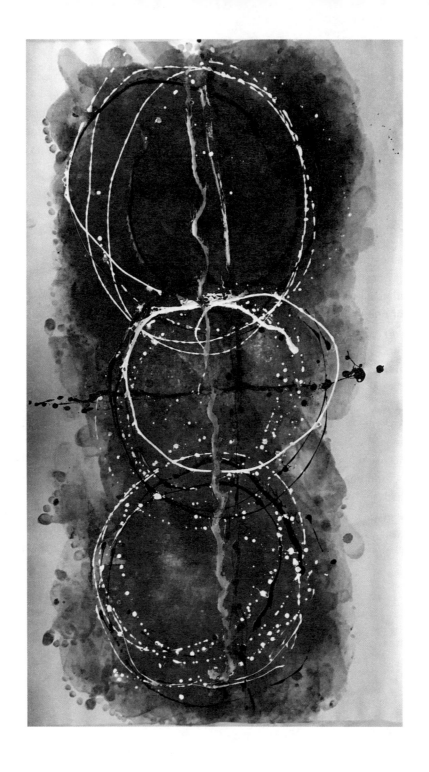

Dear Moth,

We are stars, we are literally made of the cosmos, we are what remains, what becomes, what is becoming, of that which isn't separable. We are dust blown away over the edge, Van Hunt might sing. We are difference without separability, da Silva might say. We are already past tense, against spacetime linearity.

That—that spacetime breakdown, that mood of cosmic otherwise feel and verve—is what I feel when I paint. It feels like impure possibility (impure because purity is a ruse of the epistemological substratum of western thought and desire), like absolute possibility, like anything can happen. It awaits, it rests, it calls for its own being realized. And could have been otherwise.

And since we are stars, we are also stardust, we are that which makes up the cosmos but that which also remains from being separated out from that cosmos. Perhaps we are searching, continually, for our stardust, that which holds mass while concurrently producing the occasion for feel and feeling. Perhaps love is the unceasing variation of the search for stardust. Perhaps each of us here are gathered together not through happenstance nor by random occurrence but because we have found each other, we have found our stardust. And we celebrate that being found "after" the explosion *of* and not *in* space as love, as joy, as friendship.

And imma keep doing it, not because I want to get a certain look from the pieces but because I'm constantly trying to achieve a certain feel, emotion, ecstatics.

I hope you like it,

A

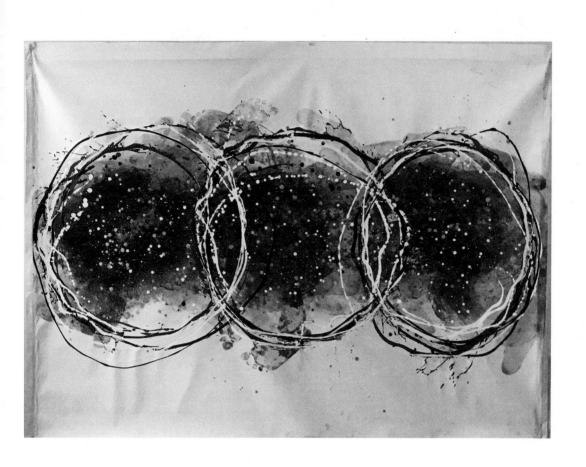

Dear Moth,

No. What I'm saying is this: Maybe we are searching for our stars, maybe love is that search. And something about that search, even when it's unfulfilled through the capture, brings me so much joy. (And so maybe the heartbreak of ghosting emerges from something like the attempt to sever connection from your stardust after its having been found "again," but for the first time too, to attempt separability "after" being gathered together in the now moment. Perhaps heartbreak is the attempted shatter of connection once the claim has been overcome. Perhaps heartbreak is the enfleshment of difference without separability.)

A

Dear Moth,

Joy is so important to me, to the traditions from which I emerge. And I want to live a joyful life, to have joy with others. It's why I sit in bars with friends until closing laughing loudly and learning and gossiping and just enjoying the presence of one another. Joy sustained against the brutalities of times past, they sustain today. I write and laugh and spend time with folks and paint not because I always have but because I want to attempt toward joy, because I wanna—as the church folks say—get happy. I want to honor the traditions from which I emerge by attempting a life of joy that is not about my personal, private, individuated experience of it but a life of joy that emerges from within a communal, improvisational practice, a joy that could only be had for *me* when shared with others, when common, when mundane and ordinary.

And I hope something of the joy I feel when I make these things is infused in them, that they are suffused with the potentiality of giving joy. I hope you have joy when engaging them, when feeling and looking and thinking about the colors and swirls and splotches.

A

Dear Moth,

So I checked it out since you said the pieces in *There is no center of the universe . . .* reminded you of M. NourbeSe Philip's *Zong!*, how the collection of voices and vocables she excavated, voices and vocables ancestors spoke through her, sounds that had to have been spoken, had to have been said, had to emerge from having been submerged.[7] You're right, there is a materiality to the sounds made that the water had to carry to the surface, that the water had to hold, had to embrace, had to care for, in order for such sounds to arrive to her as part of her practice of conjuring the noise for us to read, to hear. I get the resonance between what she attempted and what I'm attempting.

In 1781 a fully provisioned ship, the *Zong*, captained by one Luke Collingwood, leaves the West Coast of Africa with a cargo of 470 slaves and sets sail for Jamaica. As is the custom, the cargo is fully insured. Instead of the customary six to nine weeks, this fateful trip will take some four months on account of navigational errors on the part of the captain. . . . Captain Luke Collingwood is of the belief that if the African slaves on board die a natural death, the owners of the ship will have to bear the cost, but if they were thrown alive into the sea, it would be the loss of the underwriters. In other words, the massacre of the African slaves would prove to be more financially advantageous to the owners of the ship and its cargo than if the slaves were allowed to die of "natural causes."[8]

The owners of the ship, Messrs. Gregson, took their "case" to court after making a claim for insurance that was denied. There was a lawsuit. It was vulgar, doubling the violent acts against the enslaved Africans. Philip used the legal documents in order to reconstruct voices and vocables from the submerged life, the Black life that was stolen, the Black life that was rendered discardable according to western logics of politics, economy, and law.

A work like *Zong!*, although apparently authored by one person, only comes into being and fruition with the assistance and support of many others. . . . I thank the Ancestors for bestowing the responsibility of this work on me.[9]

That such a case could be argued in a court tells us something about the fundamentally settler-colonial and antiblack racist logic of western thought, that such heinous acts could be thinkable, could be thought *as* arguable. The university is the space from which we learn how to argue—through various disciplinary boundaries—the rightness and wrongness, the ethicality and legality, regarding such action. The university is a space of debate but such debate is an extension of the racial regimes and power differentials it would seek to undo. And so part of what I'm doing—with the writing, with the teaching, with the art practice—is attempting to stage an intervention into worlds by using resources of the university to speak back and against it. It might be a failed project. But I believe in the pursuit.

Philip took the text and allowed the ancestors to speak. Poetic. Because she's a lawyer and poet, she understands the intricacies of language and how it is used to construct meaning.

Poetry and the law both are about language and how language is used to construct worlds. Philip's poetry broke down words to their component parts and this in the service of a collective critique of the law, of language that makes the law. Philip took the text and was *made instrument* such that from her, ancestors would speak.

A variation on the theme. There's this artist based in San Francisco, Samuel Levi Jones, who creates works in order to critique the word, the concept of the idea *concept*, the way words and concepts are created by excluding Black life, Black flesh, from the possibility of flourishing. He takes encyclopedias, medical dictionaries, and legal textbooks in order to break them down, he takes the purported knowledge inhered in such objects in order to demonstrate the ways such knowledge production is always, to use the language of Wynter, *genre-specific*. In his series titled *Underexposed*, Jones stated that his desire was *to create something visually about what was going on in terms of representation, lack of representation within the textbooks*.[10]

Water. Submergence. Baptism. Life otherwise. Jones takes the various objects, these *very serious books*, and soaks them in water. He soaks them until they come undone, until they are—because of porosity—disoriented. He takes these disoriented objects and strips them, wants to see how they're put together by taking them apart. They are books that purport universal knowledge, that such knowledge is supposed to be universal, neutral and not produced through exclusions of categorical distinctions. But what is an encyclopedia or a medical dictionary or a legal textbook but a collection of ideas about what it means to be human? And what it means to be human, here, is what it means to be the *genre-specific* human that is gendered, racialized, classed in such a way as to hierarchize difference from white male landed gentry as deficiency. After stripping them to components to be utilized, and thus to be technologies, to be made instrument in his hands, Jones takes the skins and spines of the books and sews them together to produce panels. They are beautiful in their *an*aesthetic arrest, in their *an*aesthetic wonderment, in their *an*aesthetic unfolding.

Jones strips apart this knowledge production in order to produce a poetics and practice. Jones reanimates that which has been discarded, that which has been deemed excessive, to create art projects. Like Philip engages the "text" of the *Zong* massacre in order to expose language to its problematics, Jones's work is also poetic, is also in the tradition of critique, in the tradition of Black feminist, blackqueer imaginative possibility.

The language that constitutes the law is the language that constitutes the university. So the university is a site of struggle and contestation over language, over what is sayable, over what is deemed imaginable and impossible. And if the legal textbook and medical dictionary can be redeployed in the service of their own critique, if the legal document of the *Zong* massacre can be refashioned to allow the submerged to speak, the engagement, Black engagement with the university, circum-sacred, centrifugitive performance must also be a project of the artist, a project of artmaking, of finding joy, of producing the occasion of otherwise. Such poetics and practice are in the direction of the search for, and imagining of, peace.

But also confinement. What Philip and Jones both do is work within constraint, confinement, in order to explode it, to have confinement and constraint become the occasion for imaginative force and propulsion. Same with Reich and *M18M*. Limit is *not*. They discover within their objects the possibility for centrifugitive movement. And like them, I attempt to constrain myself to the poetics of Blackpentecostal practice—clapping, tambourine beating, shouting, leaping—in order to discover within these moves and motives the possibility for centrifugitivity. It's literally what Bishop Robert Evans says, *dancing in one spot*, how the storefront church was a constraint but also an occasion.

Black life. In the shadows. The poetic. Audre Lorde:

At this point in time, I believe that women carry within ourselves the possibility for fusion of these two approaches so necessary for survival, and we come closest to this combination in our poetry. I speak here of poetry as a revelatory distillation of experience, not the sterile word play that, too often, the white fathers distorted the word poetry to mean—in order to cover a desperate wish for imagination without insight. For women, then, poetry is not a luxury. It is a vital necessity of our existence. It forms the quality of light within which we predicate our hopes and dreams toward survival and change, first made into language, then into idea, then into more tangible action. Poetry is the way we help give name to the nameless so it can be thought. The farthest horizons of our hopes and fears are cobbled by our poems, carved from the rock experiences of our daily lives.[11]

What Lorde argues, in other words, is that poetry is a space of possibility because it allows for the dance and play of otherwise ways of existence, otherwise modes of thought. Poetry isn't a luxury, it's not something that is done because of leisure, but is done because of the urgency of our times. It is not a luxury because it produces the occasion to think that the world could be different, that we can create alternatives to what is thought to be acceptable and normal. It is not a luxury because it is the intervention into what is considered to be the acceptable and normal, and thus only, way to think. One of the most intensely felt but not necessarily recognized aspects of Europeanization and its problem of racial, class, and gender distinction is that it attacks thought and imagination. So we are charged with waging battle at the level of imagination and thought.

Epistemology is a theory of knowledge, a theory for thinking itself, and is a way to investigate how knowledge is produced in particular ways to think the world. To separate the world out through racial, classed, and gendered distinction is European in its line and root. The epistemology of dividing the world into types, types that either receive or are excluded from protection, care, is a product of European thought. Audre Lorde, through the poetic, allows us to consider how there are ways to think and produce relation to the world while also acknowledging the violence and violation that have been produced by the modern era.

Poetry, then, is not just about words on pages but is a blackqueer, Black feminist project of collective, improvisational, intellectual flow, a project of collective, improvisational, intellectual unfolding. Poetry would then be capacious enough to include singing, dancing, laughing, lovemaking, which is to say capacious enough to be about flesh, Black flesh, about a disruption to the modality of European thought and the institutions that ground themselves in such thinking, such as the university. The poetic flows, overflows, is abundant and even in the tightest quarters and cramped spaces, like inhaled and exhaled breath, the poetic a sign of life (I'm attempting the beat, the rhythm, of zero copula formations; can you feel it?) is and thus exceeds survival.

Blackness, Black Study, produces struggle and contestation with regard to knowledge and its proliferation. The university, only when yielding to the undercommon glossolalia of blackness, of Black Study, is a space from which poetic force emerges. This, the poetic possibility of the university, is the announcement and enunciation of otherwise possibility against the normative function and form of such a place of inhabitation, such a zone of institutional politic. Black Poetry is Black Study, such study is collective. This is possible in the otherwise university, the space of inhabitation that we carry in us, a way of life that extends and reaches outward for its establishment, that yearns for connection, that desires breathing in the service of being free. Long answer, and ramble, I know, to your questioning what can one do in a university. It's a site of struggle. It certainly is a space of tension and produces violence.

Trying to figure out a way to be is difficult but I'm still thinking about it,

A

Dear Moth,

Yes, sorry for forgetting to respond to that part of your message but yes, I really dug what Wynter said about Aretha too. It's like that liberating and emancipatory impulse she finds in her music, the kind with which she desires to write, is a kind of centrifugitive dance and play, the choreosonic force, of Black performance. But isn't every voice a bit of a fugitive?

The fugitive thing we hear that, once spoken, already exists in—what Heidegger would say—is the ago. And then, of course, we wait for the soon to come of the voice too. The voice is a fugitive, it steals and is stolen, it steals away home because, really, it ain't got long to stay here. "Here," of course, is in my throat. I gotta say something to you and you gotta listen to it. I tried to hold it in for such a long time but I can't. I literally—quite literally, quote literally—can't. The voice agitates from the inside, expansion of cords, suck in breath, give out life. That heavy breath, pant, sigh? That's me not wanting to say what my voice will undoubtedly say in the first place. In that space between breath pant sigh and the break when voice escapes: that is what we call the music, I think.

And I don't just mean this metaphorically. If words attempt to seize something, the voice is the release from seizure, it makes pretty (and?) plain the fact that voices try to go somewhere but never get there. So we keep on singing, we keep on moaning, we keep on whistling, we keep on keepin on, I suppose. But the voice then also enunciates what the word could not capture, what could not be captured in the word, enunciates that which remains, the residue, of thought. It's not just fugitive but centrifugitive, it spins out from its site of emergence in order to pull in toward it. Centrifugitivity is about relation, its establishment and cultivation, its establishment and care.

Anyway, I created a piece about it. Titled it "Centrifugitive Force Number 1."

The circular strokes of the brush on the multicolored surface, the white not-straight lines across, the movement, the wind, the breath of the piece. I was trying to approach something like centrifugitivity that one hears in Black singing, that one notices in the praise and prayers of Blackpentecostal saints worshipping, the kinda noise one hears at the beginning of Marvin's "Got to

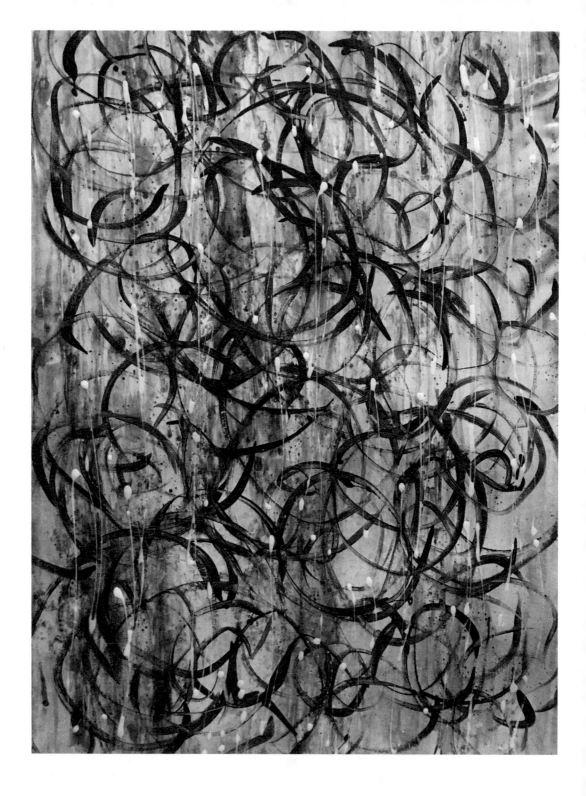

Give It Up," that one senses in various moods and moments of Black sociality. It's that common glossolalia heard at the beginning of the song, the noise of the friends talking, the speaking in tongues of Black sociality. It's centrifugitive, it's circum-sacred.

It's a kind of sacred life, a life mystical, that is about but also against the circle, its centrality. So I wanted to go in the path of a circle but break its line and root. So clockwise and counterclockwise, forward and back, cycle, cycle, cycle. It's propulsive, it's movement on the move, it's running on the run. It's the fugitive presencing of Black life.

Centrifugitivity presences (it makes present but not in a cause-effect binary along the Newtonian trajectory of time and space), it is that which, of necessity, must escape its being held, it must be given. That it escapes presences escape, presences the fact of having been held, presences *having been*. (And you know how I feel about the phrase *having been*, especially with its connection to the music we love, and to 12YAS —Northup's book, not the film.) To be as voice. On the way to voice. Friendship as a way of voice.

Voice goes on its journey out from that which contains it. The voice is a metaphor for, and material fact of, the capacity to resist being held before being held, the voice is that which is voice and *voiced* only insofar as it leaves, that it produces by way of ephemera, by what it traces, by its path, by—like the paint leaving my hand after hitting my palm or tambourine—its being carried by air. The voice is the trace of its having departed, its having been somewhere. I said or hummed or moaned or sang something and then it's gone, *it* has gone. But it, that which sends, that from which it was poured out, from which it emerged, remains.

I'm rambling.

A

Dear Moth,

What is it about modulation, about *taking it a little higher?* Think about it. Of the many songs I have directed for a choir or have played on the organ, we would want to take a song just a little higher, just a little higher, just a little higher, continually moving up the scale, recalibrating our voices, rewriting the possibilities of the song by stretching our vocal cords and widening our mouths and with each successive key change and release of a *whooooo!* just after we'd "land" in the now new tonal dominant.

It's weird: I didn't think about music and sound and location much if at all when we were together, we just sorta played it and sang it and were *there* in location together but now that all sorts of space separates us, I can't help but think about being a listener, a hearer, and from what positions I must do these things. Each letter that I think and breathe and write to you becomes just another way for me to take it just a *little* higher, revising the concepts and ideas and dreams and visions of you I have with each subsequent writing that would give you maybe a bit more knowledge of who I am, who I am becoming. Writing to you lets me modulate and defamiliarize myself, lets me understand a bit more about myself with each subsequent letter. So I'm writing to you but also, mostly and most fundamentally, writing to me.

We begin songs in one key, kinda like how we dance and shout, trying to withhold energy until the vamp, the drive. And then, finally, we let them have it, we give it a go, we exert all that we have within us. Modulation occurs in some songs, making audible migration and movement and motion, modulation as that sonorous refusal of stillness and being stilled (though, of course, being stilled is merely another "movement"). And the audience sits until they can't sit anymore, the modulations moving them so much, so the audience stands and is moved and amazed and surprised and enraptured by the heights achieved that were not initially imagined.

And there's something rather sensuous about it, something a bit erotic. It's in the ways *taking it higher* brings all of the attention to our weary flesh. Though our voices are worn out to the point of exhaustion—right there, at that broken edge, when the voice reemerges with new vigor and life and love—we sing and go higher and higher and higher, making absolute and resolutely *there, in that instance*, the very flesh that would be so discounted and dismembered in doctrines and theologies about sin and sex.

Many of our Christian theologies are—I don't have to tell you, I know—really restrictive about what our flesh can and cannot do. I mean, we both know that Blackpentecostalism was disdained and thought occult initially because of the focus on fleshly holiness and sanctification, and because of the dancing and shouting and clapping hands and stomping feet and rolling on floors and sweat, the sweat, the sweat and they didn't even have air-conditioning then, so it was likely very much also a smelly experience, and those services were in cramped spaces like storefronts where everything—sound, smell, sight, sensuousness itself—was heightened by the compression. And the speaking in tongues that was considered to be gibberish and impossible. Can you imagine a religious tradition that not only allowed for the senses to be attacked by corporeal praise but *desired* this assault?

When we sing and we go higher, the congregation hears the voices, and more. And the *more* is the way they *look* at what the voice does: to the mouths opened wider than they should be and the lips that quiver and the chins that quake and the necks twist with veins protruding and with the sometimes wagging, sometimes flattened tongues, and with the sweaty brows and foreheads. No one can keep their eyes closed with all that modulation. So the audience, of course, must attend to the visual aspects of such a—literally—moving sonic performance.

This thing called modulation in western music is the changing, moving—the transitioning—from one tonal center to another. And the notion of a tonal center is all about inhabitation and marronage, about staying and leaving. (And, still, the concept of tonal center needs to be interrogated because there is no center of the universe.)

In black, I think about the constant movement and migration and flight as what a friend's friend called the *dislocated African's pursuit of a meta-voice.*[12] Maybe not just a meta-voice but a meta-sound, a vibration that is about vibration as the fact and act of life. It makes present the fact that each of us has the capacity within us to move over and above and away from that which would keep us regulated and relegated, that which would keep us bound and belea-guered. Modulation renounces one tonal center for another, does not seek rest but, rather, seeks *occasion* for otherwise words and otherwise worlds. Mod-ulation is the chance, the encounter, the moment. Modulation is event. Modula-tion, that space between, the beatmatch, the crossfade, the break.

I don't know but when I think of modulation, and certainly when I hear it, I think of the choir arriving to a new key *together* and that arrival is but a short in-habitation in that space or field of epistemological exploration of the sonic zone, to, let's say, have a look (again, by way of throwing the voice) around at the *place* so to speak, the new space opened up by way of the always already available— and so, not new, but otherwisely possible—tonal center. But then, of course, arriving at that tonal center cannot last too long and the choir director will— exuberantly, probably a bit too excitedly—take their hands, form two fists while, with their thumbs stretched, giving the choir some sorta *thumbs up* motion; or take that one hand (for me, it was always the right hand) and point straight up, stretching from the arm through the index finger pointed, and breathe yoga-like air into and through my finger, letting the group know it was time, yet again, to *take it just a little higher.* And I think of it as arrival because it does not denote final destination but it certainly indexes that you've left somewhere, some place or space from which you sought release, somewhere you experience—as pres-ent tense—*having been* . . . A breakdown, in other words, of linear time through the modulation.

Each modulation as the event of arrival? Can we modulate together? I'd like to arrive . . . with you. I carried you in that dream after I arrived to the house. We arrived in the bedroom after I carried you across thresholds. And we arrived to libidinous joys after we arrived together in the bed. We arrived at heartbreak when joy ceased and our visages created more turmoil than butterflies. But we do not need to stay any *there* but can move to some otherwise event, some oth-erwise tonal center. Such that the center is only momentary, its gravity, fleeting. We can let go. So grab my hand.

When every voice is a bit of a fugitive, on its run away from regulative func-tion and form, modulation becomes but yet another occasion to critique the general field of normativity. If every note in Black singing is inherently unstable, given to caprice, is bent before its own being-as-*bending*, is worried previous to the occasion, then every *taking it a bit higher* is the possibility for critiquing the sonic space just evacuated and escaped. Similar to how, with melisma, several notes break the syllable when sung such that the notes are both that which breaks and that which is broken concurrently, modulation is both a *moving from* and a *moving to* (and too). Maybe Black performance is the *sense of question*. (*How does it feel to be a problem?*, Du Bois's famous question, as emerging from the general *sense of question* that blackness poses as a way of life.)

It's kinda like how Harriet Tubman escaped Eastern Shore, Maryland, arrived in New York and was, for all intents and purposes (and, yes, *intensive* purposes), *free* but returned to that very place that enslaved her only to bring others. The word, *free*, needed a Blackpentecostal, glossolalia critique from the settler notion of free as individual thing, as a xenolalic utterance. Freedom for her was fundamentally social but it was also modulatory. Constantly, freedom was being enacted by movement toward the spaces—New York, Canada, above Mason–Dixon lines—where freedom could be enacted. Double movements, we could say. Sorta like how being a runaway could very well mean (and did for someone like Harriet Jacobs in the crawlspace; or Henry "Box" Brown in a box) not *running* at all, but being stilled. Sometimes stilled movement migrates just as effectively.

I've only once heard modulation that occurred by way of declining the scale rather than—excuse my desire to sound witty—*scaling* upward. And there, too, was the element of surprise and joy by each step downward. What is it to be able to talk about reaching for heaven but not hell? If writing has taught me anything, it is that I should continue to revise and restate and recalibrate and that I can reach down, into that seemingly empty sonic space of silence, to get something. Maybe it is the echo of some such inhabitation long gone. That silence, of course, is a misnomer. That silence, of course, is noisy as hell. So I'm descending its reaches while, at the very same time, moving just a little higher. So this is me, *taking it just a little higher* in hopes. In hopes. I'm tryin to steal away, steal away home, because, I ain't got long to stay here. Gonna sing an otherwisely song in an otherwisely home sooner than you think. I'm gonna take it a little higher . . .

Love,

A

Dear Moth,

What I thought I needed to say was this: I've taken a rather romantic view of the Blackpentecostalism of my past. But I then regulated that regulation (so, would that be a full out and out deregulation? like a double negative? Or would it be a doubling, making it more insistent, more intentional, more intense? You know, when Black folks wanna do something, they say it twice: *I'm ready to eat eat,* emphasis, of course, on the first eat). The point is that I stopped short because I realized that romance and sentiment and sensuousness are deeply intimate partners, typically dismissed as the excessive and far too emotive. Sorta like how, when growing up, some of my non-Pentecostal friends would say to me something like *it don't take all that,* meaning that our praise and prayers were far too loud and uncontrolled and *getting happy* shouldn't likewise mean *getting sweaty.* It's as if we weren't ever thinking about what we were doing but were merely acted upon: by the music, by the sounds. It's as if we weren't intentional but certainly given to romance. It's as if there were nothing *in* us that was mak-ing and creating and constituting but that we were empty vessels waiting to be acted upon. We breathe in, but never exhale.

Of course you know the romantic era ended with the age of reason because reason is so reasonable and enlightenment so regulative and romance too sexual or some shit. It's like how we can enjoy champagne but not Kool-Aid because the latter is always connected to folks who are thought to have very little judgment for pure taste in the first place. As if they can't judge and have little reason to be reasonable and thus, are not. Those things which are thought romantic are supposedly purely and only *feelings* and feelings are somehow less thoughtful. So I was gonna go through this entire self-critical moment of how I romantically remember the past and how I romantically think about our romance gone awry but then I listened to some music and refused the regulation of the pleasures I enjoy by thinking pleasantly about the past. Let's just say, I got into the music. I wanted to taste it: the chords and melodies; I wanted to step into the time and the rhythm and explore.

I'm finally cool with romance and I mean romance in the fullest sense, in the capacities we all have to know through our senses and the robust deregulation of the relegation of this kinda knowledge, this sorta experience.

Like this . . .

Remember how we'd lay in bed all night talking until three or four, you falling asleep mid-sentence in my arms as I spooned you only to wake up an hour later and begin again? Me, right behind you, my left leg covering your lower body, my left arm on your stomach, your left arm right under mine, your left hand on top of mine almost getting a bit too balmy so we'd separate our hands and move our arms a bit so that cool air could surface between us because— and you know this—holding someone for a while is both beautiful and hot, the humidity emerging *between* bodies so close that "between" seemed to be a ruse.

You'd wake up and finish that sentence and you'd not even have to look at me and not even open your eyes and barely *begin* the sentence again before I was reawakened and reengaging and taking my index finger and running it along your arm and taking my head and moving it even closer and deeper still into your collar bone so I could hear you. I wanted to get into you as much as the music. To make you feel what I felt inside me, to transfer the butterflies that I thought about and saw in the pit of my stomach anytime I heard your voice. It never changed. It never changed. It has not changed. (I never said, openly I guess however, that I also really loved when you spooned me, when I was able to lie in you, with you behind me, holding me. I'm trying to practice being more tender, more vulnerable, more honest; I thought it wasn't masculine enough, manly enough, so even when you did hold me, and even though I loved it because it was so tender and gentle, I still had to fight the impulse to move myself away. Still workin this cispatriarchy bullshit out.) I want to hear your voice and still imagine it in the same ways that I'd always imagined it and even as I sit here and write to you I begin to feel that same way again and you'd smell a bit musky with that cologne and oil you wore and I'd take my finger and slip it in your briefs as you talked and play with the hair right down there, twirling and twirling my finger—and around and around and making a bit of a knot and then taking the hair and smoothing it out again.

And I would respond to your speaking but my eyes would be closed too and that was the romance. There are those that think there's no knowledge produced or created or experienced in that movement of flesh into each other—

fucking could not do what our voices and laying almost still did, though it certainly approached it, yes, indeed—but us? We learned and taught and dissented while spooning. Something about the small moans and shortnesses of breath and the snoring and the smells of our bodies—once sweaty, once humid, once balmy, now cooled and held—and the taste of your ear in my mouth and your lips with the ketchup from the fries we shared earlier that night. Remember that night? Those nights?

What happens when we remember things *as* sense and not through the senses? What if my memory of you is synesthetic? I don't want that feeling, nor that knowledge, to go. And I think that is the point of

taking it to church

or

taking it just a little higher

or

let's take it home

It's the fact that there is something there that can be taken, that has life and breath and spirit, that there is something carried, held previous to the giving of breath as song that also curiously enough remains after the last chord and note and handclap recedes.

So yes. Isn't the music the sequestering and organizing of sound that we hear? The song is an object that we use to reach things, to convey things. We turn our voices into objects, we instrumentalize our bodies for the master's use to sing and dance and pray. And with each breath—singing just makes this explicit—two things: we enunciate and articulate the weight and depth and materiality of the thing carried; and we *are* the weight and depth and materiality being carried. When we take *it*, we announce that there is something there that compels this movement, some spirited object that resists being stilled and stilling.

The looming question is: what is the *it* so carried?

The sorta simplistic answer would be the note, the key, the tonal center and I suppose those would all be correct. But what if we're talking about our romance and our lying in bed while spooning? What would be taking that *it* higher? How could we take it, to know that it needs to be carried while concurrently carrying us to some *something*? I think *it* would be that insistently unnamable presence and feeling—butterflies? effects of butterflies?—that confounds the senses while heightening their receptivity. Maybe an ongoing openness to openness, or something. I don't know.

What I do know is that we had not even begun to explore possibility before possibility seemed impossible. It's like how a lot of folks think the earth is the only place in the vastness of space that can have life, or that life can only be found and sustained when it looks like what we think it should look like. I wouldn't be surprised if some scientist somewhere in the world sometime in some future found that there were other ways to live—biologically—that simply had not been considered. I only ask because I'm all into thinking about what music would mean if there were other forms of life, other modes of being alive.

If we just pay attention to the music, then we'd know something about breathing and moving and living,

A

Dear Moth,

The problem, of course, is the relationship between being and becoming, or maybe even the possessive apostrophic and that which is possessed. You did not want to be queer—still do question it, still do wonder, still do study at the seminary—so regardless of how you felt as I'd hold you, you thought (not felt; definitely *thought*) you were being something other than your "self," as if we ever aren't nothing other than the continued movement and dissent, the perpetual suture and rupture, the dehiscence that emerges. If we are anything, if we occupy any stability, it is in that the core is itself nothing but flux, tones up, chords down, sound that cuts, and cuts sonic. You did not want to be possessed by the becoming, by the fundamental choreosonic, centrifugitive emergence of an irreducible togetherness.

And it was sensed in the ways I'd hold you and you'd get tensed up every single time. I'd put my arms around you and, ever so faintly, you'd shudder a bit, your flesh physically reacting, wanting to throw down and off and move out from that which was becoming too good. You were wary of the sustenance of such becoming, thought that emergence would eventually subside and you'd *be* some shit you didn't recognize and wouldn't be able to properly hear. But isn't that the beauty of the apostrophic possession? It's not in the possession of property as private, that's a kind of settler-colonial logic that is always also violent. What I'm thinking here is the way that possession and plurality—against singularity—tether to the other. One could, of course, say: *the shoes that belong to Betty.* Or, one could say *Betty's shoes.*

There's this wonderful little group of short stories by Faulkner titled *Go Down, Moses* and I was impressed and totally into this one character who was referenced as Tomey's Turl.[13]

In the story, he is enslaved but on the run, running—yet again in almost a dance of game and play with those who enslaved him—toward the woman he loved. He was Tomey's child. Tomey's beautiful, beautiful child. And I had a colleague who once at a conference panel argued that to be Tomey's Turl was to be a fundamental problem. Of course, I don't think Tomey's Turl thought of himself that way, he likely looked at his movement as exuberant, as ecstatic, against individuals and institutions that attempted to rob him of that possibility. On the panel, my colleague argued that because of the "status of the woman" law during enslavement, that Tomey's Turl highlighted a more general sorta irreducible dispossession of Black folks, that he made very real the fact that Black people are melancholy and abject *because* we couldn't at that time—and still can't today—possess children, property, whatever. Tomey could never claim that which she bore and this inability was the disarticulation of motherhood or some shit. Tomey's only relation to Turl would be through negation and Turl by dispossession, or so the argument went (and there were, unfortunately, a lot of affirmative nods to such declarations).

Let's just say, I never really liked that theory and I think people misread Du Bois much too much. Folks sorta skip over the fact that his explication of the "strange experience" of being a "problem" came after he said that the question "how does it feel to be a problem" was *unasked of* him, was an indirectness put *to* him, even the asking was a sorta refusal to ask (or we might say the question showed up with its own dispossessive force; he says, of course,

Between me and the other world there is ever an unasked question:
unasked by some through feelings of delicacy; by others through the
difficulty of rightly framing it. All, nevertheless, flutter round it. They
approach me in a half-hesitant sort of way, eye me curiously or com-
passionately, and then, instead of saying directly, How does it feel to
be a problem? they say, I know an excellent colored man in my town;
or, I fought at Mechanicsville; or, Do not these Southern outrages
make your blood boil?[14]

And him saying this is important, beginning with the declaration that there are worlds, plural; because how can it be *between me and the other world* if there were no world of which he could speak as his own? And he lingers with the fact of the unasked question as showing up through an indirectness of address, a kind of *angularity of racial feeling*, we might say, here the feeling being politesse. Maybe blackness is the *sense of question* and the music is the elaboration of the angularity of racial feeling? Perhaps.) You know, I don't think that Du Bois's Negroes thought of themselves—or ourselves, really—as fundamentally problems or problematics *to themselves* or in the world of his own; but it is the movement itself against the stillness and abstraction, the epistemological substratum of racial capitalism, that is posed against us in the guise of policy procedures and Rockefeller Laws and Rodney King beatings that is supposed to make us *feel problematic*. People take up Du Bois's question of the *being* of problem without thinking more about how this state of being is exteriority enforced and placed, how it befalls the one who would be so problematic. It's anterior being, it's imposed being. It ain't, then, Black being at all. If a problem, it is only so because of the *other world* that produces the unasked question.

Of course, maybe we could recalibrate—if we want to think from the position of the one so called—and ask of ourselves: what does *becoming* problematic feel like? I think that's a bit closer to what you and I were doing. And I think Faulkner was smarter than to posit Tomey's Turl as some sorta *being* rather than a fundamental *becoming* (the difference between what my friend Autumn thinks as progress versus process; where *becoming* is certain procession). And I think we can know this because the story starts with Tomey's Turl moving and running and escaping. He was reaching for something, loving for someone, creating a path, constituting as a way of life. Maybe possession by one like Tomey critiques the notion of the ways in which folks try to own their children as possession itself. It's not that Turl does not bear a relation to or have an intimacy with Tomey. Rather, when constituted, rather than constituting, as Tomey's Turl, the only thing he could do was run, not from Tomey, but from the institution that would both name and misname him by notions of self-possession. His running for love was also and likewise a giving of himself away.

When I wanted to have *becoming* with you, when I held you—though you learned to suppress or regulate it as much as possible—there was something that you had to fight, some exterior, some way of *being* that befell and continues to befall. (And I felt it too, when you'd hold me, fought it, didn't want it though I desired it. Shuddered too. Winced too. It's not that I don't understand; I understand too much.) We might call it theology or religion or history or ethics, wanting to be loved by your family, and mine. We have both been indoctrinated in a world, in language—and thus, a xenolalic utterance of settler possession and displacement and the portability of concepts—and in the idealization of the individual, one who owns and possesses oneself most fully, the ability to control oneself and the many things around us. I think your shudder was twofold: you loved my arms and the warmth but knew that yielding to such feeling would also mean throwing off the ruse that you'd gotten used to telling people, that you didn't need anyone, that you were cool with being single, that you didn't want love. *Me* would, of necessity, become *we*. And it happened ever so wonderfully and for a long while, *we* worked.

I think Faulkner is a quintessential southern writer and I don't think Tomey's Turl ever spoke but I've been thinking a lot about southern accents and the north's positing of itself as cosmopolitan. By now we're both well acquainted with that one particular former US president, how he was cast in the media as inept and stupid, and this by way of his voice, by the accent he utilized when he spoke. This happens as much in audiovisual reproductions as well as in texts and transcriptions of speeches. And I find the latter—the transcribed word from spoken to written—intriguing. Not because he didn't very often say *em* instead of *them*. He indeed did all of the time, and we both heard it. But it is curious to me because other folks who have likewise served as president or other positions of power and authority have not been transcribed with such speeched text. It's as if the media wanted to show *this is but another way to know that this guy is stupid.*

Do we even give attention to how accents are racially and class-coded ideas? I wish that *em* wasn't used to index some purported inherent inability to grasp knowledge. But I am more intrigued by how the north conceives of itself as a place that was (and is) progressive, how they lacked enslavement. Of course, we know this to be a farce and particularly after the Fugitive Slave Act, each state in the Union effectively became a slave state. But the north is often cast as progressive, often—if we pay enough attention—through the way accent is used in media. (I am, admittedly, thinking of this now because recently at a bar someone told me that I do not sound as if I am from an "urban area" because I sound "educated" and "clean." I almost had a fight, right there, in the bar.) The north can conceive of itself as cosmopolitan and progressive because they "never had slavery." And never having slavery is never having had the close, intimate relation to Blacks who share in that southern accent. The north, I think, gives itself a nonblack accent and the whites in the south are sullied because they speak with such close intimacy with Blacks.

But we already know that the north as a concept is a ruse and farce. And of course, this depends on *being* rather than *becoming*. I wonder what being is—philosophically—when it is fundamentally *becoming*, or, when it is always in process, begotten rather than made? I hope that somehow you know that I never wanted to possess you, that I only wanted to be *becoming* with you. There is a difference.

Maybe,

A

Dear Moth,

It's not that I wanted to possess you, though I certainly did enjoy and envision a future of us where we seized each other. And I never could master you but felt that each new morning occasioned things about you unexplored. Could it be possible to relate without ownership, to capture hearts while banishing jealousy?

This is where my friendships come in, especially friendships with women, with gender-nonconforming folks, with trans folks, dense and deep friendships that tell me something about how to relax the very contours of what we consider to be gender identity and even sexual orientation. I learned with you, too, that kind of relaxing, learned and am still learning how to trouble the coloniality of gender and sexual identity. All these categories have incarcerated us, have us held and bound when what we seek is liberation. My life is a blackqueer one because my friendships teach me how to love and to have intimacy and to yearn and to practice joy. They teach me about touch and the refusal of possession.

I'm a bit surprised about how upset I got about all of this last night while speaking to someone about some new sorta technology that can "perfectly reproduce" Art Tatum's piano playing. This technology has the ability to "listen" to music and re-create it. It kindasorta *sees what our brains react to* in order to infuse that in music performance. And I suppose I don't have a real issue with reproducing something. There's a guy—George Lewis, a musician and a pretty cool dude—in New York who has been using computer algorithms for years to improvise, to think about improvisation and subjectivity. And I'm down with all that because it seems he thinks of computer technology, not as opposed to human subjectivity, but as part and parcel of it. I mean, you were the one that told me that the first meaning of computer was *one who computes*, that Dells, Macs, and Gateways are only the newest mode of a really old concept.

So the issue I had with last night's conversation (aside from the fact that I was real close to my limit) was the pressure applied to the word *perfectly*, that something could be possessed, mastered sonically by machines only in order to reproduce it *perfectly*. But I wonder: what if the musician—Art Tatum, for example—

was not trying to produce perfectly? What if, following Baraka's listening to and writing about Lady Day, one tries to create failure? Or, not even failure, but what if *perfection* is not part of the sociocultural vocabulary of a world, or not a thing desired in the first place?

Nothing was more perfect than what she was. Nor more willing to fail.
(If we call failure something light can realize. Once you have seen it, or felt whatever thing she conjured growing in your flesh.)[15]

Isn't there an assumption that musicians and painters and all sorts of artists want to produce perfection? But what if they don't? Do we even think this refusal of desire is possible? That the norm could be the bending of bent notes until even the bends are bent? And what is assumed when it is thought that a new mode of some old thing now, *finally*, can create perfection? What does it say about ingenuity and emotion and drive?

Anyway, I began arguing rather forcefully against what the guy at the bar was saying about perfection and Art Tatum and his rather ridiculous assumptions. The technology he described seemed to me to be nothing other than an enactment of a desire to possess and master without accounting for the underside of such declaration. It hallucinates the idea that the "original" producers had a particular intent that could be fully realizable. Rather than asking how the technology can become another occasion to produce failure beautifully, it gets taken up to say that it can reproduce without failure. *More perfectly than even Art Tatum could've done* I think the dude said. Of course, there is likewise an assumption of an *essence* of music performance that can be found, that there is some ground zero, some foundational claim to production of emotion and thought and drive.

And there seems to be, of course, the implication of an articulation of a critique of *authenticity* because if sound technology can "hear" Art Tatum "play" without his vivid thereness, then and of course, Art Tatum becomes inconsequential to the performance of Art Tatum. His materiality, his once-there flesh, becomes discardable chaff which the wind can drive away, at best. And, if the computer can reproduce perfectly what it has captured and mastered? Well, then no one has the ability to be authentic. And I know antiessentialism is all the rage with its being against claims for authenticity but I don't even think the right questions are being posed. Like, what is perfection and how is it determined? If I said that Tatum's breath was just as consequential to his performance as his fingered weight on keys, then what?

And what about the social field that was produced when Art Tatum played? These technologies are all about reproducing and perfecting originary genius and individuality when folks like Tatum (and maybe us all?) are constantly engaging in creating ways to be with others. Then it finally hit me why dude last night was so wrong. I listened to the sermon *Let's Get It On* by Bishop Iona Locke again (for the *how-many-nth* time?) earlier this morning.[16] You know how we produce something other than but close to the concept of failure? She was preaching and in the moment of her *whooping* when the congregation is just all the way in it, screaming and clapping and providing that necessary background that isn't so backgrounded, she said

God said I will pour out my spirit . . . upon *some* flesh

and the congregation screamed back

All!

and then she came right back in

You talkin right. All! He said *all* flesh!

How would a technology account for that? She literally in her preaching moment opened up a space to allow the congregation to engage with her disarticulation of the scripture. She ruptured its flow, *some* flesh, knowing that the audience was right there with her production of something other than that which was correct. There is, of course, a world of difference between "some" and "all." But she realized the congregation as part and parcel of her preaching performance. Could the technology of perfection—rather than improvisation— *know* that she was going to exclaim *some* for the audience to respond as such? Did, and even could, *she* even know she was going to say some instead of all?

There is incalculability that is part of the performance, some aspect that cannot occur before such sitting down at piano benches or standing in pulpits. And if the organ wasn't there? And if the congregation wasn't standing and jumping and screaming?

She isn't the only one, though. It's like when folks are up exhorting the congregation, or when the organ breaks during shouting music :: there are all sorts of gaps and elisions and ruptures of sound, thought, texture, openings and forestallments that go against any such notion of "perfection" and reproduction that could ever be so termed.

These are the calling forth, not just *call and response* but *call and call*, some sorta accretion and accrual, layer upon layer upon layer, each word and phrase and scream and inhalation/exhalation engaging and revising that which came before it, affecting subsequence. Such performances are produced by the fact that the congregation has some such knowledge in them that is animated by and likewise animates any such praise leader, devotional singer, or preacher.

It's sorta like how when you'd exhort the congregation right before the preacher, or when you'd be giving words of encouragement during the momentary space between the dance and the "Yes, Lord" praise where some folks would still be praising and running while others would be hunched over and yet others still bent over with their hands rubbing on their outer thighs and over there would be Patty throwing her head back *AHHH!* and over here would be Jesse clapping incessantly and you would talk, saying something like, *Take your seat if ya can . . . hahaha!*

Or you'd say something like *I don't know what you came to do but I come to praise the . . .*

You wouldn't, of course, include the final word, the word *Lord*, but would leave the statement, if ever so minutely, open ended.

Or how you'd say *After all the things I been through, I stiiiiillll have jeeyuh . . .* and you'd throw your head back, saying *jeeyuh* quick, crisp, staccato-like and the congregation knew what that meant.

Of course, you'd have to be part of this social world to know that *jeeyuh* meant *joy* and that opening was also a space for folks to keep it going. The words don't necessarily cohere with what is desired. *We've got to move on* was as much a call for *not* moving on—for the saints to keep praising—as it was to say that it was time to *turn over the service*. These are accents on and off the beat, not just slurred speech and weighted keys, but a way to inhabit a social antiphonal world. This world isn't about perfection. It's about the *power of the Lord coming down* and I don't think you can account for that with algorithms, though algorithms can help get you there.

(And I am not against technology. The B-3 for me is quintessentially Black-pentecostal and without it, I wonder what the church world would sound like for Black folks. And I'm still waiting on someone to write about First Church of Deliverance in Chicago using the Hammond in a Black church setting, and how, curiously enough, the pastor was—what would they have said then? queer? a homophile? homosexual? gay? The technological, nonhuman machine that serves as foundational for the sound of this social world was first recognized as important by someone very queer. There's gotta be something about dispersal, spirit, and sound there. And maybe that *purported* imperfection's relation to the sound of Blackpentecost.)

It just seems that any desire for such perfection really spins out from a different sorta epistemological center altogether. Assumptions of clarity and rigor and rightness seem hella limiting to me. And there is never an accounting of how perfection—when it is achieved—may be merely another form of improv. Sometimes, I just wanna say: *leave this alone, let it do its own thing, if you wanna join it, cool but if you wanna perfect it? Stay back.*

I remember the first time I actually listened to Aretha Franklin's *A Brand New Me*. Though my parents gave all their secular music to my brother and I when we were younger, I never paid much of the music much attention, save a Michael Jackson tune here or there, a Temptations song every now and again. I'd listen to those phonographs sporadically, if I needed to feel nostalgic—and the desire for that feeling was very rare, indeed, for what had a young person to do with nostalgia when every experience was so fresh and alive and vital and who wanted to reminisce when one had not yet lived at all, but one thought they knew everything about the world and its sorrows and joys? When I did finally listen to it and not just hear it, when I was attentive in ways that allowed me to groove to the sounds of the rhythm? It was wonderful.

The short song begins with something sounding like a tap dance shoe tapping on wooden floors in a dance studio, large space with high ceilings and mirrors on all the walls such that the sound echoes with each short, staccato *taaht taaht taaht*; definitely not a mere *tap* sound but a bit more textured and lively and tarried and layered. Then the piano arpeggios and chording. *Then*, her voice's clarity and the melisma and the *dew-wew-wew-hoo!*

I finally understood why people were all into her as the Queen of Soul because whatever sorta life and love she had in her, she gave to the audience, singing with her all in studios and nightclubs and churches. With that light piano following behind her, I discovered what everyone else already seemingly knew. I was surprised that a song so short, so sweet could be so sensual and seductive because I generally think of the latter two as sounding out with trumpets and saxophones and low, melancholy voices and slurred speech, slowed rhythms. But, of course, at the end of her song, her daddy came out of her—he had breathed into her, one knows, by way of his preaching and *whooping* and the end of his sermons. Well, *A Brand New Me* inhabited the same sorta sonic space, she *took it to church* with the minor and suspended chords. Tension and release? Maybe that's where libidinal materiality resides, always in excess of the regulatory and relegated.

She knew something of moving an audience, working a crowd, engaging a congregation that she learned from what Baldwin called the *first* theater: church. And, well, church has certainly taught me to be attentive to motives and intentions with and against behaviors and actions. Some would call Aretha's sorta cohabitation between the "church" and the "world" contradictory. I'd just say: she grew up Baptist. Or (I just got finished teaching today, so theory is on my mind): there is an atheological impulse in blackness that she plays in and with and through that makes possible certain forms of seemingly contradictory living. Sister Rosetta Tharpe, of course we know, was not as fortunate as Aretha, though one could, and maybe should, though few would, argue that she was one of the first major figures of gospel to break into the "world."

While Aretha was still singing in her father's church Rosetta was already performing with her guitar, Blackpentecostal blues on stages. And COGIC was already saying that she had backslidden. Of course, when Aretha *takes it to church* in her secular music, it is thought an extension of who she is, of her life world and love. But when Rosetta did it? Not so much. She was seen as utterly problematic and in need of control and change. It's not that she saw her production of blues and honky-tonk as problematic but the social world to which she belonged, those folks around her, saw her movement from one space to another as the foil.

It's sorta like how there is the term *falsetto* that N says is the desire for *new word, new world* because the falsetto *curiously rescues and abolishes* the word (and world) as we know it. And I have this fantastic student writing a paper about Celia Cruz's voice, how it is *like* the falsetto in that it explores a new word, new world. But her voice is "lower" than expected, it reaches . . . *downward.* If there is something buried within the reaches, Cruz's voice is the limb that refuses phantasm, grasping through toward the underground, the underneath, the submerged. (I almost too quickly added *the submarined* because, let's face it, the voice shares a relation to water—no saliva, no substance, too dry to sing, maybe—and African music no doubt knows something of middle passages and boats; folks are down in the water; maybe Cruz's voice reaches for them?)

What my student and I both noticed is that there is no term to succinctly discuss the lowered voice, there is no opposite or antithesis of falsetto. Contralto might be the closest, though it is a general descriptor for the *lowest female part* though falsetto indexes what is unexpected, surprising, it is the *unnaturally or artificially high-pitched voice or register, especially in a man.* That is, there is no unnatural or artificially low and lowered voice, there is no voice submerged or buried for a woman. Of course, maybe an analysis would also think about gender as performance, always false for a man singing a *certain kinda way* but always and only possibly true for a woman?

Sister Rosetta Tharpe's actions could only be understood spatially and this spatial organization was theological. To sing the Lord's song anywhere other than the Lord's church was to eclipse the possibility of being on the Lord's side. They were interested in theological correctness and doctrinal integrity. And this rather than movement—by, of, for, in—the spirit.

This is me just being longwinded and obscure. I do, however, think there should be an analysis of the impossibility of the falsetto's opposite. And I do think there is a theology that inheres to this impossibility. If falsetto bears the trace of falsity, what such voice is true? And if truth is not possible for the voice, do women mark this by way of an irreducible contrariness (contralto, of course, is to be *counter to* the alto)? Intriguingly, though Aretha sang about being brand new, it was Rosetta who had to, of necessity, remake herself after every such performance on a secular stage. *A brand new me* each and every time she rocked in the bosom of Abraham . . . at the Apollo. She, they both really, remade themselves otherwise, alongside, as alternatives to what was deemed accepted and acceptable.

What do you think?

A

Dear Moth,

You know that when directing a choir or playing the organ, or even when I was a kid sitting in the back of the church listening, I'd laugh—and still do laugh—at the things I hear, things that don't make sense, songs that have been sung, I suppose, "incorrectly." When I was a kid, this showed up mostly when we had visitors to our church or when we went to visit other churches with whom we fellowshipped for afternoon services. My brother and I would notice how people would sing the same songs we knew but with subtle differences. Of course, you'd have to be part of the Blackpentecostal world to really appreciate it. But we loved to sing, for example, one song as

I believe god, I believe god / I believe god will do what he said
no matter what problems may bring / I believe, I believe god

but then we'd be somewhere else, some other church but they'd say

I believe god, I believe god / I believe god can do anything
no matter what problems may bring / I believe, I believe god

The slight difference between "will do what he said" and "can do anything" is illusory to most. The rhythm was ostensibly the same. The repetition and the sentiment, pretty much consistent. But my brother and I'd hear this and we'd look at each other and smirk just a bit. Not only smirk, I suppose, but we would want our *correcting* voices to be heard, so over the incorrectness, we'd say as loudly as possible—even if only to each other—*will do what he said!*—forcefully.

It was a moment to articulate difference as inherently part of the Blackpentecostal world in which we were part. It was cool because we'd notice the difference without being able to account for it or name what it meant. All we knew to do was keep singing what we knew the words to be a bit louder. It became an occasion for us to laugh with each other at them. It wasn't disparaging or anything like that. They would take our well-worn testimony service songs (this, well before the advent of powerpoint and screens, at least in our churches) and enunciate them with different lyrics. They "messed up" our song. Of course, the songs never belonged to us in the first place.

We weren't right but we weren't wrong either. The powerpoint in churches today seems to give everyone the *correct* words, seeking to eliminate the difference that only my brother and I could hear, which is cool, I suppose. I wouldn't like when Tina—and it was always Tina—got words wrong when we were singing. And she always got them wrong unless she had the words to whatever song right in front of her. But what can we laugh at now? I guess the problem for me is that there seems to be all this attention being given to regulating and removing as much of the uncontrollable and unplanned possibility, to reduce spirit to modes of acceptability and calculation.

And, I don't know, it just seems wrong and we never tried to sing those songs perfectly, we just tried to sing them so others would sing and we'd all be a part and shout together. And I know that lyrics and correction are all about doing things together but what about people who don't read as quickly or don't care about the "right" words or whatever. And no one really cared if you sang the wrong words or wrong notes and no one was concerned that you bent a note a bit or were a bit flat during your repetition. It was all about enjoyment and empowerment and boldness and bonding, about the desire to move others as you were so moved. The bishop who started our church is believed to have said that he disliked choirs and hymnals, not because they couldn't usher in the spirit, but because he felt they left most of the congregation out of the sonorous world of music and that the congregation would become an audience who had to be entertained but not engaged. Maybe he was right.

There seems to be all of this attention to who owns what sound and who wrote what song and to making sure that we sing their song the "right" way. That's why public domain songs that we sang during testimony service can be so powerful to me, that they lend themselves to being reworked and performed differently based on location. What we sing up here is different than how they sing in Oakland or New Orleans or Brooklyn or Boston or Detroit. Each location seems to have its own style. Though my brother and I smirked, we didn't get mad. It actually made us very happy to notice the differences, it let us know that there were other ways to sing the same song.

Really, it reminds me of something I'd read on a blog last week about a bishop in our church organization and how everyone knew he was a drunk . . . of course, the blogger was writing to say that the bishop wasn't "really saved" and thus is not in heaven or whatever:

My father would always tell me about how Bishop Thorogood "preached his best messages when he was drunk." I don't know how one does that but we know that holiness and righteousness makes us come out from among them and to be separated, sayeth the Lord of Hosts. How can he be saved knowing that he was drunk? I pray that he got things right before he was called home because we know that no unrighteousness shall tarry in the site of God!

I won't even go into the difference between site and sight, though they're sorta similar. I'm not in the mood to correct that anyway, but you see where I'd go with it. My father would say the same things about Bishop Thorogood, so much so that I knew he was speaking the truth. Like the blogger, I'd think it was such an odd statement to make for someone who thought about holiness as a lifestyle and not just a Sunday thing. But I think I finally get what he meant then. Or, even if I don't, I've made something from it.

What does it mean for one to produce failure against that which they espouse? Or, not really failure necessarily, but the other side, the underside, the underground, the underneath of perfection? What does it mean to try to create imperfection perfectly? Everyone who knew this bishop existed—in relation to him—by having this kindasorta knowledge of a man they kindasorta knew could not and would not live the very thing he preached and it was in that space of what we typically call contradiction that he was able to move himself and others by and into the spirit most fully. And who wants to bear the weight of being perfect anyway? It's a standard created that he—really, anyone—could never inhabit and it's sorta boring and lonely there anyway.

And I don't wanna be lonely anymore.

I'm thinking of the sermon someone preached at a church in which I was a musician a while ago. I disagreed so much of it that when he "tuned up," I didn't play anything, just kindasorta sat there staring at him, bewildered because I couldn't figure out how he'd gotten the story so wrong.

He preached about how the church is too accommodationist these days, how we should, rather, *gird up our loins* and *forge ahead* and how *we need to still preach holiness or hell*. What bothered me most, though, was his long-ass rant about how *the church has turned into a social club*, as if that's such a bad thing. Makes me wonder: do preachers actually ever pay attention to what the Jesus they say they believe in actually ever did? If anything, Jesus created what we might call a social . . . an *otherwise* sociality, an alternative way to be with others in the world that we all inhabit. The people he intentionally created this otherwise sociality with were the people you'd find in dance clubs and bars anyway. All the outcasts, the sick folks, the drunks, the gamblers, people who danced.

The problem with dude's sermon was not the characterization of the church as a social club. Instead, the problem was that he thinks this an ongoing failure, an ongoing imperfection in need of change, in need of intentional correction and regulation. He pretty much wanted to remove all of the difference that makes the social in the first place and Jesus would likely be thrown out too, I suppose.

I'm sure you're confused now about choirs and drunk preachers and social clubs but isn't the point of all that music I love, and the music we made together? That in its liveness, in the church when it is performed and you're *there* laughing at the mistakes and problems and different words atop the same structure, isn't the point of all that that sociality is created constantly by folks who recognize the beauty of imperfection and the ruse of its desired antithesis? Sociality is made *between*, is made *by difference*. This would be irreducible. Us singing at our church the same song differently—and with style—as the song they sing in Brooklyn complicates and holds up to scrutiny the notion of perfection itself. This is a gift.

Ever been in church and experienced someone, not forget the words while singing, but sing until so overwhelmed and overcome with sentiment and emotion that they *lose* words? In that very loss, just buried beneath the words' surface, emerges meaning given through a revised, a revisioned, otherwise social.

Kids smirk at each other, teenagers wail and make their voices heard from the pew to fill in the empty sonic space, Sister Joseph quickens, Deacon Jones shouts *yeeeessss*, and Missionary Davis dances. Through the singer's being overwhelmed and overcome—in the break when words are lost—spirit washes over and through and under the congregants and everyone rejoices. And I *still* don't know if I even *believe* god, or believe *in* god, but I do believe in that, that sorta movement.

Someone outside this community might say that a scene like that would be illustrative of the failure of the singer to sing. This outsider, of course, would be seeking perfection rather than the social. And that fourteen-year-old preacher wanted to shut us out. But that drunk bishop? He knew something about the beauty of imperfection, he could be included in the laity's imperfections by his own and we could be included in his, striving to make something otherwise, together. Kindasorta like love.

Wishing,

A

Dear Moth,

I recently dreamt I had a theological argument with someone in front of a bunch of kids. He was trying to teach Sunday School and they were questioning, but eager and open, teenagers. Maybe the dream emerged from me having listened to "I Believe" from the Broadway play *The Book of Mormon* recently wherein the character Elder Cunningham sings about his acceptance of everything said, everything proclaimed, from the Mormon Church with the appendage, "I Believe!" (Though I have many questions and view it as problematic the way belief, in the showtune, was held up for interrogation *because* it is belief, and because belief is *religious*; that is, I do consider other modes of thought to be grounded in, and could otherwise be cognized as, belief—from Newtonian physics to Einstein's urgent and necessary critique of Newton with "special relativity.")

But to the dream: in the disagreement, the antagonist would assert various things that happened in Hebrew Scripture—from Noah's Ark to walking across the Red Sea—with the preconditional phrase, "Well, God did this because . . ." Each time, I argued back, saying that on the one hand, one would necessarily need to believe in the concept of god generally and of the god of the Hebrew Scriptures particularly as a universal claim, and on the other hand, one would need to believe that such a categorical difference was possible to disentangle.

So maybe the dream occurred because of our conversation about music style and lyric, because the dream, too, is about difference. The dream staged the conversation about difference as categorical, pure, and possible by articulating the *god did this because* thing as a kind of pure object that could be comprehended through knowing and the range of other reasons in their infinite capacity that god did not nominate to the service of reason, presumably. And so much difference shows up in Hebrew Scripture, between, for example, a tabernacle and a temple, between a canvas and a cathedral. That difference is not one of desired practice—both were to be used for communion with the Holy One of Israel—but in how that practice was to be carried out within the religiocultural community, and how those practices were to be carried *in* the community's heart.

The tabernacle was a tent that was carried around, could be set up on any ground, whereas a temple was a designated geospatial location. The difference between a tabernacle and a tent, then, is grounded in ideas about space and time. And this difference is a kind of space of operation in which sociality opens up, a space of operation in which sociality flourishes and thrives. The difference that is considered categorical announces ideas about time, place, space, and who the people that believe in such possibility are presumed to be.

It caused me to paint.

I call it "Otherwise Possibility Number 1." Each of the panels is created with the same colors but with difference. I kept thinking about the last message you sent me, how you were talking about the lyrical content not being the only difference in the music. You're right. It's also the way musicians play the Hammond, the way chord changes are *changed* according to location, how those turn around chordal phrases can be the momentary eruption of delight and joy. All because of the difference between, say, the Brooklyn sound and the Chicago sound. They are not used to degrade the sound of others but only used to announce difference. Perhaps difference is the grounds of existence—difference, antagonism, movement. It's not about reconciling one style, one sound, with another but allowing for the difference between to be the social space upon which Blackpentecostal praise *happens*.

Connected to the dream, and to our last conversation, I wanted to show that the canvas is just a surface upon which things happen, that it is a surface, or that it's a depth, that becomes an *occasion* for joy, for love, for color, to make itself apparent. Like musicians playing the same song with chord-change differences, like the singing of those songs with different lyrical embellishments, the piece is a four-part painting that demonstrates that otherwise, alternative, difference is always possible. Such difference, such alternative, such otherwise would be irreducible, would be the *grounds* from which emerges the very possibility for life, for flourishing.

And I want work that is about flourishing, that allows me to flourish as it allows flourishing to occur *in me*. Sorry for all the italics. I'm just really moved by the way difference shows up. And instead of attempting to dispense with or discard difference, what if we worked with it, worked with and *in* it, worked

with difference as creating the possibility for thinking the world otherwise? Don't we have to figure this out? It comes back to what da Silva would say about difference without separability.

Saying the same thing, differently,

A

Dear Moth,

I dreamt I was teaching this song to a choir.[17] In the dream it'd been so long since I'd taught a choir that I had to get my groove—cussed out the choir twice, apologized—but we did it. Taught the unison part then continued on with the tenor line at *I'm reaching out to you lord* . . . then added the altos, then the sopranos. Then the thing happened, that thing that always happened when I directed choirs, it hit me.

I sorta got lost in the voices, lost myself in the sound, and almost began this sorta experience of being beside myself, vibrating to and in and with the music, letting myself go enough to ride in and between the sound, which is just the shared air breathed out, which is just breath. But I woke up right at the edge of such happening, was gonna cut the music so we could hear the three parts clearly, did the gesture and everything. But doing the gesture didn't only occur in the dream. I really did it, I moved my flesh to cut the music and the cutoff was abrupt. And abruptly I woke up, laughed when I realized what happened. But I was also sad, sad because I was finally feeling something of myself I hadn't felt in such a long time, that moment, that edge, of losing yourself completely.

Sure, I'd been painting a lot and feeling things. But this, this dream, it felt irreducibly social, like being back in the church *with others*, really feeling things *with them*, that I was part of the circle.

It's like a love, a relationship, a friendship wherein you stop worrying and being wary and just yield, give up, give in to the possibilities of vulnerability. It's about the tears that will come, sure, but it's more than that too. Something more profound, something more immanent.

And it reminded me of the other time, recently, when I woke up crying. It was a January morning, the twenty-third, and I missed someone. Some family member, or some acquaintance, or some stranger—it matters not—died in the dream, disrupting my slumber. I woke up, tears in my eyes, the tears carrying the material weight and texture of what was heard, felt, known, while asleep. Tears, the trace of another world, some otherwise reality, some perhaps soon-to-come existence. And two days later, my grandmother took her last breath.

Curious because I was not particularly close to her, yet the dream announced what was to happen not a couple of days later. The dream sensed the mood, the movement, the vibration, of existence and gave me a cue, and clue, of the soon to come. The dream was able to feel something not yet revealed. It's as if the vibration of the soon to come were already released and the dreamworld was able to feel into such vibration and make it known to me.

Dreams are curious objects of memory and mourning, of bright colorful joys and intense modulations of sadness and melancholy. You are left wanting, left wishing, left wondering. Dreams produce and contain and hallucinate both elation and ecstasy. Elations shared, flowing through the tender sweetness of air and breath and wind. Joys flowing like rivers, the comforter has come. Dreams. Dreams also produce and contain and hallucinate grief, grief that is too much to carry alone. Like lying in bed, slightly damp or perhaps even drenched because of tossing, turning. Confused mind jumping from thought to idea to brief smile to despair to fleeting pleasure to heartbreak. All this and a numbing hope, echoing the slight nothingness and almost emptiness of the image of desired stillness, a hope that rest and peace will soon come. Dreams. Dreamworlds are amplifications of possibility.

And I keep thinking over and over and over again about the dream and about how dreams in general have a sort of hallucinatory quality that is audible, vibrational, sounded out, sensed according to the gift of sensual capacity we've each been given in our individuality. (Against ableism, I want to underscore that we all do not operate with the normative five senses—some are deaf or blind, for example—but that which we've been given in our individuality allows us to detect worlds.) Resonance of vibration interrupts, resonance of vibration exists in our world, and we become attuned to such vibration. In dreams, feeling is most pronounced and we have to feel through worlds, with touch and taste and smell and sight and sound. Feeling, the ground of being for dreams, is about the liminal, about the boundary and threshold between what are presumed to be distinct, categorically separated and differentiated sense perceptions. Feeling the space between flesh and textile of quilts as you and I sleep is like the liminal space of dreamworlds.

I endure sleep paralysis a lot, you know, when the mind has awakened but the flesh remains immovable, when a person does not process the sleep stages linearly but jumps a stage. It is a temporary, momentary rupture wherein you cannot move nor speak, though you are fully conscious, fully aware, fully alive to the world around you. I sometimes wonder about the relationship between sleep paralysis and quantum entanglement. With quantum entanglement, pairs or groups of particles cannot be described independently but only as a whole system: pairs or groups of particles react to stimuli and move simultaneously regardless of their current location (and they may be far, far apart).

This simultaneity, this reaction without regard to spacetime separation, means that quantum particles react faster than the speed of light. With quantum entanglement, pairs or groups of particles cannot be said to be separate from each other but that they constitute a system, a collective, a whole. So what happens to the single particle happens to them all because of the way they are regarded as a sociality, as a relationality, fundamentally. Such that if a multiverse exists, if ours is one of an infinite range of possibilities otherwise for existence, perhaps our dreams are that which rub up against and collapse into otherwise realities, otherwise worlds. (Yes, yes, I know, I know. Quantum mechanics and multiverse theory are not necessarily the same thing; but they both allow me to imagine relation otherwise. Stay with me.) Dreamworlds are, perhaps, just a system of which we are a part. Perhaps those otherwise worlds are entangled with ours.

Dreams are the audiovisuality, the images and sounds and vibrations, of alternative structures and divergent realities. One never quite understands the juxtapositions and claims that are made as dreams until a bit after the beat, a rhythm breakdown wherein the main character realizes something's not quite right, something's a bit off, something's askew. To be in a dream is to exist within, to journey toward, to enact possibilities posited but not yet realized. Dreams are otherwise states of existence and otherwise—as always infinite, never exhausted possibility—opens and unfolds through such movement. Otherwise is an *a*nethical demand: it announces the fact of crisis in the heart of our world through the faculty of imagination, through the enactment of feeling. *An*ethical insofar as the ethical names the crisis of modern man, an entity created by western philosophy and theology, an entity that exists by the exclusion of what da Silva calls the *others of Europe. An*ethical because the modes of behavior, the demonstration of truth and justice for the others of Europe, are a performative critique of normative ethics and the man that can produce it.

What does it mean to have life within the folds and creases, within the ebbs and flows, of otherwise possibilities? To sustain such a life is to be on edge, to be engaged in a constant unfolding, a ceaseless disruption as a way of life. What life emerges in and as otherwise possibilities? Otherwise is not a place we can reach, it cannot be grasped and held or contained. Rather, otherwise announces an orientation, a posture, a journey. Like an inclined ear, like a searching eye, like a rub or glide or slide to the side.

Otherwise is not a place but a disruption into the originary scene of violent encounter, a disruption of the coloniality of being/power/truth/freedom. Otherwise is not an identity one can claim or own as property but is a practice, is a way of life, is necessarily unsettling, a process of desedimentation, a process of excavation. Otherwise is not a place though it certainly can be imagined within spatial and temporal delimitations, within crevices, cracks, loopholes of retreat. Otherwise, like dreamworlds, emerges to unsettle the seemingly settled theories of time and space as contained, enclosed, linear.

Otherwise possibilities trouble the temporality of modernity and its being harnessed as property. The disruption is such that we can be in spaces dedicated to the cause of the coloniality of being/power/truth/freedom but nonetheless gather together as an alternative structuring logic. Otherwise, like dreamworlds, feels surreal in its surround yet is very much intensely felt. As otherwise, dreamworlds demonstrate that what we desire, what we want, has already existed, indeed exists alongside and as a critique and against the currents of the epistemologies of settlement, property, and racial distinction that mark our moment of and in spacetime. Tarrying and thinking with otherwise possibility allows alternative ideas, alternative structures and realities imagined, to unfold. To unfold like sewn cloth, like sewn sound, like sewn critique.

Gee's Bend is a small Black community in Alabama, enclosed on three sides by the Alabama River. From within this community a quilting collective was discovered, a group of women that have been creating quilts for comfort and warmth, for protection from bedbugs and cold, since at least the mid-nineteenth century.

The quilts of Gee's Bend communicate a distinctively African American panoply of preferences for asymmetry, strong contrast, and affective color changes, syncopation and pattern breaks, and an improvisational flair.[18]

The various quilters are constructors, are sculptors of the cloth and textile, they put together concepts and ideas through the combination and mix, mixing and scratching cloth. Such construction is all about feel, feel on the skin and flesh, feel in the intellectual practice of construction and improvisation, feel in the name of love. Each construction of a quilt stages the very question of the possibility for construction, construction as a collective, improvisational practice. And this because these same materials could have been otherwise constructed, because the force of improvisation was first harnessed to gather pieces of material together through imagined possible combination and their necessary alternative alternating patterning.

Quilter Mensie Lee Pettway stated,

Ought not two quilts ever be the same. You might use exactly the same material, but you would do it different. A lot of people make quilts just for your bed for to keep you warm. But a quilt is more. It represents safekeeping, it represents beauty, and you could say it represents family history. . . . But not ever the same way twice.[19]

How does otherwise feel on skin, on hands that hold cloth and needle? Needles that sometimes prick, hands that sometimes bleed a bit because of mistake, because of miscalculation? And before being displayed in museums across the United States, how did such cloth feel on flesh that needed warmth and comfort? And with such warmth and comfort, a sigh, a breathing out, a breathing into. Safety. Desire. Love.

How did and does such cloth feel and smell, how does it entrap the smells of home, the food, the odor of flesh? So much feeling, so much contained there. The object of the quilt a locus of ideations and possibilities. Pettway said, *a quilt is more.* The quilt, in other words, is plural in its unfolding. The quilt is an enactment of Blackpentecostal aesthetics, they are—as Zora Neale Hurston would argue about Negro expression, Black performance—variations on a theme. And the theme is feeling. The quilts are not about the object but about the feeling that inheres in the object, that which is within and is produced by and emerges from and spreads through the object.

A quilt is more: it exists as more, exists as that which rubs up against delimitation from the outside of limitation, that which exists as excess, that which exists as plurality. With the quilt, we run back into the concept of the liminal because it is the space between dream and reality, between flesh and textile, that worlds of possibility, of entangled alternative modes of organization, are realizable. And such life and worlding between is ordinary, quotidian, everyday. Quilts on skin provide what Rizvana Bradley describes as *the haptic sense with respect to the textured life of everyday experience.*[20]

I think of the way Mensie Lee Pettway describes her quiltmaking, the process of quilting generally, as the performance of irreducible plurality, of otherwise possibility, folded into the unfolded cloth itself, the way the quilt is more, the way the quilt always exceeds that which it was constructed to be. And if such possibility to be more is internal to these quilts, then the very prompting of their being made, their being constructed and fashioned, is the desire for plurality as a way to live life, a way to be in relation to others.

Theaster Gates's artwork alongside his construction of song emerges from refusing the borders of, emerges by existing within the space between, the visual from the sonic. In his work we find an example of how visuality cannot be contained, but like an outpouring, overflows. We find how visuality must be sewn together with the aural, with the sonic, to realize its fullness. In *A Closer Walk with Thee*, Gates takes words from pottery, the pottery of an enslaved man during the antebellum era—Dave Drake, also called Dave the Potter—in order to reconstruct them into song. Living in South Carolina, Drake used his pottery work in order to place poetic couplets, he used it as a means to mark himself, his thought, his project, into that which was made by his hands, that which was constructed. Taking the etched words and constructing them into breathed sound, into song, Gates has his choir, the Black Monks of Mississippi—an itinerant group of singers and musicians Gates gathers—perform the outpouring.

Folded into the pottery, to be eventually unfolded as song through Gates, was poesis, a mode of life, a way of existing that considered pottery as able to contain the plurality, the manifold nature, of Drake's intellectual project. Captured in baked clay was the outpouring of poetry, the outpouring of thought, an outpouring that—through its being contained and held by the clay—announces for us the inability to hold and contain poetry in the head. The improvisatory resonance, the vibration and verve, the dreamworld of otherwise words, had to go somewhere, be somewhere. The poetry is the enunciative force of otherwise possibilities. Gates picked up on the refusal of categorical distinction within Drake's works, a refusal that emerges through a poetics of pottery. Gates participates in and extends Drake's theory of poetics.

The flesh and enfleshment of Drake's poesis, found in the improvisation and resonance, is reconstituted and performed by Gates and his Black Monks of Mississippi. The taking of air into and out of the flesh, the process of inhalation and exhalation, to make resonant the fact of resonance, the fact of restiveness. With song, Gates is going for something, reaching, striving for something that exceeds the concept of the singular medium, a similar reaching and striving found in the baked clay of Drake's thought. He is going for, and grounding the search in, feeling. Like cloth on flesh for warmth.

The song of the Black Monks of Mississippi emerges from a visual art practice. In the visual is the resonance of otherwise possibilities, and such resonance overflows and exceeds the boundaries and borders of containment, of the visual, outpour—like water from clay pots—into the sound, the song. Describing—and this is the part that's about both dreams, kinda sewing them together—his experience as a choir director, Gates says:

And it got to this point where like the choir stopped and then my guy, Dewayne who was on the keyboards he had this bass line . . . and it was like that moment when a Black choir director can like, let loose. That was my moment. And I remember God showing up. People call that different things: a visitation of the Holy Spirit, when your head descends in Ifa, whatever that thing is, it happened. And I found myself hot and red and balling as I continued to direct to the point where I could no longer sing . . .[21]

Gates desired, in his sonic work, to produce something on the order of constraint, a paring down of what is possible into its potentiality, into its component parts. Within the component parts, the potentiality, the alternative ordering within the object itself, is the possibility for tears and speechlessness. Another poetics, another strategy, necessary for telling, telling and bespeaking.

I understand that moment, that breaking off into something otherwise. Such a breaking off leads to an ecstatics of quietude, intense quietude where everything can be felt, pulsed, but words fail. But that quietude isn't necessarily quiet. That words vibrate, that they have multiple meanings, that, according to Andrew Benjamin, translation is the nature of philosophy, means that otherwise is within the word, within the concept, itself. Each word is given over to its plurality, to the way it vibrates up against and resonates with other words in order to produce meaning. But as vibratory, as ceaseless movement and longing, longing and yearning, words cannot contain that feeling, that rub, that texture and weight. And speechlessness emerges as not knowing what to say because such vibration overwhelms. And so sometimes, tears. And sometimes, speaking in tongues. And sometimes, clapping of hands or holy dance. And sometimes, rapt silence. Otherwise sensualities.

The Black Monks of Mississippi's poetics and song, Gee's Bend quilters—each of their practices are grounded in the stitch, in the thread, in the materiality used to arrange, to organize otherwise. Each, a quantum entanglement–like system. Each a deconstruction, a destruction, an imagining otherwise of the fabric of our lives, the place of the materiality of cloth and texture, of construction and knowledge, that constitutes the epistemology that produced for us racial distinction and its attendant violence. "The fabric of our lives" is the slogan Cotton Incorporated utilizes to advertise, to announce the importance of this textile. Yet obscured through this announcement is the way textile and texture are the foundation for the violence and brutality and horror of this world that is. The cotton gin and economy. The fabric of our lives, indeed. These artists repurpose, they seek aesthetic modalities of escape. They do not seek perfection, they do not seek the right construction of a quilt or song or book skin panel. They perform otherwise, they perform the unfolding of possibility and alternative capacity.

Otherwise is life in the flesh. To think with and as otherwise, otherwise feeling, feeling otherwise, is an apophatic conviction and connection, an apophatic yearning, ceaseless and open ended. Otherwise is a way of life predicated on interruption acknowledging the discontinuity of flesh, the open secret of open sociality. On discontinuity, Susan Buck-Morss:

The nervous system is not contained within the body's limits. The circuit from sense-perception to motor response begins and ends in the world. . . . As the source of stimuli and the arena for motor response, the external world must be included to complete the sensory circuit.[22]

The flesh is the point of convergence, the point of possibility from which sensual experience happens. The flesh is the potential, the possibility, for sense experience.

Otherwise emerges as the point between, the modality of interdiction, the life of serration, of cutting and edge. This is the audiovisuality achieved in Theaster Gates's work that spills from visual to song. This audiovisuality is found likewise in the haptic register of soft texture and weight caressing fabric squares sewn together by the Gee's Bend quilters, quilts that are more than quilts from the moment of their genesis.

The abruptness of the waking becomes a literal tear in the lifeworld because there is a feeling reached for in the dream that, now awake, I desire to capture, to have, to be carried off into. It's as if the movement in the dream set me on a trajectory otherwise than what was just moments previous. Because of course dreams feel longer than the amount of actual time, or they also disorient the possibility of Newtonian time, a different temporality altogether.

Ever dream about someone so strongly you immediately attempt to contact them? You send them a message on Facebook or a text, no matter how late or early it is, because you got a feeling in the dream there was some kinda connection you were aspiring, breathing, out toward?

What's so intriguing to me is that I woke up during the vamp, the choir singing over and over again, *I'm reaching out to you lord* . . . It's as if the song were a thread, connecting cloth of the dreamworld and the non-dreamworld, as if the reaching were from one world to another. If reaching was a conceptual object sounding out in the dream, it was reaching for worlds otherwise, reaching for enfleshment and material realization in otherwise spacetime. If reaching out, then I want to reciprocate. And if from one to another, then to plural, multiple, worlds.

Reaching still,

A

Dear Moth,

I've been watching all these YouTube videos of older Black women singing in churches and their voices have moved me because they sound, for lack of a better word quite honestly, "wet." You should know what I mean. Remember the cassette tape that I'd play in the car on our long trips up and down 95 or 85 or back and forth on 40 or 10, the tapes from convocations in Memphis and specifically the way Emily Bram Bibby (her name just sounds sanctified, holy and full . . . like she just ate a goodass meal she cooked) would walk up to the mic and would, without pleasantries—the only sound you'd hear being the movement of the microphone toward her mouth—belt out

One day at a tililililililme, sweet Jesus!

. . . that kind of voice, her kinda voice. Or even Loretta Oliver from Fellowship in Chicago singing

Wonderful savior is he!

wherein her voice sounds of its climbing out of the depths from the *wonderful*, reaching the apex by *he!*, or her singing

It's a hilililighway up to heaven . . . ooOOooOOooOOh!

Though sung with a much more rapid velocity than Bibby's, Oliver's voice likewise uses melismatic rupture as hallucinatory of a bubbling vitality, a bubbling life. Like I said, their voices sound "wet" but I'm not too sure how to translate this to "paper." Though, I suppose, if you think of the screen as "paper," then you can think of the lowercaseUPPERCASE alternation as attempting to visually represent the shaking of the voice, its refusal of being stilled, its centrifugitivity, its wayward nature, its lack of decisiveness, indexed by the repetition of interplay.

The point I'm getting at is that there are voices that, for me, sound as if they were submerged in some deep, mysterious, watery refuge for protection and care—since such voices remain alive, remain protected and kept for us to hear after such submergence is overcome—or perhaps even buried and those voices struggle for their own resurrectional capacities to be heard in and through such wet substance. To be underwater is to be, we know, beneath the surface and this below and beneath makes anyone standing above—on a ship's deck, for example—inaudible. It's not as if the sounds do not exist below the surface of a body of water; indeed, there are sciences dedicated to listening to the sounds underwater. The vibrations that produce sound, audibility, the soundscape, move more quickly and further and further still underwater. So it's not as if life is not occurring in any underneath or underwater inhabitation; it is that one must position oneself securely within the folds and underneaths that are generally considered to be listless, lifeless.

So, like I said, I've listened a lot to Emily Bram Bibby and Loretta Oliver and couldn't shake the feeling they kept giving me. I put a status on Facebook saying, simply, that their voices sounded "wet" to me, and other than a few "likes," there was no conversation that ensued, which was cool. I figured saying it out in public would make the "feeling" their voices gave me go away. But, of course, I'd been teaching about the *Zong* massacre, as you know, and I thought about it with regard to the voices.

It's like their voices are a sonic, spiritual, ecstatic parallel to such praise and lamentation. So though I was initially against it because I did not want my students to confuse the pleasure of singing in a church with the pain Philip conjures by echo (and it is indeed an echo, a hollowed-out, previous-to-situation recitation of sound that produces proximity by way of nearness to a source without ever laying claim to the conditions of such emanational force; *echo* because it is the reflection of sound *waves*, waves as in ocean and water? Perhaps), I played clips of Bibby and Oliver singing while thinking about the book. I brought it up to my students, made them recall Philip's text.

I looped several of their songs and sermons (I had no idea until this week because of YouTube that Bibby was assistant pastor of a church in New York for a while) and while we talked about Philip's poetry, their songs and sounds of watery upheaval were playing in the background (I initially wrote and deleted *blackground*, but I'm not so sure it's wrong). If Philip's poetry dives into the water to receive a word from the submerged, Bibby's and Oliver's voices attempt to extend outward from the same sorta condition of submergence.

It's not simply that their voices struggle from some sorta underwater dwelling. Their voices sound of gurgling, the flow of sonic resource that from within them—in a broken, irregular current—comes rushing out. Gurgles make me think of bubbles and bubbles are from underwater, making me consider the air necessary for such encapsulated pleas to be released to swim to the surface. The gurgle ain't nothin but the sign of life of the submerged, the sound of water currents attempting to eclipse such breath and breathing. The bubble is formed because some air from a body or organism was taken with them either as a thrown-away, discardable material substance—such as the captives aboard the *Zong* ship—or taken with them as a decision to throw oneself overboard because, as the testimony service song says, they've got a hiding place, even in the overboarded underwater world. One takes air, which is to say life, with them and the gurgle and bubble is the fact of the capacity to take things with you, in you, even in the face of conditions that would attempt to take away even your capacity to hold shit in . . .

Bibby's and Oliver's voices come to us, in all of their force and magnitude, as evidence of having been submerged but having, also and most importantly, survived any attempt at drowning. I guess the question that keeps coming to me is this: are their voices, with the "wet" sound, rehearsing a condition of the submerged that keeps coming to us again and again, an *anontological* condition? Why would such a "wet" sound be so pleasurable, why does it move the congregation in such endurational ways? What is the capacity of the "wet" voice to show signs of life even if gurgling, bubbling, from horrific conditions of drowning?

Maybe Philip's poetry, attempting to sound out something of the breath and vitality of the more than 150 drowned captives, and the "wet" voices of Bibby and Oliver are a part of the same *anaesthetic* production, a different kind of baptism. Theirs is the *sense of question* that Black performances attempt to consider, think through, stage, wrestle with, against. A kind of glossolalia, an enunciation of utterances as signs of life that demand a radically different epistemological framing to even pose questions that are suitable to and irreducible in it.

A

nothing³

Dear Moth,

I've gotta admit, I love the tendency in Black gospel music to make any rhythmic song arrhythmic, to slow down standards so that the singer can play around and toy, tinker and trouble the structure. A mundane song gains new life by way of evacuating it of any such architectonics, yielding the song to a critique of normative modes of organization itself. 4/4 time and 3/4 time and 2/4 time become 0/4 time . . . or would it be 4/0 time, marking the possibility of infinite capacity for diffusion, difference, what Derrida might call that which structures differing and deferring, *différance*? Don't mind the faux-philosophical, opaque speak. Some shit I learned—rather, "learned" (yes, the scare quotes are necessary)—yesterday (or even still, more like, some shit I *read* that didn't make much sense to me at first read, so I copied and have been trying to think about it with the things that I know). And I know I love how my own Aunt Janice would come to my church and how her "friend" Delores would play the organ for her. My Aunt Janice was queen of the arrhythmia that I'd hear in Blackpentecostal music. She'd take a song—something simple, a congregation song—like "This Is the Day"

This is the day, this is the day / that the Lord has made, that the Lord
   has made

I will rejoice, I will rejoice / and be glad in it, and be glad in it
This is the day that the Lord has made / I will rejoice and be glad in it
This is the day, this is the day / that the Lord has made

and whereas, during testimony service, we'd sing the song with the regular 4/4 structure, clapping on the two and four, my auntie would come sing during an afternoon service just before the preacher got up and she'd subject the entire song's structure to a melismatic critique. So you know how with melisma, instead of each note getting a syllable, one can sing multiple notes for one syllable of the song. So instead of saying *do-re-me-fa-so-la-ti-do* one would take the *do* and make it *do-oh-oh-oh-oooooh!* going up and down the scale. People like Kim Burrell or Daryl Coley, I suppose, are good examples.

My Aunt Janice would take that little testimony service, congregational song and sing it as a solo with Delores playing behind her. No rhythm. No structure. Rather, she built into the song ecstasy and surprise by way of the tension and release. She'd get up and say something like

ya'll pray for me, I'm hoarse, got a cold but god gets the glory on
    today.
I'm gonna sing . . . well . . . I'm gonna sing . . .

and she'd pause while Delores would play "nothing music" behind her, filling in the gaps and pauses and breaths with sweet organ music that would allow Aunt Janice a moment to think because she literally would never know what she'd want to sing but would allow the flow of the service to determine her song choice and how she'd deliver it. And Delores is such a great musician. Women organists don't get enough attention, I don't think, but she taught so many people to play in her hometown and, now, here too. Her playing was so effective and empowering to congregations, she could do everything, ear trained but also knows theory inside and out. If she was gonna play at a service, you *knew* it was gonna be a good time. She PLAYS.

Anyway. Since this one time was right before the preacher and the service was sorta dry and she wanted to give the preacher something on which to hold that would allow his sermon to escalate more easily, I'm guessing at least, she went for something familiar only to hold up its familiarity to scrutiny, only to show us that that which we thought we knew was that which we didn't know at all. Removing the rhythm while using words that we all knew very, very well meant that the substance of the song had to be found otherwise, that we had to *get into it* by her delivery, by the style she used that was, at the same time, its essence. Singing that which we all knew in a way that we did not and could know meant that we were all on a journey—with my auntie—of discovery.

So after her pondering, she came upon—which is to say, she discovered already there—the possibility for the arrhythmic version of the song, which is really, when you think about it, just another kind of rhythmic offering, rhythmic critique. Kinda like how all squares are rectangles but not all rectangles are squares. Some concepts have folded in them other concepts. Rhythm as regularity is just another way to be arrhythmic. Right? So my auntie would close her eyes right before the first word, after having looked over and nodded to Delores, Delores still playing the "nothing music" waiting for the first words, not knowing what auntie was going to sing. Of course, auntie chose a different key than the one in which Delores was playing her "nothing music," so she immediately ran her fingers up and down the white and Black notes to catch up to auntie, but so skilled she was that it took her but a quick second and she was there, right behind auntie, filling in while also anticipating.

Thi-ih-is . . . ih-ih-is oh oh oh oooh . . . the! day!

Well, to try and recount the entire rendition through typed words would only be to falsify what actually occurred. The written word can't really approach what happened live. Not at all. You would have had to have heard it. But you can at least imagine her singing this Lord's song in a familiar land but differently. It's as if my auntie would reduce the song to its component parts, examining the truth of each word and breath and note and break. The hesitant approach, I learned when I was much older, made the weary sad eyes she had whenever she sang make much more sense.

I've since learned that her best friend and organist—indeed, that Delores—was her on-again, off-again partner who was convinced as hell that hell was her destination and so life became a living purgatory for them both. Their intimate connection we'd hear as auntie sang while Delores played was nothing other than a melancholy—but also the momentary irruptions of joy, peace, hope, love—they both endured on a daily basis. (If there was melancholy, and there was—and is—it is because of the doctrine and theology of the church, not because of who they are.) The possibility for their intimate music making is that very thing that broke down all sorts of ideas about what rhythm, tune, and time could be for any song. Auntie would sing down the heavens and Delores would play the hell out of that organ until we all shouted a bit, even those who'd never danced and those who didn't want to; she might've been what she preached against but she also had something in her that she wanted to give us whenever she sat on that organ.

Delores, we'd say, was a good organist. She did not lead the song but followed politely behind. She did not dominate the song but, rather, influenced it. She did this by having all of the drawbars for the B-3 pushed in except the 8' and 4', which were pulled all the way out to eight (loudest volume). She, of course, would have the 32' bass drawbar pulled all the way out. There is nothing more soothing than the combination of the soft of the keyboard with the low bottom of the heavy bass. Carrying. Carrying as caring. The bottom and bottoming out of the testimony and song. She'd keep her setting like this while auntie sang the first two lines of the song, following, as I said before, a bit behind. Like a kind friend being led by the hand into uncharted territory. But after the dance and choreography of voice and pedal, organ and song, Delores would feel more confident and auntie would be more herself, eyes open now, having taken the microphone off the stand and holding it in her hand, prepared to walk a bit as she sang.

Delores would then pull out the 13/5', 11/3' drawbars to about four and the 1' drawbar to about two in order to add vibrancy and bounce and color to the sound. Still following, but not as far behind now. Still polite but more knowing still. After auntie'd sing "has made" in her long, drawn-out, arrhythmic manner, Delores would play the most delightful *turn around* which is like the end and beginning converging, an intro and conclusion at the same encounter. She, of course, pushed all the drawbars back in again because auntie wanted to sing the same lines again from the beginning, leaving the 8' and 4' drawbars out but now exposing the 16′ as well, moving her hands up an octave because the 16′ necessitates this move.

I'm sure none of this makes sense to you and, even if it did, you don't care about drawbar settings but at least know that by the end of auntie's singing and Delores's playing, Delores would have exposed all of the drawbars pulled out to their fullest volume and the folks in the church would be up and loud and screaming in response YEAH! YES! YESSAH! MMMMHMMMM!!! and MY MY MY and other such things because of this song and dance auntie and Delores publicly engaged.

But you, of course and no doubt, are preoccupied with the curt but any-thing-but-simple question: Why? Why does any of this matter? And why linger in such a mundane conversation as drawbar settings and lesbians who cry and curse and feign coughs when called upon to sing? This is, at least in my mind, the very question that you allowed to preoccupy you so much so that you never gave way to, or a way for, experience. You never could or would and never felt you should believe me when I'd exclaim your beauty, your brilliance. Of course, this is why you improvisationally asked me over and over again if I really actu-ally thought that, if I believed it. You were beguiling, cunning, creative with the same query asked over and over again repetitiously until I too questioned if I meant it.

So why is it you like me
  What is it you see in me
  Do you really like me
  Once someone comes around who really interests you, you'll leave
me
  You don't know anything about me
  So what do you like about me
  What things do you find attractive in me
  I am not beautiful

None of these were questions, even if some appear at first blush to be. The problem, of course, is that you considered beauty to be kinesthetic, the project of movement that has been enacted and since you had the annoying tendency to deem your actions impotent, you thought the only beauty in you that others could possibly see a farce.

To me, beauty is not kinesthetic but rather potential. It is about the set of capacities to move *toward* movement that others, quite literally, sense. And I mean *sense* in its most profound and quotidian resonance, I mean taste and touch and smell and sound and sight. Your beauty, at least in the ways I detected it, was not wrapped up in what you'd done (or, really, not done) but in the possibilities of discovering worlds together. This was the beauty of Delores's playing behind and with my auntie: the possibility for discovering, for happening upon something, for invention and improvisation. But my auntie's breaking the song into components also sounded out a similar concern that you'd announce each time you'd ask me the same question differently. She did not believe the words she was singing, so she exposed them to newness and revision to see—maybe hear?—something *in* them that would portray and tell and prophesy some truth. She wanted the kinesthesia of the words rather than to live in their potential. The funny thing is, the congregation *got* it, they felt the potential and praised accordingly. But for auntie and Delores, the potential was simply not enough, they needed some action, some movement.

But, of course when I think about it now, kinesthesia and *potentia* are not that different. Or, rather, they are both constructed from our social worlds and just like silence does not ever exist outside of a desire for it, and just like emptiness (of jugs, for example) is a ruse (a jug that is empty, Heidegger would say, is full with all the mixed properties that make air; to proclaim it empty is really to say that air is "nothing" but we know that this is not the case), so too is *potentia* a kind of movement (and likely that kinesthesia is also *potentia* with *différance*). I mean, everything is always moving, in a state of flux. So even the notion of potential does not fully encapsulate the ways in which *potentia* is a form of movement. It is the motion of possibility, it is the stirring up (the gift? was I Paul to your Timothy?) of occasion, it is the flow of withholding.

What I mean is that *potentia* for me makes audio-visible the anticipatory nature of hearing. What we'd hear in auntie's announcement of a cold? The possibility for failure and not just of the song, even if not primarily the song, but the possibility for failure to produce the holy, sanctified, and set-apart subject deemed necessary for singing the Lord's song. What we'd hear in the first, hesitant, melismatic word *this* that she'd sing? The stirring up of a world of holy trouble. We knew, with that word, that the power of the Lord was sure to come down. The surprise would be in how, not in the fact of us getting there because there was determined as achievable and achieved before she began. My auntie doesn't sing much these days and isn't invited out much either. Delores still plays, thankfully, but they are rarely seen together from what I understand. Both of them got "delivered." Too bad they're no longer saved.

In potentia,

A

Dear Moth,

Another dream in which I woke up remembering. This time, I woke up, quite literally, singing one of my favorite congregational songs

send it on down lord, send it on down
lord let your holy ghost come on down
send it on down lord, send it down
lord let your holy ghost come on down

which, of course, must be finished with

power, power lord, power, power lord
power, power lord, power, power lord

but I think I was thinking and feeling and dreaming about it because we'd sing it and sing it and sing it sometimes for ten and others fifteen minutes. And that doesn't *seem* to be a long time at first blush until you realize that it is the same melodic structure the entire time and the lyrics do not really change. It's something so cool about singing around and around and around again, expecting something to come to you, expecting inflection and intensity to build and explode.

In the dream, I realize now, Mother Burke was in it with her white head covering, habit, and stockings. So it wasn't so much a dream as it was a reminiscence that took place during my sleep. She always sang *that* song, especially but not only when the service was—what we'd say—"dead" or "dry." She'd start singing from the pulpit when she was gonna preach, banging on her tambourine, and her voice was, I suppose, contralto, teetering on tenor, gravely, full of conviction and emotion.

She wouldn't just delicately sing *send it on down* but would add accent and texture send it ooown down lode, send it ooooowwwwn down!

and the congregation would have no recourse but to follow with just as much intensity and intention, clarity and conviction. And she'd bang that tambourine, and when she really got into it, she'd stand up from her seat and with the *shack-a-lack shack-a-lack* of the rings and pig skin held tightly together by wooden rim, nails, and thumbtacks, she'd close her eyes, throw her head back, and sing even louder. And the only way for me not to become bored on the B-3 was to become creative with the chording, sometimes *laying into it* and staying on one chord and then following with another, line by line, and other times switching chords and bass notes *back forth back forth back forth*.

What I love about the song, of course, is the fact that the Saints would be moving and moving and moving in order to bring the Lord's power down. You know I'm all into migration stories and have read entirely too many slave narratives where folks would escape from the conditions of enslavement by moving their bodies to above the Mason–Dixon Line, and to New York and to Boston and to Canada, which is all well and good. But I don't like the idea that seems to animate at least some people's thoughts about the folks who never "ran" but remained. There's all this moral judgment that is a little too close to implying that *it couldn't have been that bad if people stayed, if everyone didn't just drown themselves in the sea throwing themselves overboard.* Or sometimes, the moral judgment shows up as a critique of the enslaved, stating that they existed in conditions so very limiting that the very idea of escape was an impossibility.

Bullshit.

It's easy to make pronouncements about *well, what I would've done if I was a slave? I would've beat every goddamn muthafucka who tried to touch me.* Just seems a bit vulgar and wrong to me.

And so I love the song because it changes what movement does, and conceives of an alternative, social, radical mode of personhood and flight. The Lord's power *coming down* is about the recognition that we can use movement *or* stillness in order to bring something to ourselves. The Lord's power *coming down* means that the singing and testifying and dancing and speaking in tongues is so moving and persuasive and powerful that not even the Lord can stay on the outside, up above or somewhere away unaware. The Lord would be compelled to move to where the sound and movement is going on.

The song implies a knowledge of what we know and give, of that which we have in us, that can move things around us, that can bring things to us. Movement is not always about going, but is likewise about things coming. I sometimes wonder, of course, just what we attempt to bring to ourselves. Folks who read and take up Orlando Patterson would say something like because one is marginalized and enslaved that they have no honor, that this lack is irreducible.[1] Of course, they think that this notion of honor is what individuates and what makes a subject and so those who do not have honor do not have proper subject positionality, are violated of the possibility of being a citizen. So they think that performing certain rituals and behaviors brings honor, respect, and respectability and, thus, the ability to be a citizen, a part of this great nation and world.

Needless to say, I disagree with all that social death shit. If people are trying to bring anything to themselves—otherwise movement—it is attention that is sustained and engaged. *Power, power lord* is singing *with* power about the power. It is not a demonstration of fundamental lack or irreducible—and thus, impossible—dishonor. Rather, it says that honor as so defined by "social death" by those that have "it" isn't desirous in the first place. Desiring the *coming down* of the Holy Ghost ain't nothing but knowing that there is something here, with us, in us that moves us. Every song ain't about heaven. And I'd be all nerdy to say that this desire for the *sending down* is the repudiation of humiliation, shame, and abjection in which some theorists and scholars would so relegate Black social life. To say *send it on down* rather than *take us on up* is another way to think movement and motion, migration and flight. So no, folks did not have to leave conditions in order to critique conditions, or to even *have* a critique of the conditions, that marginalize and oppress.

Maybe this is a follow-up to what I wrote you about ecstatic asceticism, about being outside oneself *together with others*, away and removed from linear temporality. So if away and removed from linear temporality, then it can be and is and has always been here and now. And I said that Foucault would probably be against this sorta asceticism because it is a seeming renunciation of pleasure. But only seeming. What if asceticism itself functions as a mode of pleasure? What if renunciation feels good? What in asceticism can require us to think pleasure differently? There was always pleasure in Mother Burke's voice, she was convinced and convicted that the Lord's power could and, indeed, would come down. I guess the vulgarity is in the idea that a particular *becoming together with others* in a sorta ecstatic asceticism isn't possible, it's in the idea that she would only aimlessly repeat these phrases without such movement on the part of the Lord, it's in the idea that there ain't nothin here that the Lord might desire.

A

Dear Moth,

I have been rather obsessed with New Dawns music lately, listening to recordings of us, though we only performed for a little over two years. And I have of course been listening to it lately because our anniversary is quickly approaching—not of our coming together but of our breaking apart. I've been watching these recordings, listening to them with the volume on up as high as possible because I've been trying to rediscover you, so to speak. I wanted to know if there was something in your gestures, in your face, in your smile that I could know and seize, on which I could think and meditate. So I've been looking and listening to instances and inflections.

You know I don't necessarily believe in soulmates but something certainly happened that first day we went to the diner. The shy eyes, the reticent gestures, the bashful but ongoing pleasure of jumping headlong from one conversation to the next. Who knew that that sorta calm conversation and knowing comfort were possible between strangers? Who knew that that sorta wordplay and game, inflection and voice were attainable for two people not even yet acquaintances? I had butterflies.

And of course, and thus, I knew. And of course, you told me you trusted me. And of course, that made no sense if we were bound and restricted to some sorta linear time progression. Our meeting, I think, at least for me, was the disruption of such linearity. It's as if I'd known you many moons ago, some half life gone, that our communion and conversation could be traced back to some such agora. (And I've been quietly working on this speculative fiction about a character named Xenith who finds life and love after he comes to earth as a created human being . . . the life and love he finds is with the king's son but they'd "known" each other before their birth or whatever. It's like, rather than meeting for the first time, they "found" each other on their planet. But the whole fucked-up part was because they were both of similar kind and species, people couldn't understand it and so they had to make all sorts of cosmic conclusions about the nature of love and sex and connectedness that precedes time and exists long after time ceases. Anyway, our love was the inspiration.)

What was most weird and cool and most interesting was that that nondate—whatever it was—was the first time you asked me, right before you left, if we could pray together and it made me quite afraid. I was not one prone to pray. Of course, I grew up saying grace and going to *prayer and bible band* on Tuesday nights and Wednesday-night prayer meetings (Mingus was entirely too correct), so I knew and know how to pray. I just didn't then. And don't now. I did not then because I felt it inefficacious, a joke, folly that tried to escape this life. Prayer was infelicitous at best, a performative utterance that did not do what it purported.

Then I met you and our communion, at the very least, introduced me to the notion of focus. Of course, other traditions privilege meditation as a means to focus thought and breath though I had never conceived of those loud prayers from my mother and father that way. But you showed me and whispered to me and spoke in tongues to me and demonstrated for me how wrong I was. *Just because we're loud doesn't mean we're not focused or not contemplative* is what you said to me. Focused thought and breath is not only found in the quietude of Buddhist meditational practice, in the soft hum or brush of yoga chaturanga poses and the like. It is found when my mother would be in the microphone and I'd be on the organ backing her up, her saying something like

Satan! The Lord rebuke you!

wherein she'd punctuate words with the letter *t* and the sound *tuh!* along with the intentional singularity of such words that were plural (think of *rebuke* rather than *rebukes*) for dramatic purpose and pause. So it'd sound like she was saying

Satan'tuh! The Lord rebuke'tayuh!

as some sorta melismatic break of word and augment with new sound. *What do you think prayers are?* you'd ask me, then making me listen to my mother a bit differently because, well, she did not say *satan'tuh* when she was speaking, only when she was praying or preaching or, generally, when she was convicted. So, and of course, you forced me to think about the intentionality of such breath and vocable-ic rupture and suspension.

We stood outside the diner, and you asked *can we pray right quick? I mean, before we leave?* and there was no way I could say no to you. You were insistent while asking but tender. You were energetic by some sorta withdrawal. It was in your face. You became gravely serious as we stood out there, not knowing how to say *goodbye*, whether we should shake hands or hug or kiss, right there, in the lot, outside, for all to see. I wanted to do all those things but I did not yet really even know you, I just knew that I felt things that were either dormant or dead or demonic, all concurrently, all for you. So much boldness displayed by your query. So much strength. And conviction, I suppose. I just sorta stood there and you just continued by standing right in front of me, looking me clear into my eyes—I almost began to have tears forming right there, in the bottom of my heart—grabbing my hands with your hands, you lowered your voice a bit and said, ever so gently, *we should . . . we should pray. I know this may seem a bit strange but I'd like to pray with you. For me? Please?*

I did not say a thing. I sorta stood there stunned by what was happening, loss of control. Then a tear, before you even uttered a word, a tear formed and it dropped and, I suppose because you did not want me to feel embarrassed, you bowed your head and closed your eyes. The dropped tear, you felt and were correct to know, was assent and ascent. I bowed my head, closed my eyes. Then we stood there. And the wind blew a bit. And the streetlamp overhead in the parking lot buzzed a bit, almost backgrounded to the edge of nothingness. Faint, ever so faint. You began to moan a bit, really quickly. Then *Father, I'm thankful for the two of us having met today. Keep him and me as we leave here. I would certainly like to see him again. In Jesus's name. Amen.*

But all I heard was *I would certainly like to see him again.* And you hugged me. Then got in your car. I never told you but I stood in that parking lot for nearly ten minutes after you drove off. I could not figure out what had just occurred with me, with you, with us. I just knew that I'd see you again. And so, I was very, very happy. So happy that I cried. And then, of course the text I sent: *you're beautiful.*

These thoughts of that first experience and prayer came to me today as I listened to the first song our group sang at that first concert some years ago, the one I'd written, "Prayer for Zelophehad's Children." To say that Mt. Zion Church of God in Christ knew not what to make of this group of singers, musicians, and songs is no misstatement. I don't think most of them had even heard of Zelophehad so they were confused about who we were singing to or for. This mattered less when I descended the scales on the B-3 but, still, most of the congregation remained wary of us throughout the two songs we rendered. (Render, of course, is the best word for what we did because we had decided—you, I, Salim, Jaylah, Jalisa, and Bobby—that we would literally improvise our way through the entire song; we made it up on the fly, though we practiced the structure of the song and knew the keys, we would allow you to lead us from tonal center to tonal center, and the harmonic progressions were up to us to provide as you gave the melody [I think about it as emerging from the long tradition of hymn lining and fervent Blackpentecostal prayers during weeknight services, honestly]; I did what I could do on the B-3 in order to cut and augment the sounds you all made. Zelophehad, and his daughters I suspect, would have been proud. I love, still, that though it was called "Prayer for Zelophehad's Children," the song we sang was an arrhythmic run of "We Have the Victory" and "Victory Is Mine" and "What Do You Think About Justice?," testimony service songs we turned inside out to redeploy them.)

Breathing into our microphones and using the atonal sound of our breath as much as the harmonies, Bobby's percussive operations and the sonic architectonics provided by your melody and my response? Well. We gave the meaning to Zelophehad's daughters going to Moses, telling him that he should be open to the spirit, to give them what rightfully belonged to them, even if the laws and customs of their time dictated that women were not able to inherit land. Our song was all about contesting conventional notions of the sacred, of the gospel, of the love of Christ and the power of community, changing the words mostly so they could be freedom songs instead of about Jesus.

We breathed a bit on and off, before and after the beat. We sang harmonies that clashed. And we hummed and buzzed. The congregation wasn't ready but neither was Moses, so we were all right. The video is funny, you can see the congregation sorta just sitting there and you can see us not paying them any attention. Just kept singing, kept insisting, kept pushing through with improvisation. After a while, they got with it, got with what we were doing, we sounded churchy enough that they began to praise. I miss that sorta blending and disagreement, that kinda sound and sociality, that prayer, that praise.

Still,

A

Dear Moth,

I'm thinking about New Dawns because I want to approach the kind of decentering that occurs when the lighted edge cuts darkness with the new day, shifting every second, barely detected by eyes naked. Our group was similarly concerned with tonal centers and energetic fields, we tried to sing of the divine by modeling an otherwise social of intimacy and warmth and love and religiosity. We wanted to decenter the center, make the center centrifugitive, against itself. This meant dwelling with tones and singing slow songs with layers and new atonal harmonies and listening to "world" music and Islamic prayers and Gregorian chant for the chance and occasion for old new things, for things otherwise. And because of the intentional rhythms and arrhythmias we chose for our songs, as the organist, I was able to explore and plunge the bass pedal points in ways I did not know possible that only matched and heightened the ways in which we plunged and explored each other's bodies.

My friend—who listened to our music, attended and recorded every concert and appearance—said she was recently watching a video of New Dawns and how, for her, the music we created sounds like the residue of a constantly haunting dream, how our singing and humming and moaning and instrumentality and cadence and structure and harmonies and melodies are similar to when one is abruptly awakened and how one so awakened immediately notices the loss of the material content of the dream the more one tries to recall, so one attempts to reconstruct the dream by rhizomatic feeling, that tendency of using the last sensation and emotion because, we know, it, if anything, remains. But she said it also *awakened* her, made her alert to possibility she did not know she was seeking, sent her on a search for more. A sense of question.

We use whatever such final feeling there is to take us back into that which seeks to escape, a gathering and organizing of ephemera, if you will. So, for instance, you wake up with tears in your eyes and you are astonished at such tears. But the materiality of such tears leads you to a feeling of loss and abandonment. But that feeling of the gap and hole leads back to the question: *why do I feel this way* and based on that question you reconstruct that, in the dream, your best friend from childhood—whom you've never met; this is important information—that friend is left standing, waving to you as you—that's it! you remember—as you drive away with your father in his red Cougar with the top down and you see your friend becoming smaller and smaller but on the trunk hood you see the dance of sunlight reflection and shadow of trees quickly animated because of your father's speed; and then you remember that you had had friends before you began moving all over the country but that this dream served as premonition (you began having this dream before you'd even met your father) because now that you move from place to place with such insistence you trust people less and less and have few that you can call friends. (The *you* here, of course, is me.)

This recall, working from a tear or smile or laugh or itch toward that which it hallucinates, then toward some question or general concern, further still to the even broader general field from which any emotion or sensation comes? That is how we'd sing. We were a difficult group to understand because we were after something so anoriginal and base and foundational and moving, something *an*aesthetic and full and free. And it was Blackpentecostal only insofar as it was open to moving by the spirit. And tongues.

A

Dear Moth,

Filmmaker Arthur Jafa has a concept he calls Black Visual Intonation:

How do we make Black music or Black images vibrate in accordance with certain frequential values that exist in Black music? How can we analyze the tone, not the sequence of notes that Coltrane hit, but the tone itself and synchronize Black visual movement with that? . . . What [Black Visual Intonation] consists of is the use of irregular, nontempered (nonmetronomic) camera rates and frame replication to prompt filmic movement to function in a manner that approximates Black vocal intonation.[2]

One of the reasons I'm thinking and reading about mysticism and sorta medieval spiritualties is because I'm interested in the construction of selfhood present there. Does it model a soon-to-come modern liberal subject (and its racialized, gendered, classed hierarchies)? And this intrigues me because whiteness has to be considered a spiritual condition, something that is extrarational but that presumes itself to be rational. And I'm thinking about this all, mysticism and its resonances for modern thought, because Black Visual Intonation denotes a different epistemology of operation regarding Black visuality, for Black movement, for Black audiovisual emergence and encounter. Jafa's after a *way* to do what Black folks do as breathing life, as filmic practice. It is to enflesh film with the presence of what a kind of European mystical tradition would seek to evade.

Ever think about the relationship between *imagine* and *margin*? I keep thinking about it because they're so close to each other, enunciating them, breathing out the strange utterance and babel of such words, reveals a sort of affinity, a closeness that yesterday struck me as perhaps having more to do with each other than I first thought. I keep thinking about, for example, the history of what gets called mysticism, even in western theological traditions, and how lots of folks that we'd today consider mystics were marginal to their traditions, how they were at times shunned, at times thought to be too dangerous in the ways they thought their relations to the divine. What's so intriguing is that even if they are sorta presaging the logics of western man, that the way they do so still presents a method otherwise, a threat to normative religious man, because they rub up against the idea that there is something deeper and more urgent and more affective that can connect us to something intangible, perhaps unseen, perhaps undetected except through a search. This ain't nothin but the imagination. So how does being marginal prompt imagination?

It is simply undeniable that there are social worlds that invite others to join in. It's not an essentialist claim but neither is it an antiessentialist claim. It's something Arthur Jafa describes as the "materialist retentionist" strain or grain that runs in and through and over Black folks. The retention of material that could performed, material that could be—for example—danced, musicked, played, eaten, enjoyed. Such retention is made material through the fact and act of performance. A European mystical tradition would be against the retention of the materiality of the funk, of the flesh, it would be produced through a warding off, a renunciation, of the material blackness seeks to retain.

Jafa thinks that there are "levels" of culture that are enacted and performed based on materials retained. That material is often that which is in the head—a style, a gesture, a line, a root. He says that when the enslaved were transported to the Americas, whatever culture they could carry in their heads—the patterns, music, dance; the ways of breathing and doing, ways of caring and sharing, ways of conjuring and conceiving—could more easily be passed from generation to generation as well as dispersed amongst people. It's a pretty sophisticated argument to say something like *we remember*.

But you know I've been talking about Blackpentecostalism as if it's some sorta monolithic group. But there are all kinds of Pentecostals with all sorts of doctrinal beliefs. But what I find most curious and most interesting is how there is a pretty consistent theme of movement, motion, migration, that most Blackpentecostals—even if they do not themselves individually engage—do no balk at the sight of what others find unseemly praise.

Of course, there's something seemingly a bit problematic in the construction of the above paragraph, beginning every statement as if it is some such would-be adversarial conjunctive utterance. But the rhythmic feeling I was going for in that paragraph with all the *buts* is the same sorta quality which, if anything, New Dawns aspired toward, a sorta Blackpentecostal open-ended-like resistance to resolve. Each utterance of the *but*, not contradicted or stood in contradistinction, but opened up a way, a way of escape, widened the ever widening circle of thought, emotion. And it is exactly how New Dawns would perform.

But Bobby would introduce a rhythm. But you'd follow, with the bare *architect-aural* blueprint, the bare bones, so to speak, of what would eventually become song. But what you'd hum or moan or line out was both more and less than melody, it was evacuative structure, withdrawn breath, tendency and tentativity of the voice, hesitance and reticence, giving sound and words while remaining ever so wary of them being somehow conclusive. But stuttering, scatting.

We achieved a kind of poetics of Blackpentecostalism, even if not the doctrine or theology: just as one *plays at* shouting, initiates by that slight and jubilant dance—deliberative—ever so, and a bit, lightly, not glibly but with eyes open, looking around while the feet *tap-tap-tap-dip, tap-tap-tap-dip.*

Your singing would begin with some kind of chant or repetition. But we'd hear. But Jaylah would come first with that alto, full of vibrato and conviction, sometimes in a minor, plaintive strain against your melody though it was difficult to know. But it was not until Jaylah's entry that I would begin to figure out a way, a way toward harmonics, following and creating harmonic phrasing, clicking the *tremolo* then the *chorale* and back again. But Jalisa would enter, with her soprano register, often changing the tonal center with her voice, cutting, augmenting what was already there. But Salim would round out the voices, tenor holding some such thread of melody. But then, and only after the entry of all voices; but then, and only after I was chording, would I end phrases with the bass pedal points. But of course there were tambourines, but much, much later.

I remember one of the first times we sang like that, each one entering the sonic conversation from the pew, wherever we were seated, and the congregation seemed dumbfounded. Dumbfounded but they could not also help but be moved by our hollers and wails and tonalities. We revised "Prayer for Zelophehad's Children" to "Zelophehad's Daughters," and with the revision of the title was also the introduction of 5/4 rhythmic pacing and spacing, some new inheritable but nonreproductive call and call against response. Our voices didn't so much respond to the other as much as the voices called out in recognition *for* the other (it's like the difference between *glossolalia* and *xenolalia* . . . the former is *for* the other, utterance as commons but incomprehensible; the latter is *for* a "self," an assumed possible core stability that we call identity . . . but more on that some other time). Each voice was allowed to occupy its sonic space, a field or zone of voiced movement, wherein the voices tried not to *touch and agree* as much as they tried to detect distance and dwell together by buoyant engagement. The rhythm, of course, was Bobby's fault, but we made do and did something otherwise. And true to form, voices simply fell out when they were exhausted from singing. The congregation would always and undeniably be *in it* by the time we were done, so the open-endedness worked, they filled in the space where our sound once occupied, we moved them and were so moved.

So I get angry when folks tell me, as did a couple of acquaintances after one of our performances—you were there; you remember, I'm sure—*It don't take all that!*, that what we did was a shade on the side of excessive, too expressive and unnecessary. Pretty much the same sorta critique I heard about growing up at the storefront Blackpentecostal church, where services were too long and we were too tired to do anything once we got home Sundays except sleep. *It don't take all that* is really a claim about authenticity, saying that, as my friend reminded me of Gertrude Stein's statement, *there's no there there.*

It's a claim that approximates the idea that since it does *not* "take all that" to have an encounter with the divine, that which happens there, the "all that," that excessive and expressive strain is nothing other than posturing that posits something that is anything but "real." I can almost hear someone saying *if I can be quiet and composed and have an encounter with the divine, your sweat is merely performance.* The weird thing is this, though: I think most Blackpentecostals would agree and say, no, it doesn't "take all that." But whereas the former is critique, the Blackpentecostal claim is to say *but we still do it*, and most importantly including the idea, *and you can join us if you so desire, it is available to us all, there is nothing that I do that you cannot do and let me show you, this is a social thing, it does not belong to me but to the community that practices it together.*

I'm pretty cool with the idea that Blackpentecostals don't get everything right. What I love about the tradition, though, is that it is fundamentally invitational, it constantly says to come in, eat, have fun, shout even if you don't know how to, tarry, sweat with us. The music of New Dawns was seeking that notion of joining and togetherness. We never "finished" our songs but left them undone on purpose. It's like this: Blackpentecostalism is about transfer, the in-between. Things don't end, energy just modulates from moment to moment. We did not aspire toward perfection but toward pursuit, toward journey, toward carrying. Sure, we could've sung normal songs and sung with staid composure. The performances toward the divine we created did not necessitate the excess. But the excesses were the best parts of the performances, I think.

Love,

A

Dear Moth,

Maybe this will help. I've been rereading Saidiya Hartman, especially *Lose Your Mother*, and what she stages are a set of angularities, something like an angulation of thought, of Black thought, of thought gathered from dispersed materiality, of thought gathered from dispersed matter. It shows up first, for me at least, in what she recounts as what she first *heard* in Elmina. The sonic sets off the narrative, is what releases all that is to come. What she recounts, what she heard, what is remembered with sonic force? *Obruni*. She tells us that *obruni* means stranger in the tongue of the folks she encountered, a word and plea and call meant to mark her difference from the ones of the would-be nonstranger.

And it got me to thinking: From where does the knowledge of the stranger emerge? One has to have two kinds of knowledge—of the familiar and of the strange—in order to make a declaration of what is and is not, who is and is not, strange, a stranger. From where does such knowledge of the familiar and the strange emerge? What sorta epistemology is grounded in such a call and encounter? It is the knowledge of the unfamiliar now of inhabitation, a knowledge of having known, a knowledge of having desired. Such that the word *obruni* to name one as stranger, as strange, perhaps might also produce a counterfactual claim. To make such a claim about a Black person, yes even from America, is to make a juxtaposition that is not expected, is to produce angulation, the movement of otherwise spacetime. Frederick Douglass knew something of such angulation through the pairing of the unexpected:

The slaves selected to go to the Great House Farm, for the monthly allowance for themselves and their fellow-slaves, were peculiarly enthusiastic. While on their way, they would make the dense old woods, for miles around, reverberate with their wild songs, revealing at once the highest joy and the deepest sadness. They would compose and sing as they went along, consulting neither time nor tune. The thought that came up, came out—if not in the word, in the sound;— and as frequently in the one as in the other. They would sometimes sing the most pathetic sentiment in the most rapturous tone, and the most rapturous sentiment in the most pathetic tone. Into all of their songs they would manage to weave something of the Great House Farm. Especially would they do this, when leaving home.[3]

They'd sing, he says, the most pathetic sentiment in the most rapturous tone, the most rapturous sentiment in the most pathetic tone. What he recounts, in other words, is the angular nature of Black performance, the way it can arrive to us through the unexpected, how the expected and the peculiar form a unique bond, another relationality, otherwise sociality. Black performance not as a series of resolutions and solutions but the *sense of question* that angularity makes evident. Such angularity is space making, is spacetime making, is a disruption of the normative space and time of Newtonian physics. Because not only did they walk and march and go to the Great House Farm, they used sound and song to mark territory with the ephemeral sounds and songs that were improvised. It was all about the moment, the moment of encounter with the woods, with the path, with each other, it was all about the moment of performance as the possibility for establishing relation otherwise than what was deemed accepted or acceptable according to western musical traditions of time, meter, scale, harmonics. Because, and this is important to me, what is the measure of the *pathetic* and the *rapturous* in song and sound? This is not a key signature with which we are familiar and yet one gets a sense of what Douglass meant even if one doesn't have a particular sound signature in mind. The sentiment produces for us by way of Douglass the *sense of question* of black key signatures, marked by relation to mood and movement.

Anyway. What's so intriguing to me is the pairing and the doubling of the pairing and the undoing of the doubling of the pairing—rapturous and pathetic—such that any iteration of them is always more than double, always exceeding the limits of western rationality. What I'm trying to say is, I get this sense in Hartman too.

The African-American residents of Elmina had complained that the refurbishment of the castle offended the dead and "whitewashed the

Black man's history" by camouflaging the foul character of the place. But the paint was like perfume on a rank body; it exaggerated the stink rather than diminished it. The castle was picturesque in a way that made you cringe, unless, of course, you forgot the cost of its grandeur. And it was easy to forget the slaves crushed under the weight of all that monumentality.[4]

Perhaps the pairing of rapturous with pathetic is about exaggeration, about making real the key signature of enslavement, the sound of the peculiar institution, the sound of violence and ongoing violation. And its afterlife. Hartman, here too, recounts a similar angularity, a placement of juxtapositions—here, white paint, violence of terror. Such that the aesthetic encounter is one that has to be interrogated, the aesthetic form has to be something that cannot be taken, excuse the phrase, at face value or by merely attending to the surface of things. The angularity of it all, the juxtaposition, opens up the already available disruption to normative spacetime to consider other possibilities. Against the aesthetic, we have to have a preferential option for the *anaesthetic* performance.

And so, Adrian Piper again. She has this piece titled *Art for the Art-World Surface Pattern* that I keep coming back to, that I keep thinking about over and over again. She says of it,

Art for the Art-World Surface Pattern surrounds you with the political problems you ignore and rationalizations by which you attempt to avoid them. . . . Art for the Art-World Surface Pattern was one of the first of a series of works I did that attempted to confront this "depoliticizing" or neutralizing effect of the aesthetic stance in contemporary art on the issues raised by minority and other politically concerned artists. My intention was to bombard the viewer with political information concerning various catastrophes and situations around the world, and simultaneously to block recourse to the "aestheticizing" response, by incorporating it satirically onto the work itself. Hence, in order to distance oneself from the work, one would be forced to adopt some critical stance that did not itself express the aestheticizing response.[5]

That the piece had to be constructed in a literal room, in a literal space of inhabitation, is important, of course. What Piper does is spatialize the problem of aesthetic encounter when it is the grounds for engagement, the way the aesthetic becomes a category that is a strategy of containment, a way to racialize and dispense with difference. So back to obruni. Maybe the kids are artists, concerned with politics and catastrophes that are ongoing. Maybe it shows up as the call and encounter enunciated with the sonic force of obruni. Maybe they are announcing an entanglement that western civil society would have be *merely aesthetic* and by naming an aesthetic encounter—a stranger—they are compelling otherwise thought about relation. They produce an angulation of thought, a disruption, a moment of astonishment, a performance of disruptive capacity. A different relation has to be produced when the aesthetic judgment is foregrounded. So perhaps obruni is a concern of aesthetics, one that compels us to consider relationality differently.

So the relation perhaps is about the judgment of aesthetics, and an *anaesthetics*—through astonishment and exacerbation—can happen. Such an *anaesthetic* force—produced through the charge of obruni—disrupts western aesthetics and western metaphysics. To name as stranger, in other words, is to name through a kind of defamiliarization, but such defamiliarizing does not exhaust the possibility of relation but becomes the occasion, the edge and horizon, from which relation must be otherwise considered. It is a metaphorization of knowledge, the metaphorization that is the grounds of knowledge, a distancing that is also about a certain claim of and for knowledge production, a distancing from what has been done toward what can possibly be.

A

Dear Moth,

Remember that show *Out All Night* that starred Patti LaBelle from a few years ago? The show about Chelsea—played by Ms. LaBelle herself—owner of the "Club Chelsea" nightclub?

Well, there's one episode, in particular, that I remember. She sang the song "You Are My Friend" and the song is that sorta on-the-edge kindasorta inspirational, kindasorta secular tune about being friends and having love and sharing it with the world. The song slipped into words that were familiar to any gospel ear, so much so that my father was excited and possibly sorta on the edge of saying that Ms. LaBelle was not only showing that she'd grown up in the church but that—and he'd say this with a bit of enthusiasm right in the bottom of his voice, restrained a bit—*you know she knows the Lord, right?* The words in the song *I've been looking around and you were here all the time* resonated with him but it was also the appearance of Ann Nesby—kindasorta known for singing with the kindasorta gospel-inspirational choir Sounds of Blackness. Ms. Nesby and Ms. LaBelle screaming and wailing and walking the floor and waving hands and stomping feet was as reminiscent of "church" as it could get for my father, so he was pleased. Something happened right there after the song ended when Ms. Nesby threw her hand up and almost said—almost but restrained herself from saying—*hallelujah!*

And I've always tried to figure out that moment, that break when things transition from one mode to another. It's like when a gospel singer or group—think the Clara Ward Singers or Shirley Caesar or the Clark Sisters—is performing at a decidedly non-gospel awards ceremony and they say *let's take it to church* which means you're gonna hear someone wail in the microphone, there will be an organ filling the air with sustained and minor chords and arpeggios and there might be a tambourine struck here and there, now and again.

Pretty much, taking it to church indexes some sorta building of tension sonically in order to be released. You also hear this when people are dancing and shouting at church. At first, folks may just stand and clap, or dance but really playfully. But the music builds and swells and builds and swells and then—

pop!—snare drum struck and the organist grinds, sliding up or down the keys, breaking. And the people fill the instrumental gap with the sounds of their feet and their voices and their clapping. The release is the moment of encounter, the moment of the ever-so-faint exceeding and overflowing that occurs right after the tension built is outpoured.

Or it can be much simpler. Like when singing congregational songs during testimony service, when we go from one song to the next because they have the same form, the same chord structure. Going from

"This Is the Day"

to

"In the Name of Jesus (We Have the Victory)"

to

"Victory Is Mine"

to

"Bless That Wonderful Name of Jesus"

to

There is power, power, wonder working power in the blooooood of the laaaaamb . . .

The point? The point is that, at least in the social world and social life of the curious churches in which I've been a member or in which I've been a musician, there is a much more general disposition toward transition. Transition is the occasion. Life in and as transition. In the transition—after tension is released, or from song to song—one descends and ascends simultaneously, one gets down by going higher. That is, one creates centripetal and centrifugal—centrifugitive, circum-sacred—space to dwell and inhabit and move into the tiniest cracks and crevices. Getting down, going higher, descending and ascending in small space dissolves and erodes the limits of location itself, lays bare the ruse of boundaries.

To have a disposition toward transition is, to me at least, the realization that transition is the relinquishment of position and location, it is movement on the move that is constantly moving and never arriving (or, more precisely, arrival is about *staying* rather than possessing). I mean, what was most intriguing about the transition from song to song was the aspect of and ability to be surprised, to be inspired and struck with awe and wonder with the *way* the transition occurred: what chords did the musician play, how did we clap, did the drummer keep going or pause if only in an infinitesimal beat?

It's like that time I heard someone leading praise and worship sing

We worship Christ our Lord / we worship Christ our Lord
We lift our hands to Him today / we worship Christ our Lord

and transitioned to

We worship Christ our Lord / who is worthy to be praised and adored
So we lift up holy hands with one accord / we worship Christ our Lord

Not just a surprise but also the absolute joy and beauty of mixing the second song—"Blessed Be the Name of the Lord"—literally pouring the contents of the second song into the first to create something otherwise from something old at the point of transition. Something I read recently said something like: the great thing about Black Church musicians is that they have to fulfill a role normally thought only reserved for "composers" in western classical music.[6] One must be adept with a range of sonic ideas, chord structures, and progressions in order to cohere with singers. But one must be able to do this while learning and creating at the moment of performance. This is not just reserved for organists, though. This singer created a new song from splicing two old songs. And the congregation was pleased. And he was pleased because we were pleased. And we all emerged from the situation differently, thinking about the possibilities of mixing old things, things never thought to cohere.

Transition, in the break, is a relinquishment, an opening and being vulnerable. Relinquishment is a concept of relationality. It is not what someone is, it is what we do. But we let things go only in order to receive. We exhale in order to inhale, we dispense with that which is within us so that we may constantly receive more. If we do not engage in the constant relinquishment of seizure and ownership, we will never have anything, we will cease to be. If I try holding my breath, it won't work. Gotta give up that shit that I want and need the most. But giving it up, relinquishing, allows for renewal, for refreshment. Just like chorus, the refrain within transition, the otherwise.

The "Blessed Be the Name of the Lord" surprise and pleasure came by releasing the expected toward some old but wholly other thing. Relinquishment and breathing, it seems to me at least, are part of the same unbroken circle. Like Marvin Gaye said

I gotta give it up,

A

Dear Moth,

So about this painting practice . . .

Christina Sharpe ends her book by talking about care. She says that care is all we have. To end with care, to end with a point of departure, is to not end at all. It is instead to call, to seek, to journey, to request, to manifest desire for relationality—for sociality—and thus to resist the imposition of modern western thought that would have us severed one from another. To end with care, as Christina Sharpe does, is to open rather than close—to think directionally and, possibility, otherwise.[7] To care about that which is considered impossible to care for, to offer care—as concern, as tending to, as love, as abiding with—is to disrupt the time and space of western logics: its history, its present, its futures.

The philosopher Georg Wilhelm Friedrich Hegel is famous for having said that Africa does not belong to history. And though lots of philosophers have attempted to explain away such racism—though it was precisely antiblack racism that allowed such an assertion—I want to attend to the complexity that emerges when one considers history as something that is not axiomatic, that is not self-evident, as something that can be categorically refused to a people, as a mode of thinking relation that can function by exclusion. I want to consider those excluded from history philosophically because to belong to, to be captured by, to be engulfed in history-philosophical is to be placed within the strictures and constraints of the normative world and, following the line and root of Sylvia Wynter's poetics, *its* overrepresentation.

We might say that overrepresentation itself is a problem, if not *the* problem, of the mood and movement against the flourishing of Black life, against the flourishing of Black flesh. In other words, what if the perennial problem of our current political moment—its crisis of meaning, its ongoing reproductions of settler colonialism and antiblack racism as dual nodal forces of its globality and violence—is rooted at least in part by desiring a history, at least in part by desiring a Being that belongs to history?

What if the History Hegel marks, and thus then perhaps the history of *western thought*, and thus also *thought-western* itself—that big and wide and capacious category that seeks to claim everything within its reach, that attempts to leave nothing unfurled in its wake—is created through an aversion to difference, an aversion to the disruptive capacity of Black life and flesh and Black language, the desire to create smooth, linear, progressive, and forward-moving time? (It leaves *nothing* unfurled, that which it considers to be nothing is also that which is not considered, that which is not thought, and, thus, that which is its own thing.) To produce history by averting blackness is to produce through exclusion and violence, such that to want to belong to it, to desire it, would be something that must be refused. How to attend to the fact that what befalls blackness, what befalls Black flesh, is what is produced by the exclusion of and aversion to blackness, that which remains after overrepresentation of Man?

Her book points us there, in that direction, to that restive questioning, that restive calling that is also a solicitation for response. She calls us to think about the necessity, the urgency, the practice of care. And if care—of braided hair before ecological crises that have the fingerprints of *Man* on them; of delicate and gentle and intentional placements in boats—is that which cannot be liquidated or quelled, then how does one practice care when a neoliberal logic of inclusion and exclusion, of monetization and financialization, can utilize the concept of care itself as a means to further exploit, exclude, and produce violence against Black flesh? That is, how can we practice care as reflex and gift and outpouring against the imposition of having to care, of being forced to care, of being made to care as a juridical practice of antiblack violence? Can we practice care against the logics of violence and exclusion that mark care as all that we "have"? What is care to overrepresentation?

To ask about care is to consider how to be together, how to forge a way otherwise, how to imagine life and love and possibility. It's about how to be, how *we* be.

African American Vernacular English—or Black English—has different roots than Standard American English. Linguists argue that the speech patterns, intonations and inflections, grammatical rules and behaviors, derive from Niger-Congo roots. Harriet Joseph Ottenheimer says,

Notice that while African American Vernacular English [AAVE] uses
tense markers in exactly the same way as the other Niger-Congo

languages do, it also makes use of English kinds of tense-marking strategies. . . . AAVE speakers are adopting some grammatical elements from English but they are using them in accordance with correct AAVE tense markers.[8]

With zero copula, instead of "Where are you?" one can ask, "Where you at?" Or, instead of "Who is she?" it can be rephrased, "Who she?" The habitual *be* refers to a behavior that may or may not be occurring at the present moment but happens perpetually. "He be at the store" does not necessarily assert that the person is currently at the store but the fact that the person goes to the store consistently. It is not a question of presence but of habit, of action continually. It is a question and concern of presence, relation, sociality, *care*.

Black English is the enfleshment of care, yet it is often considered "slang" at best and "lazy speaking" at worst. It is often raised to the level of ridicule and lambast, dismissed as inconsequential and improper. The delegitimizing of speech, of communication, is to delegitimize ways of existence, modes of inhabitation, forms of omission and habit. Delegitimizing language delegitimizes a way of thinking, a way of relation, a form of care. But produced by otherwise traditions, otherwise ways to think and imagine, we can think about Black English with its improvisation on presence as concerned fundamentally with care.

I've been thinking about my grandmother, how she was unable to remember most of her family the years before she died. It was difficult, certainly. But what if Black Vernacular English also gives us a way to think about forgetfulness and the working of memory? What if instead of thinking of gaps in knowledge as loss, we considered it as an occasion for thinking the being of social life, the being of sociality, that does not take deletion as degradation? I've seen *Coco* twice and what's so lovely about it is how Miguel sings to Mama Coco but previous to that situation, he still engaged her as someone worth loving, worth caring for.

What's this gotta do with the painting practice? It's about the space between, kinda like what Miles Davis is known to have said about music, playing what's not there. The painting practice I'm engaging is trying to think about space and placement and improvisation and randomness, and it's trying to think of what occurs between color gradations and movements of handclaps, foot stomps. I'm trying to think the visuality of Black Vernacular English, trying to think the visuality of Black speech. It's about portals and chambers and dwellings. These are not practices about representing something, it's not about representation. It's an opening, a tear, a rip, an occasion to be vulnerable as a way of life.

What do you think?

A

Dear Moth,

It's like this: to carry a service. To be underneath, underground, underwater sounding out and through. Background and surplus. The gift. This is *nothing*. Nothing, not the absence but the overwhelming presence of some otherwise possibility, in this moment—this here and now moment. Exorbitance of the plural event of the alternative in wait. It wanders and precedes and follows, presences and flows. It sets atmosphere and mood and agrees and dissents. Descends and ascends. At the same time, the very same time. Arpeggiated creativity and sustained discovery.

S P A C I N G
T I M I N G

Triggers the mind, reflection. Recollective holy. It's there, it's here. How to put it together? This is that *nothing*.

What are you playing

they'd ask before we'd sing . . . before the service would begin.

Oh . . . nothing

I'd say, a bit with a smile. Knowing that I'd moved them with this putting together of something that is called *nothing*. I'd say it with joy, undulated joy. Both erstwhile and post. With each enunciative declaration of *nothing* is its underside, its truth, its improvisational meaning. Improvisational and provisional. Somewhere between those two words, those two concepts is where that *nothing* is. *Nothing* as fullness, as birth, as

L   I   F   E

More abundantly*lylyly*. This service, its acoustemology, comes from nothing but to know this nothing, you must come from and eternally return to that there.

Hold the foot pedal, sustained.

Play with the chords on top. Make them sound different. Vibrate variously in flesh, through pews and carpeting and wooden floors. Because of sustained bottom, playful top. Dramatic changes from loud to soft, the interplay of dynamics, intensely. And all this before anyone gets on the mic and says *praise the Lord* anticipatorily.

Funny. Funny how *anticipatory* and *participatory* are harmonic, the former waits and desires the latter as a kind of fulfillment. All this because *nothing* was and is being played, figured out, invented. Something full is being emptied in order to be refilled. The organ, the Hammond, the B-3 breathes. It exhales and inhales, fill again.

But. Also. Laying pretty beautifully apparent: *nothing* is not ever true, it is always the index of the lack of some propriety or given structure or epistemology or center. Even while being rehearsed from within a normative claim or mood.

So. Centrifugitivity announcing the refusal of center, also the fullness of *nothing*. Something is there, there in nothing.

I've been writing nothing all this time. Like the music. Not a song. A series of sounds attempting a feeling, a mood through astonishment, tension and release. It's about how chords are put together, what occurs between two to make folks gasp for breath, clap, nod their heads, quicken, throw up hands and say *ooooh, Jesus!* It's nothing, but so full. Full of content.

Some call it chord progression but that's the ruse; one immediately, enthusiastically realizes that digression is foundational to this form of nothing. That word—*nothing*—curious, indexes faith, sonic substance of things hoped for, immaterial acoustic evidence of things unseen. Faith is forward, futureward but so often is talked about through some sorta observed empiricism. Not faith in the least.

Faith is the uncapturable, though in standard testimony and theological reflection, it is put forth as a happenstance past event, always working through a tense situation. It's like when Mother Smith would say

and if he NEVER does anything else, he's already done what he's said he
would do!

or Deacon Jones would say

I know God is real because he saved me!

or we'd sing the song

Look what God has done / mastermind is he!

What often is glossed over is the past tense of such reflection, hindsight
reflections about a past; they are empiricist judgments, they tend toward the
ago, the *gone*. Faith, however, is the antithesis of such claims to knowledge and
is not an empiricist possibility. The enslaved had faith in a freedom they had
not tasted but knew was both available and possible, and not based upon a past
deliverance but a futureward contemplation and injunction of justice as necessary. But that seems wrong too, futureward. It was otherwise, the mark and index of a refusal of cause and effect, linear spacetime. The freedom they had not
yet experienced enfleshed the liberatory practice that they were already living,
the liberatory practice juridic universality nor self-determination could give nor
withhold. They found—as happening upon as well as were the basis from which
emerged—an otherwise liberation.

Faith, otherwise, is the *soon* of Heidegger, how he argued that time is nothing but a succession of nows, always being approached by the *soon*, always re-
ceding into the *ago*. Heidegger, I'm sure, wasn't talking about anything I'd play
in church, he wasn't thinking about the Blackpentecostal *nothing music* that
would animate pretty much everything that happens in a service. But he picked
up something, some *nothing* that the musician was already engaging. The musician in search of the *soon*. The musician playing in and as and for anticipation.
But then, in such a play, it's not about the ago, the now, or the soon. It is about
the gestation of otherwise possibility.

That's the *nothing*, the counterclaim of predestination, the interest in building as we climb or play or listen. That *nothing* is faithful, full of conviction that the *because to-come*, the irreducible agnosticism of nothing, will entangle with the now moment to affect change.

What I mean is this: it's sorta like when Paul would say that it wasn't as though he'd already attained something but that he would press anyway, that he would strive and lift and move and ascend or descend or something. He pushed things behind while reaching before. (Is it clear yet, after all this time and all these letters, that this might perhaps be my favorite scripture passage?) It's like William Seymour and Charles Harrison Mason itinerating all over the country, not even primarily to preach . . . but primarily to seek, to find that greater, more in-depth experience. They kept moving all over the country because they wanted experience meaningful and full and free. This? This is that *nothing*, that search, that movement. Their walking and sitting on trains and talking and eating with others? That's what it sounds like.

Maybe something, or nothing at all,

A

Dear Moth,

I had the dream. Again. With such precision and clarity and I'm really fatigued from having had it. Again. With such precision and clarity from seeing the same scenes replay over and over again. I get the message, I get the content, but it leaves me depleted, really bothered. This time, it began poolside. I was drinking out of a red cup so it must've been homemade. I'm thinking a Moscow Mule. It feels right to say that and dreams are all about feeling. So I'm drinking and my now much former pastor, it's been over ten years, is baptizing people in the pool. But then, a sharp turn of events, they are taking communion. I am standing on the side drinking out of the red cup. They take communion singing their songs and I sing along because I know the words but also keep sipping out of my cup.

Anyway.

So things end abruptly and I try to speak to some of the so-called Saints. Some of them do speak but sorta at arm's length, not really warm or kind or inviting at all. It now dawns on me—I'm trying to remember everything without forgetting while typing it all out as quickly as possible—that I was at the pool because I wanted to go swimming, wasn't really expecting to see them at all. Maybe I wanted my own sorta baptism that wasn't so bound to harmful theology that makes so many of us feel shame and embarrassment.

So I go in to give the pastor a hug—it's been a long time, remember—and she turns away, says, *no, we don't do that here,* referring to my cup and offers me not even as much as a hello. And then an abrupt change in scene again and we're in the sanctuary. I know it's the church because of all of the blue.

I no longer have the cup but I'm sitting in the back, sorta like how I was on the side of the pool. It feels like, at least now trying to recall it, that the so-called are staring at me, sorta upset I'm there. And this because I'm unrepentant. This caused one of the so-calleds to get on the microphone to definitely speechify about me.

No, no, no. Someone needs to say this. Someone needs to call this
out. We do not accept sin here. We will not pretend that he is ok. He is
on his way to hell.

Others of the so-called affirmed and amen'd her, some nodded and clapped.
It's not like I believe in hell anymore, or heaven if we're being honest, so that's
not what bothers me. People believe what they will to get them through the day.
Autonomy of thought. We all need to have it.

What bothers me so much is that ten years later the so-called Saints are at
the same hypocritical place they were then, that there's a sorta self-righteous
egotism to having purportedly "unshakable" "faith." I could talk about the person that voted for Bush because "Bush is protecting the family from gay people"
(and that's a direct quote), a person involved in their own terribly abusive clan-
destine behaviors. But that person was repentant. Me? I ran outta desire for re-
pentance when I realized that the shame I was told I had to endure was simply
not mine to carry, when I realized that I could live otherwise, that I could live
truthfully and I could do so because so many had come before me to challenge
doctrine and dogma, so many modeled what genuine community not based on
fear of hell and self-loathing was like. They opened community to me in ways I'd
never felt when I carried the burden of the always possible discovery and calling
out publicly of my supposed sin.

Yet here they are, only able to wax poetic about what the Bible says, unable
to live in the current world in ways that do justice, love mercy, and walk humbly.
Because being sanctimonious so often feels better than struggling to make the
world better for everyone, because being sanctimonious allows the so-calleds
the ability to cast glances at folks they've deemed unlovable such that nothing is
required of *them*. It's a fascinating hustle, when you really think about it.

Of course there's value there, that a lot was learned and felt there. But that
doesn't absolve them, or any of us, from being held accountable for the harm
we do or desire to inflict. And I can talk about this world because I know its inner workings and have experienced just how hypocritical things are, how self-
serving it is to talk about the sins of others, how really egotistical it is to declare
an entire class of people fundamentally flawed. And that's just not a game I can
be part of anymore, haven't been for some time. I'd begun coming out to people,

slowly, surely, before I'd even left the place but I can't pretend I don't feel some resentment, still, for lots that's transpired since those days.

Anyway, this dream keeps happening and I'm tired of it. Perhaps it's a caution to me, to us, to never become self-satisfied. Sanctimony shows up in all kinds of packaging and presuming to be "progressive" is its own seductive narrative. And the loneliness, the intense sense of displacement I have felt, I now realize, has a lot to do with religious community, spiritual nomadism, feeling outside the communities of care I once knew so well. I haven't been to weddings or birthday celebrations or funerals of people I have known and loved deeply. Their world, literally, is no longer mine, and I feel such a feeling of severance from it. The loneliness of the interpersonal is one level, certainly real and felt and known. But there is the loneliness of the social world, the spiritual community, that feels sharper and more fundamentally hurtful. And the dream, this dream that keeps happening, finally let me be able to articulate this. But still, I'd be happy to not have this dream anymore.

Maybe one day,

A

Dear Moth,

The occasion of the political climate, the occasion of the old but for many new thing about politics and disorganization, gave me a sorta explicit example. This Instagram video is what I meant by renouncing the one for the many; check it out.[9]

These are folks that own and/or work at bodegas in New York City, all kindsa folks gathered together to argue in favor of their flesh, for the protection of their collective, improvisational, nondivisional, nonsingular identity, they moved and worked in the favor and protection of a nonliberal subjectivity, an intersubjective otherwise as possible. This prayer in the park, in the open, is beautiful to me.

Look at the sorta gracefulness with which they stand, then bow, then bend. Listen to the quiet, the quiet that makes the sound of wind and street noise apparent, a quiet that is not about the evacuation of sound but a refilling, an indwelling, of otherwise sound. Listen to how in that silence is the anticipation for the sounding out, the call, to bend again. It's, I don't know, beautiful to me.

They withdrew into the world, into worlds, made themselves available, open, by retreating into the outside. There, in the outside, they found through performance, the secret place of the most lowly, the secret place of blackness— to echo a friend a bit—lowly against exaltation, they withdrew into the clearing. And there they worshipped. And there other theys stood and watched, rapt. They ascended into dissent, into descent. They left the bodegas and made themselves secret in public, and in such doing undid the distinction between private and public. They made apparent otherwise in flesh in the *thennowsoon* and *whenwhere* of spacetime. Entanglement. Entangled. They were not lonely. It is a mysticism of the social, the mysticism of sociality.

I've been listening to my breathing more as I sleep. Or, not necessarily listening but have become more aware of it as sound, as making noise, as displacement continually. I listen as I sleep or as I run on the treadmill or even as I walk down the street. Something about the constant movement of air in and out, in and out. Something about how we have to keep doing it to keep alive, how it is a biogenic fact, how flesh needs air to revive itself, sustain itself. That something from the so-called outside's gotta come and dwell with us, in us, maybe the dissent and descent of the Holy Ghost was just making this explicit: what keeps us alive, what holds us in embrace of the living, is something available and common and collective and social and outside oneself. It is ecstasy in the most explicit sense.

And I get this feeling as I watch these people pray in the middle of the city, as I watch them pray as staging protest. They're praying from positions physically, and from stations of life sorta theologically and philosophically, that are considered in the United States to be discardable, unnecessary, in need of conversion. But what their praying in the sorta secret place of blackness shows me is that they breathe and in the fact of such breathing we should cherish it.

I'll say more soon but this is getting to be too long,

A

acknowledgments

And there are so many ways to be thankful, to practice a kind of delight and joy of sociality that makes the work—any work—not only possible but plausible. *The Lonely Letters* is produced through social engagement with the world, with the fact of friendship as the grounding wire and way out from the mundane and quotidian and ordinary modes of exclusion and disconnection and violence. The many ways one can be thankful are hopefully felt with each page of each letter, each a solicitation to practice joyfulness of gratitude to be able to try, to be able to try again, to be able to enter into friendship as a way of life.

And I am grateful. And I am thankful.

I am thankful to the many people I have encountered that have encouraged me to keep writing, to keep painting, to keep thinking and feeling and hoping and wishing that the otherwise than this was not only possible but able to be practiced in, and thus against, the normative world. Each encounter with the world, with worlds, leaves me breathless, leaves me thinking and feeling and hoping and wishing for the continual unfolding of otherwise possibility. And this, the thought and feeling and hoping and wishing, emerge because of the practice of journeying with others, friendship as the way of life for me to be sustained, to be held and to hold, to be loved and to love.

And I am grateful. And I am thankful.

Ronald Sr. and Roxann Crawley, my parents. I love you each day and learn from you continually and am thankful for the fact that relationship grows and changes and turns and moves and unfolds and is never *done*, is always able to be augmented. Without you I would not have breath and being, without you I would not have been able to detect worlds that your commitment to Black-pentecostalism makes possible for me daily.

And to Ronald Jr., my brother and friend. I love you, too, and am thankful for our continually growing friendship. Thank you for all that you are. Time tests our lives, it changes us, it compels us to search deeper still for stillness and happiness and love. You stand tests, you endure, you continue.

And I am grateful. And I am thankful.

To my friends Imani Perry and Nicole Fleetwood, thank you for the love and care and tenderness and generosity with which you read and engaged and thought with this work. Thank you for the words offered in reply, the questions and suggestions, for the thoughtfulness and gentleness with which you handled the letters telling something about loneliness, letters seeking connection, letters bespeaking intimacies as possible and plausible. I am appreciative for your charitable readings.

To Ken Wissoker, I am grateful for the vision and clarity you provided during the editorial process. It was a great pleasure to work with you. To Olivia Polk, Nina Foster, Toni Willis, Susan Albury, Aimee Harrison, and the entire Duke University Press staff, thank you for all you provided to help make this book, for ushering it from manuscript to design and publication.

For continued mentoring and friendship, Fred Moten, Maurice Wallace, Louise Meintjes, Willie James Jennings, Ian Baucom, I am always grateful, forever indebted, always in communion.

To Desiree Thompson: this, quite literally, would not be a project without your care and love and pushing and friendship. Thank you for suggesting that I write to myself, that I send emails to myself in order to get out whatever it was that was trying to be said, that was trying to say itself into the world. Thank you for knowing and caring for my heart, for knowing that whatever it was needed to come through me, needed me as a conduit. Thank you, forever.

To Nicole Ivy, Crystal McElrath, and Alexis Yancey, I love you each deeply and am appreciative for your friendship.

Thank you to Akira Drake, the only person I talk to just about every day since at least about 2001. You have been such a constant support and sounding board and such a consistent and caring person to me. I will always be in your corner and care for you. Thank you for all that you are.

Words cannot describe my friendship and siblinghood with Kendal Brown and Jonathan Adams. You both know so much about me and my affect and mood and my mourning. You celebrate with me and care for me. It is astounding, really. Thank you.

I'm grateful for the friendship of Amaryah Armstrong, Kyle Brooks, and Jamal Calloway, thankful for the enduring friendship, the *endearing* friendship. Thank you for practicing openness and care for me and for allowing me to practice these things with you.

It is a wonder, your friendships you practice with me, Amey Victoria Adkins-Jones, Jasmine Johnson, and Jennifer Morris Brockington. At different times, at different occasions, each time unanticipated by me, you each let me cry on the phone or at dinner or at the bar with you, you never let me feel shame or embarrassment but encouraged me to share and breathe and be. Such a gift, your friendships. Such an honor to call each of you friend.

I am grateful to you too, Khalilah Liptrot, for all that you encourage me to be, for how you continually support me, for how you listen and sense for me. And to Shydel James, I am glad that our friendship, since high school, continues to grow and unfold.

And to SA Smythe, thank you for encouraging my art practice, for sensing that it is about something, that it is about the worlds we make with one another, that we can practice friendship as encouragement and joy and love of one another. And thank you for being there and saying that, yes, the outline for this work should be in conversation with BPB, thank you for encouraging me to move in this direction.

My friends at UVA, AD Carson and Meredith Clark, thank you for allowing for life here to be a place where friendship could happen and flourish. And thanks for putting up with my cooking too much food and keeping you here for hours to laugh and talk and learn. I appreciate you. And to Donna Auston, Sylvia Chan-Malik, Kameelah Mu'min, and Naomi Washington-Leapheart, thank you for being my sisters.

And to Sofia Samatar for encouraging these letters from the very beginning, for the care with which you read and engaged and wrote to me about them.

And I am grateful. And I am thankful.

Ayanna Abi-Kyles, Timothy Adkins-Jones, Lindsey Andrews, Maile Arvin, Crystal Baik, Moya Bailey, Melissa Bethea, Felice Blake, Rizvana Bradley, Daphne Brooks, Jayna Brown, Rosa Echols Brown, Simone Browne, Courtney Bryan, Anthea Butler, Amalia Cabezas, Leslie Callahan, Letitia Campbell, Michelle Commander, Nahum Chandler, Allison Curseen, Jessica Davenport, Cathy Davidson, Keri Day, Jennifer Doyle, Carol Duncan, Alethea Dunham-Carson, Erica Edwards, Eve Ewing, Roderick Ferguson, Julius Fleming, Mona Ford, Max Foxx, Erica Fretwell, Jamila Garrett-Bell, Eddie Glaude, Alexis Pauline Gumbs, Sarah Haley, Donna Hampton, Stefano Harney, Laura Harris, John Hester, Leah Hobson, Karla Holloway, Jonathan Howard, Jennifer Hughes, Cora Ingrum, Arthur Jafa, Regine Jean-Charles, E. Patrick Johnson, Imani Johnson, Damon Jones, Feminista Jones, RA Judy, Mariame Kaba, Ronak Kapadia, Elleza Kelley, Robin Kelley, Jodi Kim, Aliya S. King, Mariam Lam, Susannah Laramee-Kidd, David Lloyd, Nathaniel Mackey, Summer McDonald, Katherine McKittrick, Nick Mitchell, Matthew Morrison, Mendi+Keith Obadike, Laura Nasrallah, Mark Anthony Neal, Fari Nzinga, Imani Owens, Yumi Pak, Leigh Patel, Courtney Patterson, Ann Pellegrini, Jade Perry, Jeremy Posadas, Ann Powers, Guy Ramsey, Shana Redmond, Kathryn Reklis, JT Roane, Abdul-Hamid Robinson Royal, Anthony Bayani Rodriguez, Dylan Rodriguez, Britt Rusert, Regina Scarbrough, Sarita See, Setsu Shigematsu, Denise Ferreira Da Silva, Candace Simpson, Jordan Stein, Andrea Smith, Damien Sojoyner, David Stein, Pamela Sutton-Wallace, Leonne Tanis, Keeanga-Yamahtta Taylor, Todne Thomas, Elizabeth Todd-Breland, Kyla Wazana Tompkins, Trudy, Rosaline Valcimond, Deb Vargas, Shakera Walker, Kentina Washington-Leapheart, Kirsten West Savali, Terrion Williamson, Autumn Womack, Bryant Woodford, Nikki Young, I am thankful to you all.

To the many Moths, the ones that have come and gone, those that have caused butterflies and dense, deep, unexplicable sadness, thank you, too, for giving me an occasion to attempt to care, to learn more about my place in the world, to give me a reason to stop and breathe and try and attempt and grow and apologize and laugh and cry and . . .

Friendship. What an absolute gift and treasure and joy. Friendship. What an amazingly beautiful and lovely form of relating to worlds of possibility heretofore undiscovered. Friendship, the unfolding of a way of life that takes comfort and care and concern and camaraderie as the first operations. Thankful. Absolutely thankful.

notes

and[3]

1　Manthia Diawara, "One World in Relation: Édouard Glissant in Conversation with Manthia Diawara," *Nka Journal of Contemporary African Art* 2011, no. 28 (March 20, 2011): 5.

2　Nahum Chandler Dimitri, *Toward an African Future—Of the Limit of World* (Living Commons Collective, 2013).

breath[3]

1　"Mahalia Jackson—How I Got over LIVE. YouTube, accessed September 3, 2019, https://www.youtube.com/watch?v=l49N8U3doBw.

2　TheClarkSistersTV, *Twinkie Clark & Richard White Clean—Accept What God Allows*, accessed August 23, 2018, https://www.youtube.com/watch?v=sceCHxTroLs&feature=youtu.be&t=9m6s.

3　Meister Eckhart, *Meister Eckhart, from Whom God Hid Nothing: Sermons, Writings, and Sayings* (Boston: New Seeds, 2005).

4　Talal Asad, *Formations of the Secular: Christianity, Islam, Modernity* (Stanford, CA: Stanford University Press, 2003).

5　Quoted in Amy Hollywood and Patricia Z. Beckman, eds., *The Cambridge Companion to Christian Mysticism* (Cambridge: Cambridge University Press, 2012), 83.

6　Preface by Rebecca Chopp in Nancy L. Eiesland, *The Disabled God: Toward a Liberatory Theology of Disability* (Nashville, TN: Abingdon Press, 1994), 11.

7 Julian of Norwich and A. C. Spearing, *Revelations of Divine Love*, trans. Elizabeth Spearing (London: Penguin Books, 1999), 3.

8 Denise Ferreira da Silva, "On Difference without Separability," in *32a São Paulo Art Biennial, "Incerteza Viva" (Living Uncertainty)*, exhibition catalog, 57–58, accessed March 7, 2018, https://issuu.com/amilcarpacker/docs/denise_ferreira _da_silva.

9 Jason W. Moore, *Capitalism in the Web of Life: Ecology and the Accumulation of Capital* (New York: Verso, 2015).

10 Leanne Betasamosake Simpson, *As We Have Always Done: Indigenous Freedom through Radical Resistance* (Minneapolis: University of Minnesota Press, 2017), 33, 36.

11 Cheryl I. Harris, "Whiteness as Property," *Harvard Law Review* 106, no. 8 (1993): 1707–91.

12 Michel Foucault, "Friendship as a Way of Life," in *Ethics: Subjectivity and Truth*, ed. Paul Rabinow, trans. Robert Hurley (New York: New Press, 1997), 136.

13 Foucault, 137.

14 "Hortense Spillers Interview with Tim Haslett for the Black Cultural Studies Web Site Collective in Ithaca, NY," Black Cultural Studies website, February 4, 1998, http://www.blackculturalstudies.net/spillers/spillers_intvw.html.

15 Rev F. W. McGee, *Rev. F.W. McGee*, vol. 2 (Document Records, 1992).

shouting[3]

1 Steve Reich, *Music For 18 Musicians* (Nonesuch, 2005).

2 Nahum Chandler Dimitri, *Toward an African Future - of the Limit of World* (Living Commons Collective, 2013).

3 Hymn Choir Channel, "He Set Me Free," May 3, 2007, YouTube video, 7:54, https://www.youtube.com/watch?v=skEzQq2ySRA.

4 Nathaniel Mackey, *From a Broken Bottle Traces of Perfume Still Emanate: Bedouin Hornbook, Djbot Baghostus's Run, Atet A.D.* (New York: New Directions, 2010), 14.

5 Moya Bailey and Trudy, "On Misogynoir: Citation, Erasure, and Plagiarism," *Feminist Media Studies* 18, no. 4 (July 4, 2018): 762–68.

6 Audre Lorde, *Sister Outsider: Essays and Speeches* (Berkeley, CA: Crossing Press, 2007), 9.

7 Steve Reich, *Writings on Music, 1965–2000* (Oxford: Oxford University Press, 2002), 87.

8 Reich, 87–89.

9 Harriet A. Jacobs, *Incidents in the Life of a Slave Girl, Written by Herself* (Boston: Bedford/St. Martins, 2009).

10 Toni Morrison, *Playing in the Dark: Whiteness and the Literary Imagination*, William E. Massey, Sr. Lectures in the History of American Civilization; 1990. (Cambridge, MA: Harvard University Press, 1992).

11. James Baldwin, *Just above My Head* (New York: Dial Press, 1979), 566.

12 Iona Locke—Topic, "Let's Get It On (Sermon)," October 8, 2015, YouTube video, 57:57, https://www.youtube.com/watch?v=SCxyYTE6k2o.

13 TheClarkSistersTV, "Twinkie Clark & Richard White Clean—Accept What God Allows," June 20, 2008, YouTube video, 10:01, https://www.youtube.com/watch?v=sceCHxTroLs.

14 hammondxc3, "We Have Come into This House," May 8, 2011, YouTube video, 7:20, https://www.youtube.com/watch?v=NFXSL_zGOQc.

15 Gospel Today Volume 4—Topic, "Praise Break," July 4, 2015, YouTube video, 4:18, https://www.youtube.com/watch?v=WFVBgsvqix4.

16 Edmund Burke, *A Philosophical Inquiry into the Origin of Our Ideas of the Sublime and Beautiful* (New York: P. F. Collier and Son, 1909–14; Bartleby.com, 2001), http://www.bartleby.com/24/2/.

17 Aelita Andre, "Aelita Andre—Prodigy of Color Exhibition in New York City," May 16, 2011, YouTube video, 13:45, https://www.youtube.com/watch?v=23hWMvSrZx8.

18 Gregory Schroeder Jr., "Apostle Robert Evans, Jr. 'Dancing in One Spot' (Audio Snippet)," February 7, 2013, YouTube video, 5:17, https://www.youtube.com/watch?v=5sGokTGgQ9A.

19 Giorgio Agamben, *Profanations*, trans. Jeff Fort (New York: Zone Books, 2007).

20 Sylvia Wynter, quoted in David Scott, "The Re-Enchantment of Humanism: An Interview with Sylvia Wynter," *Small Axe* 8 (September 2000): 126.

21 Mackey, *From a Broken Bottle*, 51.

22 Philip Gibbs, "Where Is the Centre of the Universe?," Physics and Relativity FAQ, 1997, http://math.ucr.edu/home/baez/physics/Relativity/GR/centre.html.

23 Mackey, *From a Broken Bottle*, 11.

24 Cedric J. Robinson, *The Terms of Order: Political Science and the Myth of Leadership* (Chapel Hill: University of North Carolina Press, 2016).

25 Denise Ferreira da Silva, "To Be Announced: Radical Praxis or Knowing (at) the Limits of Justice," *Social Text* 31, no. 1 114 (March 20, 2013): 43–62.

26 Sylviane A. Diouf, *Slavery's Exiles: The Story of the American Maroons* (New York: New York University Press, 2014), 8.

27 hammondxc3, "We Have Come into This House."

28 Reich, *Writings on Music*, 21.

noise[3]

1   Werner Heisenberg, *Physics and Philosophy: The Revolution in Modern Science* (New York: Harper Perennial Modern Classics, 2007), x.

2   Karen Barad, *Meeting the Universe Halfway: Quantum Physics and the Entanglement of Matter and Meaning* (Durham, NC: Duke University Press, 2007), 19.

3   Ferreira da Silva, "To Be Announced."

4   Denise Ferreira da Silva, *Toward a Global Idea of Race* (Minneapolis: University of Minnesota Press, 2007).

5   Sylvia Wynter, "Unsettling the Coloniality of Being/Power/Truth/Freedom: Towards the Human, After Man, Its Overrepresentation—An Argument," CR: *The New Centennial Review* 3, no. 3 (2003): 257–337.

6   Heisenberg, *Physics and Philosophy*, 1.

7   Robinson, *Terms of Order*.

8   Lindsey Andrews, "From Inside a Black Black Box," *Lute and Drum* 8 (2016): n.p., http://issue8.luteanddrum.com/#!andrews/.

9   Mackey, *From a Broken Bottle*, 34.

10 Cedric J. Robinson, *Black Marxism: The Making of the Black Black Radical Tradition*, Third World Studies (London: Zed Press, 1983).

11 Robinson, 2.

12 Wynter, "Unsettling the Coloniality," 271.

13 Bernard McGinn, *The Foundations of Mysticism: Origins to the Fifth Century* (New York: Crossroad, 2004), 136.

14 McGinn, 194–95.

15 See part 2 in Robinson, *Black Marxism*.

16 *Moonlight*, dir. Barry Jenkins (A24; Plan B Entertainment; Pastel Productions, 2016), film.

17   Paul F. Kisak, ed., *Quantum Entanglement! ". . . Spooky Action at a Distance"* (n.p.: CreateSpace, 2016), 1.

18 Stephen Morgan, "Scientists Show Future Events Decide What Happens in the Past," *Digital Journal*, June 3, 2015, http://www.digitaljournal.com/science/experiment-shows-future-events-decide-what-happens-in-the-past/article/434829.

19 Baldwin, *Just above My Head*, 189, 197, 213, 566, 576, 340.

20 Hortense J. Spillers, "Mama's Baby, Papa's Maybe: An American Grammar Book," in Black Black , White, and in Color: Essays on American Literature and Culture, 203–29 (Chicago: University of Chicago Press, 2003).

21 Toni Morrison, *Beloved: A Novel* (New York: Vintage International, 2004), 88–89.

22 Adrian Piper, *Out of Order, Out of Sight* (Cambridge, MA: MIT Press, 1996), 27.

23 Fred Moten, *In the Break: The Aesthetics of the Black Black Radical Tradition* (Minneapolis: University of Minnesota Press, 2003), 253.

24 Lorde, *Sister Outsider*, 56.

25 Samuel R. Delany, *The Jewel-Hinged Jaw: Notes on the Language of Science Fiction*, rev. ed. (Middletown, CT: Wesleyan University Press, 2009), 4.

26 "The Little Girl Who Sold the Sun (La Petite Vendeuse de Soleil)," Riverfront Times, accessed September 5, 2019, https://www.riverfronttimes.com/stlouis /the-little-girl-who-sold-the-sun-la-petite-vendeuse-de-soleil/Film?oid=2707330.

27 Fred Moten, Wu Tsang, and Denise Ferreira da Silva, *Who Touched Me?* (If I Can't Dance, I Don't Want To Be Part of Your Revolution, 2016), 7.

28 Terence Nance, *An Oversimplification of Her Beauty*, Apple, accessed August 23, 2018, http://www.imdb.com/title/tt2073520/.

29 "Knitting History," The Knitty Gritty NYC, accessed August 23, 2018, http:// www.theknittygrittynyc.com/knitting-history/.

30 Alice Walker, *In Search of Our Mothers' Gardens: Womanist Prose*, repr. ed. (Orlando, FL: Mariner Books, 2003).

31 Ferreira da Silva, *Toward a Global Idea of Race*, 9.

32 Martin Heidegger, *On the Way to Language* (New York: Harper and Row, 1971).

33 Fred Moten and Stefano Harney, *A Poetics of the Undercommons* (New York: Sputnik and Fizzle, 2016), 14–15.

tongues[3]

1 Jeremy Fernando, "On Stupidity—or, on Love and Valentine's Day. | Treehouse," February 9, 2015; accessed September 6, 2019, https://tembusu.nus.edu.sg /treehouse/2015/02/on-stupidity-or-on-love-and-valentines-day/.

2 Hollywood and Beckman, *Cambridge Companion to Christian Mysticism*, 16.

3 Hollywood and Beckman, 43.

4 W. E. B. (William Edward Burghardt) Du Bois, "Last Message to the World," in *W. E. B. Du Bois Speaks: Speeches and Addresses, 1890-1919* (New York: Pathfinder, 1970), 355.

5 Katherine McKittrick, ed., *Sylvia Wynter: On Being Human as Praxis* (Durham, NC: Duke University Press, 2014), 11.

6   Greg Thomas, "PROUD FLESH Inter/Views: Sylvia Wynter," *ProudFlesh: New Afrikan Journal of Culture, Politics, and Consciousness* 4 (2006): n.p.

7   M. NourbeSe Philip, *Zong!* (Middletown, CT: Wesleyan University Press, 2008).

8   Philip, 189.

9   Philip, xi.

10 PAPILLION, "Samuel Levi Jones Artist Talk," December 18, 2014, YouTube video, 40:15, https://www.youtube.com/watch?v=3x2brzqisvc.

11 Lorde, *Sister Outsider*, 37.

12 Mackey, *From a Broken Bottle*, 50.

13 William Faulkner, *Go Down, Moses* (New York: Vintage, 1990).

14 W. E. B. Du Bois, *The Souls of Black Folk* (n.p.: CreateSpace, 2010), 4.

15 LeRoi Jones, *Black Music*, reissue edition (New York: Akashic Books, 2010), 28.

16 Iona Locke—Topic, "Let's Get It On (Sermon)."

17 Kadeem Graves, "Where Can I Go—DFW Mass Choir," July 4, 2012, YouTube video, 7:07, https://www.youtube.com/watch?v=Lp43JVkzJlo.

18 Paul Arnett et al., *Gee's Bend: The Architecture of the Quilt* (Atlanta, GA: Tinwood Books, 2006), 31.

19 Arnett et al., 37.

20 Rizvana Bradley, "Introduction: Other Sensualities," *Women and Performance: A Journal of Feminist Theory* 24, no. 2–3 (September 2014): 129, https://doi.org/10.1080/0740770X.2014.976494.

21 anxiouscatfilms, "Theaster Gates and the Black Monks of Mississippi, Eindhoven 2008," January 24, 2011, YouTube video, 14:46, https://www.youtube.com/watch?v=GWE3iXYptrc.

22 Susan Buck-Morss, "Aesthetics and Anaesthetics: Walter Benjamin's Artwork Essay Reconsidered," *October* 62 (Autumn 1992): 12–13.

nothing³

1   Orlando Patterson, *Slavery and Social Death: A Comparative Study* (Cambridge, MA: Harvard University Press, 1982).

2   Arthur Jafa, "Black Visual Intonation," in *The Jazz Cadence of American Culture*, ed. Robert O'Meally, 264–68 (New York: Columbia University Press, 1998).

3   Frederick Douglass, *Narrative of the Life of Frederick Douglass, an American Slave, Written by Himself: Critical Edition* (New Haven, CT: Yale University Press, 2016), 20.

4   Saidiya V. Hartman, *Lose Your Mother: A Journey along the Atlantic Slave Route* (New York: Farrar, Straus, and Giroux, 2007), 69.

5   Piper, *Out of Order, Out of Sight*, 161, 164–67.

6   Salim Washington, "The Avenging Angel of Creation/Destruction: Black Music and the Afro-Technological in the Science Fiction of Henry Dumas and Samuel R. Delany," *Journal of the Society for American Music* 2, no. 2 (2008): 235–53.

7   Christina Sharpe, *In the Wake: On Blackness and Being*, repr. ed. (Durham, NC: Duke University Press, 2016).

8   Harriet Joseph Ottenheimer and Judith M. S. Pine, *The Anthropology of Language: An Introduction to Linguistic Anthropology* (London: Cengage Learning, 2018), 322.

9   Simone Leigh, "#bodegastrike yesterday. Repost @pchza," Instagram video, February 3, 2017, https://www.instagram.com/p/BQDRUKCD-Tw/.

index

Du Bois, W. E. B., 45, 70; *Black Reconstruction*, 141, 142; "problem" question by, 167, 173–74

Eckhart, Meister, 21–22, 92, 97, 121
Einstein, Albert, 91, 190
Ellison, Ralph, 91
Enlightenment thought, 122, 168
entanglement, 36, 63–64, 95, 103, 111, 114–15, 124, 132, 134–35, 232, 248; quantum, 97, 110, 118, 123, 196
epistemology, 8, 37, 181, 224, 229, 242; defined, 159–60; "epistemological substratum" (Robinson), 92–94, 98, 121, 152, 174; limitations of western, 10, 27, 32, 64, 79, 88, 95, 121, 138–39, 141, 201; sonic, 5–6, 166
ethics and "the anethical," 88–89, 196–97
ethnocentrism, 93
Evans, Robert, 56, 159
evaporation, 19
excess, 4, 26, 42, 45, 59, 63, 64, 133, 158, 168, 199, 227–28; *excessus mentis*, 146; gift of, 95; libidinal, 18, 182

Faulkner, William, 172–75
feeling(s), 4, 5, 7–8, 36–38, 76; Baldwin and, 106; blackness and, 10, 36, 37; dreams and, 195; *Moonlight* and, 106–8; quantum physics and, 87; quilts and, 199; romantic, 3, 168; as thought, 37
Ferreira da Silva, Denise, 27, 70, 88, 141, 152, 193, 196
"fiery prayer," 146–47
Flash, The (TV series), 19
forgiveness, 103–4
Foucault, Michel, 29, 31
Franklin, Aretha, 149, 161, 181–82, 183–84
friendship, 5, 10, 11, 29–30; Foucault on, 29

Gates, Theaster: and the Black Monks of Mississippi, 199–201
Gaye, Marvin, 161, 163, 236
Gee's Bend quilting collective, 197–98, 201
George, Stefan, 142
Gibbs, Philip (quoted), 65
glossolalia, 70, 160, 163, 165, 201; vs. xenolalia, 147, 167, 174, 226–27
gospel music, 1, 5–6, 36–37, 140, 145, 149, 161, 163, 165, 182–83, 204–6, 207–13, 214, 233–34; falsetto in, 1, 64, 140, 183; melisma in, 140, 167, 182, 204, 208; modulation in, 164–67; rhythm in, 207–9; variant lyrics in, 185–88. *See also* Hammond B-3 organ
—songs: "Accept What God Allows," 19, 43; "Blessed Be the Name of the Lord," 235; "Bless That Wonderful Name of Jesus," 234; "He Set Me Free," 36, 39; "How I Got Over," 19; "In the Name of Jesus," 234; "Send It on Down," 214–16; "Spread the Word," 129; "There's a Storm Out on the Ocean," 56; "This Is the Day," 207–9, 234; "Victory Is Mine," 234; "Where Can I Go," 194, 202
Goudy-Johnson, Keith Darnell, 43
Grindr (website), 25

Hammond B-3 organ, 5, 19, 32–33, 43, 56, 64, 77–80, 82–84, 112, 181, 191, 215, 221; drawbars on, 56, 78, 112, 210–11; Leslie speakers with, 81; playing "nothing" on, 241–42
Hartman, Saidiya V., 1, 229, 230–32
Hebrew Bible, 190–91
Hegel, Georg Wilhelm Friedrich, 237
Heidegger, Martin, 142, 143, 161, 212, 243
Heisenberg, Werner, 88, 89–90
Holiday, Billie, 178
Hollywood, Amy, 24
homophobia, 4, 10, 37, 44, 99, 101, 103–4, 107
homosexual panic, 96, 99

northern vs. southern states, 175–76

Northup, Solomon, 163

Oliver, Loretta, 204–6

Open Door, 32, 70, 102

Ottenheimer, Harriet Joseph, 238–39

Out All Night (TV series), 233

"overrepresentation of Man" (Wynter), 28–31, 71, 90, 93, 143, 196, 237–38

Oversimplification of Her Beauty, An (film), 133

painting, 46–61, 237, 239

passing chords, 77

patriarchy, 4, 10, 27–28, 105, 108, 138, 169

Patterson, Orlando, 216

Paul, Saint, 244; and Timothy, 212

perfection (in performance), 177–81, 186; beauty of imperfection, 189

performance studies, 1, 9

Petite Vendeuse de Soleil, La (film), 129–31

Pettway, Mensie Lee, 198–99

Philip, M. NourbeSe, 91, 156–57, 158, 205–6

Piper, Adrian, 14, 120–22, 231–32

poetry, 159–60

pottery, 199–200

praise breaks, 50, 61, 70

quantum physics, 8, 10, 87–89, 97–99, 110–11, 122–23, 132–33, 196. *See also* entanglement

queer antagonism. *See* homophobia

queerness, 25, 138–39. *See also* blackqueerness

quilts, 197–99

refusal concept, 28

Reich, Steve, 35–37, 39–42, 43–45, 50, 61, 77, 78–79, 158–59

relationality, 8, 10–11, 22, 63–64, 98, 137, 196, 230, 232, 235, 237

religion, 28–29, 64, 92–94, 246; in *Book of*

Mormon, 190; in *Moonlight*, 108. *See also* Black Church culture; Blackpentecostalism; mysticism

Robinson, Cedric, 31, 67, 76, 89, 94–95; on Marxism, 92–93, 141–42

Rockefeller Laws, 174

Ross, Bob, 46

Rule of Saint Benedict (Benedict of Nursia), 22

science, 8, 27, 59, 96–97. *See also* Newtonian physics; quantum physics

selfhood, 224

sexism, 4, 10, 37

Seymour, William, 244

Sharpe, Christina, 237, 238

shouting, 1, 19, 36, 39–40, 44, 56, 59–60, 65, 70, 83, 165, 226

Simpson, Leanne Betasamosake, 28

Sister Outsider. See Lorde, Audre

slavery, 28, 76, 141, 142, 148, 156, 167, 175–76, 215–16, 229–30, 243; "status of woman" law in, 173

social death, 216

sociality, 29; religious rejection of, 22–23, 94–95. *See also* Black sociality

Spillers, Hortense, 1, 25, 30, 119

stardust, 152, 154

Stein, Gertrude, 227

strangers, 229, 232

Sufism, 103–4

Superman, 125–29

synagogues, 82

Tamar (biblical), 146

tambourines, 61, 81, 106, 159, 214–15, 233

Tatum, Art, 177–79

Temptations, The, 181

Teresa of Ávila, Saint, 22, 24, 92, 121

Tharpe, Rosetta, 182–84

thing: etymology of, 59; slang use of, 144; thingliness, 143–44
Till, Emmett, 1
touch, 145, 147
transitions, 234–36
Tsang, Wu, 133
Tubman, Harriet, 167

universities, 29, 157, 158, 160

voice, 161, 163–66, 204–6; "wet" sound of, 204–6

Walker, Albertina, 129
Walker, Alice, 49; *The Color Purple*, 91, 137–38; "In Search of Our Mothers' Gardens," 138
whiteness and white supremacism, 27, 28, 67, 108, 138, 224
wrestling, 104–5
Wynter, Sylvia, 27, 28, 63, 71, 93, 157, 237; on Aretha Franklin, 149, 161

"yonderworld," 120–21, 122